A Commentary on Cicero, De Divinatione I

A Commentary on Cicero, *De Divinatione I*

Celia E. Schultz

University of Michigan Press
Ann Arbor

Published in the United States of America by the
University of Michigan Press
Manufactured in the United States of America
⊚ Printed on acid-free paper

2017   2016   2015   2014   4   3   2   1

A CIP catalog record for this book is available from the British Library.

Library of Congress Cataloging-in-Publication Data

A commentary on Cicero, De divinatione I / Celia E. Schultz.
        pages   cm — (Michigan classical commentaries)
    Contains the Latin text of Cicero's De divinatione, Liber 1 and commentary in English by
Celia E. Schultz.
    Includes bibliographical references and index.
    ISBN 978-0-472-11939-4 (hardcover : alk. paper) — ISBN 978-0-472-03608-0 (pbk. : alk.
paper)
    1. Cicero, Marcus Tullius. De divinatione. Liber 1.   2. Divination—Early works to 1800.
I. Cicero, Marcus Tullius. De divinatione. Liber 1.   II. Schultz, Celia E. Commentary on
Cicero, De divinatione I.   III. Series: Michigan classical commentaries.
PA6296.D15   2014
203'.2—dc23
                                                                    2014031383

For
Liam and Eli

Preface

Not until I decided to teach Cicero's *De Divinatione* several years ago did I finally sit down and read the whole text. I had used it for years as a quarry—pulling out what I needed for other projects—but like many historians of Roman religion, I had never given much thought to the work on its own. I thought I knew it well, but I was wrong. As I worked my way through the dialogue, I realized two things: first, that it would support a reading different from the standard view that Book 2 represents the true opinion of the author and, second, that although Pease's 1920–23 commentary, the most recent commentary on the Latin text, is still useful for scholarship, it is not suited to most readers who approach the text today—not only classicists, but scholars of religion as well. Thus I have set out to provide an accessible commentary that validates the first book's contribution to a meaningful debate over the validity of divination.

Many people have contributed to this project. My colleagues and students at Yale University—especially Christina S. Kraus, Verity Harte, John Oksanish, and Caroline Mann—gave advice that has kept me from many errors. Many of the ideas I worked out in conversations with them were tested out on my new colleagues and students at the University of Michigan in a seminar on Cicero and Roman religion taught with Sara Ahbel-Rappe in winter 2011: John Daukas, Harriet Fertik, Jacqueline Pincus, Amy Pistone, Andrea Brock, Alexandra Talarico, and Bram ten Berge. Siam Bhayro, Susann Feingold, David Potter, and Ruth Scodel commented on portions of this project. David Wardle, Gil Renberg, and John P. F. Wynne generously shared their published and unpublished work. In 2009, I learned a great deal during a delightful weekend spent at Georgetown University at a Commentary Writers' Workshop on Latin prose works with Alexander Sens, S. Douglas Olson, Charles McNelis, Salvador Bartera, Luca Grillo, and Ben Weston. Kate T. Allen went through the manuscript and corrected many mistakes. Troy Leonard ensured that the Latin text is accurate. Ellen Bauerle and the staff at the University of Michigan Press kept the project moving forward. I am also very grateful to John N. Dillon, who read *De Divinatione* with me and greatly improved the commentary. He has a precision of thought I can only hope to achieve. Most of all, I owe thanks to Julia Gaisser, who has read more drafts of this commentary than she planned. Through her suggestions and corrections, she has injected a lot of life into this book. Since my time at Bryn Mawr College, she has been the kind of teacher and scholar I strive to be. All errors and opinions in what follows are my own.

I regret that Federico Santangelo's *Divination, Prediction and the End of the Roman Republic* (Cambridge, 2013) appeared after this book had gone to press. I have not been able to incorporate it into my discussion.

This book is dedicated to my sons, Liam and Eli Driscoll, who are always eager to know what comes next and who help me to see the future.

Contents

Abbreviations

Some works cited in this study are noted with the following abbreviations. All journal citations in the bibiliography follow the abbreviations in *L'Annee Philologique*.

Ax   W. Ax. 1938. *M. Tulli Ciceronis Scripta Quae Manserunt Omnia*. Vol. 46, *De Divinatione, De Fato, Timaeus*. Stuttgart: Teubner.

Bailey   C. Bailey. 1947. *Titi Lucreti Cari: De Rerum Natura Libri Sex*. 3 vols. Oxford: Clarendon.

BNP   H. Cancik and H. Schneider, eds. 2002–. *Brill's New Pauly*. Leiden: Brill.

CAH²   *Cambridge Ancient History*. 1982–. 2nd ed. Cambridge: Cambridge University Press.

CHI   *The Cambridge History of Iran*. 1968–91. 7 vols. Cambridge: Cambridge University Press.

CIL   *Corpus Inscriptionum Latinarum*. 1863–. Berlin: de Gruyter.

FrGH   F. Jacoby. 1923–58. *Die Fragmente der griechischen Historiker*. 3rd ed. 3 vols. in 7. Leiden: Brill.

FRH   T. J. Cornell, ed. 2013. *The Fragments of the Roman Historians*. 3 vols. Oxford: Oxford University Press.

G&L   B. L. Gildersleeve and G. Lodge. 2003. *Gildersleeve's Latin Grammar*. Reprint of 3rd ed. London: Macmillan.

IG   *Inscriptiones Graecae*. 1903–. Berlin: de Gruyter

ILLRP   A. Degrassi. 1957–63. *Inscriptiones Latinae Liberae Rei Publicae*. 2 vols. Florence: La Nuova Italia Editrice.

ILLRP Imagines   A. Degrassi. 1965. *Inscriptiones Latinae Liberae Rei Publicae Imagines*. Berlin: de Gruyter.

ILS   H. Dessau. 1892–1916. *Inscriptiones Latinae Selectae*. 3 vols. Berlin: Weidmann.

Inscr. Ital. *Inscriptiones Italiae*. 1916–. Rome: Libreria dello Stato.

IPerg. 3   C. Habicht. 1969. *Die Inschriften des Asklepieions.* Altertümer von
             Pergamon 8.3. Berlin: de Gruyter.
Kühn   K. G. Kühn. 1821–33. *Claudii Galeni Omnia Opera.* 20 vols.
             Leipzig: Knobloch. Reprint, Hildesheim: Olms, 1964.
LIMC   *Lexicon Iconographicum Mythologiae Classicae.* 1981–97. 8 vols.
             Zurich: Artemis.
LTUR   E. M. Steinby, ed. *Lexicon Topographicum Urbis Romae.* 6 vols.
             Rome: Quasar, 1993–2000.
MRR   T. R. S. Broughton. 1951–52. *The Magistrates of the Roman
             Republic.* 3 vols. New York: American Philological Association.
NLS   E. C. Woodcock. 1959. *New Latin Syntax.* London: Methuen.
NTDAR   L. Richardson, Jr. 1992. *A New Topographical Dictionary of Ancient
             Rome.* Baltimore: Johns Hopkins University Press.
Oakley   S. P. Oakley. 1997–2005. *A Commentary on Livy, Books VI–X.* 4
             vols. Oxford: Clarendon.
OLD   P. G. W. Glare, ed. 1968–82. *Oxford Latin Dictionary.* Oxford:
             Clarendon.
Pease   A. S. Pease. [1920–23] 1963. *M. Tulli Ciceronis* De Divinatione.
             Darmstadt: Wissenschaftliche Buchgesellschaft.
Pease *N. D.*   A. S. Pease. [1955–58] 1968. *Marci Tulli Ciceronis* De Natura
             Deorum. 2 vols. Darmstadt: Wissenschaftliche Buchgesellschaft.
Peter   H. Peter. 1914–16. *Historicorum Romanorum Reliquiae.* 2nd ed. 2
             vols. Leipzig: Teubner.
RE   A. Pauly, G. Wissowa, and W. Kroll, eds. 1894–1978. *Real-
             Encylopädie der classischen Altertumswissenschaft.* Stuttgart:
             Metzlerscher.
Ribbeck   O. Ribbeck. 1897. *Scaenicae Romanorum Poesis Fragmenta.* 3rd ed.
             2 vols. Leipzig: Teubner.
Rose   V. Rose. 1886. *Aristotelis qui ferebantur librorum Fragmenta.*
             Stuttgart: Teubner.
RRC   M. H. Crawford. 1974. *Roman Republican Coinage.* 2 vols. London:
             Cambridge University Press.
SBA   D. R. Shackleton Bailey. 1965–70. *Cicero's Letters to Atticus.* 7 vols.
             Cambridge: Cambridge University Press.
SBF   D. R. Shackleton Bailey. 1977. *Cicero*: Epistulae ad Familiares. 2
             vols. Cambridge: Cambridge University Press.
SBQ   D. R. Shackleton Bailey. 1980. *Cicero*: Epistulae ad Quintum
             Fratrem et M. Brutum. Cambridge: Cambridge University Press.
Schäublin C. Schäublin. 2002. *Über die Wahrsagung.* Düsseldorf: Artemis and
             Winkler.
Skutsch   O. Skutsch. 1985. *The* Annals *of Q. Ennius.* Oxford: Clarendon.

Timpanaro   S. Timpanaro. 1999. *Cicerone: Della divinazione*. Milan: Garzanti.

TLL   *Thesaurus Linguae Latinae*. 1900–. Leipzig: Teubner.

Wardle   D. Wardle. 2006. *Cicero:* On Divination *Book I*. Clarendon Ancient History Series. Oxford: Clarendon.

Wehrli   F. Wehrli. 1953. *Die Schule des Aristoteles*. 10 vols. Basel: Schwabe.

Outline of Books 1 and 2

De Divinatione is less tightly organized than many of Cicero's other philosophical works. The following outline sketches the main divisions of the argument of Book 1, but the reader should bear in mind that Quintus's argument does not flow in a strictly linear manner. The structure of Book 2 is less complex.

Book 1

Prologue, including doxography (1–7)
Narratio: setting the scene and introductory conversation (8–11)
Partitio: Quintus's organizing principles (11–16)
Results, not causes, are important (17–33)
Exempla of natural divination (34–71)
Oracles (34–38)
Dreams (39–59)
Exempla of technical divination (72–81)
Divination as a sign of the gods' concern for mankind (81–89)
Divination among the nations of the world and at Rome (90–108)
The tripartite causation of divination: *a deo, a fato,* and *a natura* (109–31)
Conclusion (132)

Book 2

Prologue, including catalog of works to date (1–7)

General objections (8–26)
Technical divination: haruspicy, thunder and lightning, prodigies, auspices, sortition, astrology (26–99)
Natural divination: prophecy and dreams (100–146)
Conclusion (147–50)

Concerning the Text

The text of *De Divinatione*—along with that of *De Natura Deorum, De Fato,* and several other works—is based on three manuscripts of the ninth or tenth century from France (A, B, and V) and one late eleventh-century manuscript from Italy (H). Since the focus of this commentary is the content and context of Book 1 of the dialogue, I have not sought to provide a new text but have worked with an eye to A. S. Pease's 1920 edition and W. Ax's Teubner text of 1938. I have retained Ax's archaic orthography, which prefers *u* to *i* in open medial syllables before labial consonants (e.g., Iuppiter optumus maxumus). Below is a list of passages where the text presented here diverges from Ax's text.

AX		THIS EDITION
1	p. Romani	populi Romani
3	nam ut omittam . . . conplexus est	. . . . conplexus est!
	et [in] monstris	et monstris
4	rem p.	rem publicam
6	quom	cum
16	quor	cur
17	⟨de⟩ consulatu	consulatu⟨s⟩
20	generosa stirpe	generosa a stirpe
24	rei p.	rei publicae
27	quoius	cuius
30	, id est . . . invenit	[id est . . . invenit]
34	divinitatem	divinationem
35	rei p.	rei publicae
36	et * motibus	[et motibus]
37	quis ignorat.	quis ignorat?
43	prop[r]iora	propiora
	Acci[us]	Acci
45	veruncent	verruncent
46	ipsa [Phalaris] domi	ipsa domi

49	praecepisse[t]que	praecepisseque
58	huius somnii mihique	huius somnii, mihique
62	modo [ait] hoc modo illud	modo ait hoc modo illud
66	praesagatio	praesagitio
	obsequi?	obsequi!
68	sanguine[m]	sanguine
71	potest [et] officium	potest officium
72	quod [et] Etruscorum	quod Etruscorum
77	rei p.	rei publicae
	censere[n]t	censeret
79	qui est campus agri Lanuvini	[qui est campus agri Lanuvini]
89	permotione divina.	permotione divina?
	[ut] testis est	testis est
	rem p.	rem publicam
91	Iami[n]darum	Iamidarum
92	x singulis Etruriae populis	x ex singulis Etruriae populis
95	dum habent auspicia	[dum habent auspicia]
96	rem p.	rem publicam
108	[et] simul aureus	simul aureus
110	contagione	cognatione
111	re p.	re publica
113	vaticinationes cum somniis	[vaticinationes cum somniis]
116	somniorum [Antiphontis] interpretatio	somniorum interpretatio
122	quo quem . . . quaerimus,	(quo quem . . . quaerimus?)
	[Epi]Cyrum	Cyrum
132	exclusa[m]	exclusa

Introduction

De Divinatione (*Div.* hereafter) is a multifaceted work, important for the study of Roman religion, history, and intellectual life, as well as Latin literature and Cicero himself. The work has long been used as a resource for scholarship in these areas, but little attention has been paid to its own merits. This commentary aims both to assist the reader in seeing *Div.* as a cohesive whole and to make it accessible—not only to classicists, but also to scholars of religion and to philosophers who may not be familiar with the historical and intellectual backgrounds that are the focus here. The cases made for and against divination in *Div.* closely follow arguments made by Greek philosophers, but many of the *exempla* illustrating them reflect Cicero's preferences in literature, his own poetic efforts and political experience, and his expertise as an augur. The result is a very personal work closely tied to the author's own experience.

A scholar should write without bias, and when she cannot, she should make her biases clear—especially when they pertain to the central critical issue raised by the text. Because of space constraints, this commentary deals only with Book 1 of *Div.*, but it assumes that both books of the dialogue are of equal importance to understanding the whole. In this regard, this commentary departs from the orthodox understanding of *Div.* that sees Book 1 as a straw argument constructed in order to be knocked down by Book 2, which is taken to be Cicero's personal opinion. The orthodox position has been taken by Pease (1920–23), Guillaumont (1984, 2006), Timpanaro (1999), Wardle (2006), and many others. The more integrative reading followed here has been advocated by a smaller group of scholars, most important among them Beard (1986), Denyer (1985), Schofield (1986), and Krostenko (2000).

It is significant that Cicero chose to write *Div.* as a dialogue with opposing voices rather than as a treatise where only one position is represented. By structuring *Div.* as he has, Cicero keeps open the question of the validity of divination. By not resolving the debate at the end of the work, he leaves us to come to our own conclusion: he declares at 1.7 that he himself is not certain what to think about divination. To assume that the opinions expressed in

Book 2 are entirely the author's puts too much emphasis on the fact that the character that delivers the argument is that of the author. For this reason, this commentary distinguishes between the literary figure called Marcus in the dialogue and the historical person Cicero. A detailed argument for separating the two can be found in Schultz 2009.

Life of Cicero

Cicero's personal experience, especially his circumstances in the years 45–44, and his intellectual interests shape the content and structure of *Div*. Thus it is necessary to offer an evaluation of his contribution to the Republic and to Latin literature. To that end, I offer a brief overview of his life and work. For those desiring more detail, several excellent English-language biographies of Cicero are available. The view of Cicero presented here most closely matches that of Elizabeth Rawson's *Cicero: A Portrait* (1975).

Like other young men of good families from towns outside the capitol, Marcus Tullius Cicero (b. 3 January 106 BCE and his younger brother, Quintus, were brought to Rome from their home in Arpinum to receive an appropriate education in rhetoric and law, but their studies were interrupted by the outbreak of the Social War between Rome and many of its former Italic allies in 91 BCE. During the conflict, Cicero served on the staffs of L. Cornelius Sulla (*Div*. 1.72, 2.65) and Cn. Pompeius Strabo (*Phil*. 1.2.27). It is likely that, during his service under Strabo, Cicero met Strabo's son, Cn. Pompeius Magnus, better known in English as Pompey, who was the same age as Cicero. Cicero and Pompey were destined to become major players in politics in the decades to follow. Also on Strabo's staff was L. Sergius Catilina (Catiline), whose path would cross with Cicero's in the sixties.[1]

When the war ended in 88, Cicero, still too young, at eighteen, for important public service, returned to his studies in rhetoric and philosophy, particularly of the skeptical Academic and Stoic schools. After some important initial successes in the law courts in the late eighties, Cicero chose to hone his oratorical and philosophical skills through study in Greece and Rhodes. He would later claim that he departed for the East in 79/78 to improve his strength

---

1   Both the younger Pompey and Catiline appear as members of Strabo's *consilium* on the Asculum inscription (*ILLRP* 515 = *ILS* 8888 = *CIL* 1².709 = *CIL* 6.37054), a text, partially preserved on two bronze plaques (now in Rome), that records grants made to Strabo's Spanish auxiliaries. The absence of Cicero from this list may suggest that he was with Sulla when the grants were made (probably in 89), although the possibility remains that he was with Strabo but too unimportant to merit inclusion on the *consilium*.

for public speaking (*Brut.* 313–15), but Plutarch insists that the reason was fear of the dictator Sulla (*Cic.* 3.4).

When he departed for Greece, Cicero left behind not only Rome and his budding career but also his young family: the wife he married in around 79, Terentia, who came from a wealthy patrician family, and his daughter, Tullia, who had been born not too long after their marriage. A son, Marcus, was born a year or two before Cicero's consulship in 63. His long marriage to Terentia survived political turmoil and exile but eventually came to an end in 47/46. A brief marriage to the much younger and much wealthier Publilia quickly followed but lasted only a few weeks. Tullia died in 45, and her devastated father sought consolation in philosophy, as he had always done in times of distress.

POLITICAL CAREER

Cicero achieved the rare feat of advancing to each rung of the political ladder in the first year he was eligible. This accomplishment is even more impressive since Cicero suffered a significant political disadvantage: he was a *novus homo*, the first in his family to reach the Roman Senate. With no family connections to help him, the chances of a man reaching the pinnacle of political power in this period were slim. Cicero's popularity with voters no doubt had much to do with his success in the law courts. His early forensic speeches tackled the popular issues of corruption and unfair use of power, and he recounted in later years that applause from onlookers sometimes interrupted him while he spoke (*Or.* 107). On returning to Rome from serving out his quaestorship in Sicily, he continued his career in the courts, hitting a high mark with his successful prosecution of Verres, a corrupt former governor of Sicily, in 70. Cicero was victorious even though Verres's defense was argued by Q. Hortensius Hortalus, up to that point the leading orator in Rome.

Cicero was elected to the consulship in 63 at age forty-three. It is important not to give too much weight, as is sometimes done by modern scholars, to Sallust's claim (*BC* 23.5–6) that Cicero achieved this highest office only because he was perceived as a safe alternative to the other candidates: the disreputable Catiline and C. Antonius Hybrida. The former had escaped conviction for extortion just the year before (probably by bribing the jury), and the latter had been thrown out of the Senate several years earlier. Cicero, however, had long been popular with voters.

The crowning glory of his consular year was Cicero's suppression of a conspiracy, led by Catiline, that aimed at the overthrow of the government and the elimination of private debt. Catiline fled to his supporters in the north, while Cicero, with the backing of the Senate, put to death those conspirators remaining in Rome. Out of relief and gratitude, the Senate awarded Cicero the honorific title *parens patriae* (*Pis.* 6; *Phil.* 2.12). But the golden moment was brief. Talk soon began that Cicero had acted illegally. Anti-Ciceronian sentiment came to a head when, in 58, the tribune P. Clodius Pulcher (long one of Cicero's detractors) revived a law that exiled those who executed citizens without trial. Cicero avoided prosecution by leaving Rome for Macedonia, but Clodius persisted in having his exile voted into law. Clodius's power waned quickly, however, and Cicero returned to Rome in September 57.

The political landscape to which he returned was dominated by an alliance of Pompey, Caesar, and Crassus. Having little part to play in politics during these years, though he joined the college of augurs after Crassus's death in 53, Cicero turned to writing philosophy. It is to this period that we date such important works as *De Oratore* and *De Republica*. In 51, he grudgingly left behind his books and accepted the governorship of Cilicia (*Att.* 5.15.1 = *SBA* 108.1), as the hostilities between Pompey and Caesar escalated. Cicero avoided taking sides for a time (his indecision is clear in his letters from this period), but he eventually sided with Pompey and the republican forces in the Civil War of 49. After the republicans lost at Pharsalus, Cicero was pardoned by Caesar but was again excluded from political life.

The final act of Cicero's life began with the murder of Caesar in 44—a conspiracy to which he was not party but that gave him cause to rejoice (*Ad Fam.* 12.3.1 = *SBF* 345.1 and 10.28.1 = *SBF* 364.1). He was once again a leading figure in the Senate, supporting Brutus and Cassius, actively working against Antonius, and cultivating a friendship with Caesar's heir, Octavian, whose political acumen Cicero underestimated (*Ad Fam.* 11.20.1 = *SBF* 401.1). Eventually, Octavian sided with Antonius, and as a favor to his new ally, he did not object when Antonius put Cicero's name on a list of political enemies marked for death. Shortly thereafter, on 7 December 43 BCE, Cicero was murdered by Antonius's soldiers. Livy's version of the event is preserved by the elder Seneca (*Suas.* 6.17).

> . . . *taedium tandem eum et fugae et vitae cepit regressusque ad superiorem villam, quae paulo plus mille passibus a mari abest, "moriar" inquit "in patria saepe servata". satis constat servos fortiter fideliterque paratos fuisse ad dimicandum; ipsum deponi lecticam et quietos pati quod fors iniqua cogeret iussisse. prominenti ex lectica praebentique immotam cervicem caput praecisum est. nec satis stolidae crudelitati militum fuit: manus quoque scripsisse aliquid in Antonium exprobrantes praeciderunt. ita relatum caput ad Antonium iussuque eius inter duas manus in rostris positum, ubi ille consul, ubi saepe consularis, ubi eo ipso anno adversus Antonium quanta nulla umquam humana vox cum admiratione eloquentiae auditus fuerat.*

[... in the end, he wearied of life on the run and turned back to his villa, the one mentioned earlier that sat just over a mile from the sea. He declared, "I will die in the fatherland I have so often preserved." It is generally agreed that his slaves bravely and loyally prepared themselves to fight on his behalf, but that Cicero himself ordered his litter to be set down and instructed them to endure in silence the constraints of unjust fortune. He leaned forward out of his litter and offered his assassins his neck without flinching; they beheaded him. Nor did that satisfy the soldiers' senseless cruelty: they cut off his hands as well, since those hands had written censorious things against Antonius. Cicero's head was brought to Antonius and on his order was set between his two hands on the rostra where he had been heard so many times—as consul and often as a former consul, indeed even in that very year against Antonius—with more admiration for his eloquence than had ever been given to another mortal voice.]

LITERARY CAREER

Cicero has long been valued as a great Latin writer and stylist. Quintilian (*Inst.* 10.1.112) saw him as the pinnacle of Roman eloquence: *Quare non inmerito ab hominibus aetatis suae regnare in iudiciis dictus est, apud posteros vero id consecutus ut Cicero iam non hominis nomen sed eloquentiae habeatur* (Thus it is not inappropriate that he was judged by his contemporaries to rule the courtroom, and that in succeeding generations Cicero was considered the name not of a man, but of eloquence itself). Cicero left behind him a monumental corpus of speeches, letters, poems, and rhetorical and philosophical works.

The man himself is best revealed in his letters, more than nine hundred of which were published after his death. The most authoritative editions of the various collections (arranged by recipient) are those of D. R. Shackleton Bailey (*SBA, SBF, SBQ*). Because many were written without a view toward eventual publication, the letters present a more honest, sometimes less flattering portrait than do Cicero's more carefully crafted works. They are also an invaluable source for the history of the last decades of the Roman Republic. Their preservation is owed to Atticus, Cicero's close friend and frequent correspondent, and to Cicero's slave and personal secretary Tiro, whom he freed in 53 (*Ad Fam.* 16.16.1–2 = *SBF* 44.1–2) and who lived well into the reign of the emperor Augustus. Cicero's long career as an advocate and politician is also documented in more than forty extant speeches, some only in partial form, and in the titles and fragments of another thirty.

Plutarch's report that Cicero had an early reputation for being not only the best orator at Rome but also the best poet (*Cic.* 2.3) is probably based on the reception of his *Aratea*, a youthful translation of the *Phaenomena* of Aratus, a

Greek poem about constellations and weather signs, written in the early third century. Cicero seems to have been the first to translate it into Latin. Many others followed his example,[2] indicating the importance of not only Aratus's original but also Cicero's translation, as texts to be rivaled. Several fragments are preserved in *Div.* 1 as part of the argument that there are signs in the natural world that portend changes in weather. *Div.* 1 also preserves long passages of his two later historical epics, the *Marius* and his *Consulatus*, as part of the argument that the gods send signs and predictive dreams to mortals. These epics were far less popular than the *Aratea*: in particular, the *Consulatus*, written to celebrate the suppression of the Catilinarian conspiracy, was widely ridiculed by contemporaries and later generations for its pretentiousness and for excessive self-praise (e.g., *Pis.* 72–73; Quint., *Inst.* 11.1.24; Mart. 2.89.3–4).

Nearly all of Cicero's rhetorical and philosophical work dates to the two periods of his retirement from political life: namely, to 57–51, in the aftermath of his exile, and to 49–44, the period of Caesar's ascendancy. Indeed, Cicero often presented his work as an alternative method of serving the public good when more active means of political participation were denied him (*Div.* 2.1, 2.7; *Tusc.* 1.3; *N. D.* 1.6–7; *Off.* 1.1). Acutely aware of the ongoing deterioration of traditional forms of government, Cicero sought to address matters of governance of the state and the training and obligations of its leaders.

Divination at Rome

The Romans communicated with their gods through sacrifice, prayer, and material offerings. In turn, divination allowed the gods to communicate their pleasure or displeasure to men and, for this reason, was critical to the functioning of the Roman state. Divine approval was a requirement for the undertaking of important events in public and private life, among them military campaigns, political elections, meetings of the Senate, weddings, business transactions, and travel. If the gods expressed displeasure through the signs they sent, the Romans would try again to appease them with rites in their honor. If successive attempts were unsuccessful, the Romans would abandon the project or delay progress until the gods were amenable. It appears that, over time, the purpose of divination evolved from checking on the gods' immediate attitude to predicting the future. This shift in emphasis can be seen as a logical outgrowth of the

---

2   The other translators include Cicero's younger contemporary Varro Atacinus, Germanicus (it is not clear if this is the nephew of the emperor Tiberius), possibly the emperor Gordian III, and the late antique poet Avienus.

desire to know what the gods felt: future success was impossible without the gods' approval of the present course of action.

Average Romans had access to a wide range of diviners for hire who assisted them with quotidian decisions: itinerant lot diviners, soothsayers, dream interpreters, and astrologers. Rarely are their tools and manuals preserved (see 34n. *aequatis sortibus ducuntur*). There is, however, a significant number of inscriptions that record instances when Romans had dreams or waking visions in which their gods spoke to them directly. Throughout the Roman world, there were also some temple complexes (most famously those of Asclepius) where worshippers sought medical cures revealed to them in dreams.

We have only traces of divination in daily private life, and we know almost nothing about the people who provided professional divinatory services. We are much better informed about the priests who served the Roman state. The college of augurs, of which Cicero was a member from 53 BCE until his death, practiced augury, the most distinctly Roman method of divination. Augural law laid out detailed rules for reading the *auspicia* (auspices), signs sent by Jupiter in the flight, song, and behavior of wild birds (the most comprehensive treatment is Linderski 1986). In some cases, caged domestic fowl were observed. Augury was central to Roman identity—it played a prominent role in the story of Rome's foundation and its early history—and along with sacrifice, it formed the core of most public rituals, that is, observances performed *pro populo*. As with all public priesthoods, the augurate was held in great esteem and was, in practice, open only to men who had distinguished political careers. In a letter consoling Cicero on the death of Tullia, Servius Sulpicius Rufus cast Cicero's augurate as the pinnacle of a career that had brought father and daughter much pride (*Fam.* 4.5.5 = *SBF* 248.5).

Signs requested from the gods, such as when the augurs asked the gods' approval for the opening of a military campaign or for public elections, are called impetrative (*signa impetrativa*). When the gods sent signs of their displeasure without being asked (*signa oblativa*), the Romans resorted to two other groups of priests, the *quindecimviri sacris faciundis* and the *haruspices*—usually one or the other, but occasionally both in concert. When prodigies (events that violate the natural order, like a statue bleeding or a cow talking) or natural disasters, like floods and lightning strikes, were reported to the Senate, that body would turn to the priests to learn how to appease the gods and restore the *pax deorum*, the delicately balanced relationship the Romans had with their gods. The *quindecimviri sacris faciundis* had exclusive access to the Sibylline books, a collection of prophetic utterances of the Sibyl, priestess of Apollo, in Greek hexameters compiled after the burning of the Capitoline temple in 83. This collection was a replacement for an original that was thought to have been acquired from the priestess herself by Tarquinius Priscus, the fifth king of Rome. The *haruspices*, diviners brought in from Etruria, were experts in the *Etrusca disciplina* (*haruspicina*, haruspicy), a divinatory science that dealt primarily with but was not limited to lightning strikes and signs appearing in the entrails of sacrificed animals (see 3n. *haruspicum disciplina*).

For public matters, the Romans preferred methods of divination that allowed interpretations to be tested and verified. All the forms of divination mentioned thus far are types of technical, or artificial, divination: their practice involved the application of developed principles and rules for interpreting signs. Largely absent from Roman public life were all forms of natural divination, that is, signs sent by the gods directly to men through dreams, prophetic frenzy, and inspired oracles without the use of an intermediary. There are only three instances in the history of the Roman Republic when the state was prompted to action because of an individual's dream (*Div.* 1.4 [cf. 99], 55; Granius Licinianus, *Annales* 33.22), and the Romans rarely consulted the great oracles of the Greek world for public purposes. Consultation of the Sibylline books is the closest the Roman state came to practicing natural divination on a regular basis, but even then the uncontrolled aspect of the Sibyl's prophecies was tempered by the fact that the books were brought out only when the Senate ordered it and by the fact that the Sibyl's words were selected and interpreted by a board of fifteen priests.

Cicero the Philosopher

Although young Roman aristocrats often received, in addition to traditional education in rhetoric and law, some basic training in Greek philosophy, Cicero's engagement with philosophy was greater than most of his contemporaries' (*Brut.* 306–15). Teachers were readily available in the eighties: frequent military conflicts in the East ensured a steady stream of Greek intellectuals fleeing to Rome. When Philo of Larisa, the head of the skeptical New Academy, arrived in Rome along with other Athenian refugees in around 87, Cicero quickly became a devoted student. In his writings, Cicero frequently announces his allegiance to the Academy, which preferred the suspension of judgment rather than dogmatic adherence to unfounded beliefs. Also in the eighties, Cicero studied with the Stoic Diodotus, who eventually came to live in Cicero's house. Cicero's philosophical education continued in 79/78–77, when, while on tour in the East, he attended lectures by Antiochus, now head of the New Academy at Athens, and by the Stoic Posidonius in Rhodes.

Throughout antiquity and beyond, Cicero's philosophical works were highly regarded and widely read. He fell out of favor only in the mid-nineteenth century, due partly to historian Theodor Mommsen's dismissal of Cicero's works as derivative cribbing of Greek philosophy.

> The treatise *De Republica* carries out, in a singular mongrel compound of history and philosophy, the leading idea that the existing state constitution of Rome is substantially the ideal state-organization sought for by the philosophers; an idea indeed just as unphilosophical as unhistorical . . . The scientific groundwork of these rhetorical and political writings belongs of course entirely to the Greeks. (*The History of Rome*, trans. W. P. Dickson [1898], 5.508)

Fortunately, the tide has turned, so that Cicero's philosophical writings are now recognized as having made a genuinely valuable contribution (see, e.g., the essays in Powell 1995). Cicero created a vocabulary for concepts not previously expressed in Latin that would continue to be used through the Renaissance, and he introduced the form of the philosophical dialogue into Latin. Most important, Cicero forged a distinctly Roman style of philosophy as he sought to combine philosophical argument with rhetorical virtuosity. Through his rhetorical technique and his skill at persuasion, Cicero aimed to make the learning of the Greeks accessible to his fellow Romans.

The overarching theme of Cicero's philosophical works is the effect of philosophy on human behavior and the functioning of society, though this theme plays out differently in the works from the two periods of his philosophical output. The writings from the fifties share the aim of making Greek ideas about the nature of public life and institutions accessible to a Roman audience, highlighting the role of the orator as statesman and philosopher. Cicero takes up theoretical issues raised by Plato, whom he held in the highest regard, and sets them firmly in a practical Roman context. This is seen most clearly in Cicero's *De Republica* and *De Legibus*, which were inspired by Plato's dialogues *Republic* and *Laws*. Whereas Plato discusses the ideal state and a utopian code of law, Cicero grounds his consideration of the optimal form of government and law firmly in the historical Roman Republic.

Cicero's philosophical writings from the forties stand apart from his earlier works in several respects. They make less of their Platonic models and more frequently present the arguments of rival schools of Hellenistic philosophy (the Stoics, the Epicureans, and the Academics), providing the reader with an encyclopedic introduction to the main subjects of Greek philosophical inquiry: logic (*Acad.*), ethics (*Fin.*, *Tusc.*), theology (*N. D.*, *Div.*, and *Fat.*), and physics (which, for Cicero, overlaps considerably with theology).[3] The political

---

3   Schofield 1986, 48.

relevance of treatises on the nature of the gods and the existence of free will is not obvious: we tend to think of belief as an internal matter. Cicero's decision to write on divination, not a major topic addressed by Greek philosophers, also requires some further explanation.

De Divinatione

It may seem odd that a man whose life was consumed by politics and who does not seem to have been particularly devout should turn to writing about the gods, but for the Romans, politics and religion were inextricably linked. The success of their state depended largely on the Romans' success in pleasing the gods. Theology constitutes a greater share of the philosophical oeuvre for Cicero (a total of three works written in the same period)[4] than it does for Plato and Aristotle, and Cicero was not alone among the leading men of Rome in writing on the subject.[5] The flowering of Cicero's interest in questions of religion in the midforties was due not only to his need for consolation at the death of Tullia but also to his distress over Rome's turbulent political situation.

Div. was intended, along with the now fragmentary *De Fato*, to complement Cicero's more ambitious theological project, *De Natura Deorum* (N. D. hereafter).[6] In *N. D.*, Cicero lays out Epicurean and Stoic ideas about the nature of the gods and their role in the world and subjects them to a thorough Academic critique delivered by the pontifex C. Aurelius Cotta. Cotta criticizes the Epicurean notion of gods completely removed from the concerns of men, for making the gods useless (Book 1), and he criticizes the Stoic belief that the gods actively govern the universe and take the needs of mankind into consideration,

---

4   There has been broad consensus over *Div.*'s date of composition since the evidence was compiled and assessed by R. Durand in 1903. The catalog of Cicero's philosophical works that prefaces Book 2 of *Div.* indicates that *Div.* was written after *N. D.* (which is mentioned as being in process in a letter of August 45 [*Att.* 13.38.1 = *SBA* 341]) and before *Fat.* (May–June of 44). This leaves open the question of the chronology of *Div.* and Caesar's assassination on the Ides of March, 44 BCE. In an effort to accommodate references in *Div.* to Caesar's death and several passages (e.g., 1.11) that are more sensible if they refer to a time when Caesar was still alive, Durand proposed that some, if not all, of *Div.* was composed before Caesar's death, with portions of it revised shortly thereafter.

5   For a summary of the evidence for religion and divination as subjects of intellectual investigation among Cicero's peers, see Rawson 1985, 298–316. We know of works on divination by two of Cicero's augural colleagues, Ap. Claudius (*Div.* 1.29–30) and C. Marcellus (*Div.* 2.75), and by two other late republican scholars, Tarquitius Priscus and A. Caecina, both of whom held no elected office but circulated in the highest social circles at Rome. The exact nature of these works is not known.

6   The relationship among these three works is made explicit at *Div.* 2.3.

for failing to account adequately for the ills humans suffer (Books 2–3). At the conclusion of Book 3, the character Marcus voices support for the Stoic position, though he does so in quintessentially Academic terms (*mihi Balbi ad veritatis similitudinem videretur esse propensior*, 3.95).

Div. comprises a debate, in two books, on the validity of divination. The topic had been addressed in *N. D.*, but not in great detail; Cicero's brother Quintus (on whom see 8n. *Q. fratre*) proposes at the beginning of *Div.* that they discuss divination precisely because it had received only cursory attention in *N. D.* (1.8). Cicero applies the same method he used in *N. D.*, of exposition (in Book 1) and critique (in Book 2), to the Stoic argument defending the validity of divination. The Epicureans, who dismissed divination altogether, do not appear in *Div.* Like Cicero's other dialogues, including *N. D.*, *Div.* follows an Aristotelian model that allows speakers to deliver extended speeches without interruption. Though less lively than Platonic dialogues, with their frequent interchanges among the interlocutors that allow the conversation to flow toward revelation and true understanding, the lengthy dissertations in Cicero's works give each of the two opposing schools of thought thorough treatment.

In the first book of *Div.*, Quintus makes the case for divination, arguing that he need not explain how the gods send signs to mankind, so long as he can demonstrate that they do. The belief in the existence of divination is closely tied to the Stoic notion that the gods care for the well-being of men: the gods convey information to human beings through signs in order to benefit them. Quintus's Stoic argument is subjected to skeptical critique by the figure of Marcus Cicero himself in the second book: Quintus cannot prove that any instance of divination he has adduced as evidence was not the result of coincidence, rumor, or outright fakery by the people involved.

Prior to this dialogue, divination had not often been the subject of serious philosophical inquiry, perhaps because it was not as central to civic life for the Greeks as it was for the Romans. Most of the Greek philosophers known to have treated the topic had extensive interaction with the Roman elite, and Cicero has made use of their work. There is good reason to think that Quintus's discussion draws extensively on the work of the philosophers Cratippus and Posidonius, both of whom were known to Cicero personally and are named explicitly as sources at several points (*Div.* 1.5, 70, 113, 125, 130). Their works, however, do not survive. There are points in Book 1 where Quintus also draws on Plato and Platonic sources. Marcus's reasoning in Book 2 closely follows known Academic views and criticisms of Stoic beliefs. Carneades, the leader of the skeptical Academy in the second century BCE, left no writings to posterity, but Cicero mentions Carneades's student Clitomachus in Book 2. It seems likely that Clitomachus, who wrote extensively, is the main source for the Academic counterargument. The Romanness of the dialogue comes largely from the fact that many of the *exempla* are drawn from contemporary politics and the recent past: they derive from Cicero's own experience.

OVERALL PURPOSE OF *DE DIVINATIONE* AND OF THE COMMENTARY

Div. is intended to supplement the discussion of *N. D.* by taking up divination as an important aspect of the gods' interaction with men that was not fully addressed in the earlier dialogue; indeed, Book 1 is shaped partly in response to portions of Cotta's Academic critique in *N. D.*[7] Cotta had raised two challenges for the Stoic Balbus, whose argument about the gods rested partly on examples of divination: how did divination develop, and can it really be placed alongside other *artes*, such as medicine, that can offer rational explanations for links between seemingly unrelated events and outcomes? Quintus's long speech in *Div.* 1 takes up each question. He emphasizes the antiquity and ubiquity of divination throughout his argument and repeatedly highlights that technical forms of divination were developed through observation over long periods of time (*observatione diuturna*). He provides many instances of successful divination that demonstate that valid empirical forms of divination exist and that humans also possess an ability to divine while asleep or in a frenzied state.

The traditional approach to reading *Div.* has been to dismiss Quintus's Stoic argument of Book 1 and to give priority to the Academic counterargument of the second book as a straightforward statement of Cicero's personal view that divination is nonsense. This reading of the second book draws a direct connection between the literary character Marcus and the author Cicero, a dubious methodological assumption. No rule requires that a character express the personal views of the historical person whose name he bears. Indeed, the character of Quintus in *Div.* gives the Stoic argument for divination, but the historical Quintus is known to have adhered more closely to the Peripatetic school (*Div.* 2.100; *Fin.* 5.96).

The assumption of identity between character and author in the case of *Div.* has repercussions for reading the dialogue as a whole, prompting many readers to see it as a rationalist's argument against both popular enthusiasm for divination and aristocratic manipulation of the practice for political gain. Distinguishing between the author and the character allows Book 1 to stand on par with Book 2; *Div.* then appears as an open debate that reflects the author's stated uncertainty. Cicero's decision to use himself and his brother as interlocutors can be understood as an effort to make the dialogue as intimate as possible. This aspect of *Div.* is further enhanced by Cicero's decision to have

---

7   The relationship between the treatments of divination in *N. D.* and *Div.* is laid out carefully in Wynne 2008, 138–287.

Quintus (Q. in the commentary) support his argument with many episodes from Cicero's life and many passages from his other writings. In *Div.*, Cicero comes very close to arguing with himself. To emphasize the distinction made in the commentary between the historical person and the literary character, I refer to the consul of 63 as Cicero (C. in the commentary) and to his fictional counterpart as Marcus (M. in the commentary).

This commentary strives for a more integrative reading that starts from the premise that the two books should be put on a par, and it does not overlook the fact that the dialogue does not point toward any obvious conclusion. Instead, *Div.* achieves its stated aim of offering a comparison of the arguments for and against the validity of divination (1.7), leaving readers to make up their own minds and obfuscating the question of Cicero's personal opinion. Elsewhere, when Cicero wants to suggest to his reader his own preference, he does so, as at the end of *N. D.*, where his character offers a qualified endorsement of the Stoic argument. The absence of any explicit statement of the author's opinion in *Div.* is significant. The dialogue should be understood as a debate designed to provoke reflection by the reader about the validity of a ritual practice of the utmost importance to decision making at an official level in the Roman state. Cicero is particularly concerned about the role of divination in contemporary politics, an issue that must have seemed of pressing importance in 45 and 44. His preoccupation is underscored by the prevalence of contemporary (as opposed to Greek and historical) *exempla* throughout the dialogue.

This commentary also strives for a more unified reading in another respect. Portions of *Div.* have attracted the attention of historians of religion, philologists with an interest in early republican poetry, and, to a lesser extent, philosophers. It is common for scholars to focus on a single layer of the text, such as its relationship to its philosophical predecessors. Others use it as a resource for anecdotes and fragments that contribute to arguments that do not bear on the dialogue itself. It is easy to forget that Cicero wrote *Div.* as a unified literary project that drew on his personal knowledge of a wide range of material. The present work tries to keep before the reader the multifaceted nature of the text and to consider in multiple ways the many *exempla* presented therein. Because the numerous fragments it preserves have already been treated extensively elsewhere as evidence for lost works, the emphasis here is on how they further the argument of Book 1. The result, it is hoped, is that the reader will see *Div.* as a rich and intriguing work in its own right.

Text

M. Tulli Ciceronis *De Divinatione* Liber Primus

1 Vetus opinio est iam usque ab heroicis ducta temporibus eaque et populi Romani et omnium gentium firmata consensu, versari quandam inter homines divinationem, quam Graeci μαντικὴν appellant id est praesensionem et scientiam rerum futurarum. magnifica quaedam res et salutaris, si modo est ulla, quaque proxime ad deorum vim natura mortalis possit accedere. itaque ut alia nos melius multa quam Graeci, sic huic praestantissimae rei nomen nostri a divis, Graeci ut Plato interpretatur a furore duxerunt. **2** Gentem quidem nullam video neque tam humanam atque doctam neque tam inmanem tamque barbaram, quae non significari futura et a quibusdam intellegi praedicique posse censeat. principio Assyrii, ut ab ultumis auctoritatem repetam, propter planitiam magnitudinemque regionum quas incolebant, cum caelum ex omni parte patens atque apertum intuerentur, traiectiones motusque stellarum observitaverunt, quibus notatis quid cuique significaretur memoriae prodiderunt. qua in natione Chaldaei non ex artis sed ex gentis vocabulo nominati diuturna observatione siderum scientiam putantur effecisse, ut praedici posset quid cuique eventurum et quo quisque fato natus esset. eandem artem etiam Aegyptii longinquitate temporum innumerabilibus paene saeculis consecuti putantur. Cilicum autem et Pisidarum gens et his finituma Pamphylia, quibus nationibus praefuimus ipsi, volatibus avium cantibusque certissimis signis declarari res futuras putant. **3** quam vero Graecia coloniam misit in Aeoliam Ioniam Asiam Siciliam Italiam sine Pythio aut Dodonaeo aut Hammonis oraculo, aut quod bellum susceptum ab ea sine consilio deorum est?

Nec unum genus est divinationis publice privatimque celebratum. nam ut omittam ceteros populos, noster quam multa genera conplexus est! principio huius urbis parens Romulus non solum auspicato urbem condidisse sed ipse etiam optumus augur fuisse traditur. deinde auguribus et reliqui reges usi et exactis regibus nihil publice sine auspiciis nec domi nec militiae gerebatur. cumque magna vis videretur esse et inpetriendis consulendisque rebus et monstris interpretandis ac procurandis in haruspicum disciplina, omnem hanc ex Etruria scientiam adhibebant, ne genus esset ullum divinationis quod neglectum ab iis videretur. **4** et cum duobus modis animi sine ratione et scientia motu ipsi suo soluto et libero incitarentur, uno furente altero somniante, furoris divinationem Sibyllinis maxume versibus contineri arbitrati eorum decem interpretes delectos e civitate esse voluerunt. ex quo genere saepe hariolorum etiam et vatum furibundas praedictiones, ut Octaviano bello Cornelii Culleoli, audiendas putaverunt. nec vero somnia graviora, si quae ad rem publicam pertinere visa sunt, a summo consilio neglecta sunt. quin etiam memoria nostra templum Iunonis Sospitae L. Iulius, qui cum P. Rutilio consul fuit, de senatus sententia refecit ex Caeciliae Baliarici filiae somnio.

5 Atque haec, ut ego arbitror, veteres rerum magis eventis moniti quam ratione docti probaverunt. philosophorum vero exquisita quaedam argumenta cur esset vera divinatio collecta sunt; e quibus, ut de antiquissumis loquar, Colophonius Xenophanes unus qui deos esse diceret divinationem funditus sustulit, reliqui vero omnes praeter Epicurum balbutientem de natura deorum divinationem probaverunt, sed non uno modo. nam cum Socrates omnesque Socratici Zenoque et ii qui ab eo essent profecti manerent in antiquorum philosophorum sententia vetere Academia et Peripateticis consentientibus, cumque huic rei magnam auctoritatem Pythagoras iam ante tribuisset, qui etiam ipse augur vellet esse, plurimisque locis gravis auctor Democritus praesensionem rerum futurarum conprobaret, Dicaearchus Peripateticus cetera divinationis genera sustulit, somniorum et furoris reliquit, Cratippusque familiaris noster, quem ego parem summis Peripateticis iudico, isdem rebus fidem tribuit, reliqua divinationis genera reiecit. **6** sed cum Stoici omnia fere illa defenderent, quod et Zeno in suis commentariis quasi semina quaedam sparsisset et ea Cleanthes paulo uberiora fecisset, accessit acerrumo vir ingenio Chrysippus, qui totam de divinatione duobus libris explicavit sententiam, uno praeterea de oraclis, uno de somniis; quem subsequens unum librum Babylonius Diogenes edidit eius auditor, duo Antipater, quinque noster Posidonius. sed a Stoicis vel princeps eius disciplinae, Posidoni doctor, discipulus Antipatri degeneravit Panaetius nec tamen ausus est negare vim esse divinandi, sed dubitare se dixit. Quod illi in aliqua re invitissumis Stoicis Stoico facere licuit, id nos ut in reliquis rebus faciamus a Stoicis non concedetur? praesertim cum id, de quo Panaetio non liquet, reliquis eiusdem disciplinae solis luce videatur clarius. **7** sed haec quidem laus Academiae praestantissumi philosophi iudicio et testimonio conprobata est. etenim nobismet ipsis quaerentibus, quid sit de divinatione iudicandum, quod a Carneade multa acute et copiose contra Stoicos disputata sint, verentibusque ne temere vel falsae rei vel non satis cognitae adsentiamur, faciendum videtur ut diligenter etiam atque etiam argumenta cum argumentis comparemus,

ut fecimus in iis tribus libris quos de natura deorum scripsimus. nam cum
omnibus in rebus temeritas in adsentiendo errorque turpis est tum in eo
loco maxime, in quo iudicandum est quantum auspiciis rebusque divinis
religionique tribuamus; est enim periculum ne aut neglectis iis impia fraude
aut susceptis anili superstitione obligemur.

8 Quibus de rebus et alias saepe et paulo accuratius nuper cum essem
cum Q. fratre in Tusculano disputatum est. nam cum ambulandi causa in
Lyceum venissemus (id enim superiori gymnasio nomen est), "perlegi" ille
inquit "tuum paulo ante tertium de natura deorum, in quo disputatio Cottae
quamquam labefactavit sententiam meam, non funditus tamen sustulit."
"Optime vero" inquam; "etenim ipse Cotta sic disputat ut Stoicorum magis
argumenta confutet quam hominum deleat religionem." Tum Quintus
"dicitur quidem istud" inquit "a Cotta et vero saepius, credo ne communia
iura migrare videatur; sed studio contra Stoicos disserendi deos mihi videtur
funditus tollere. 9 eius orationi non sane desidero quid respondeam; satis
enim defensa religio est in secundo libro a Lucilio, cuius disputatio tibi
ipsi, ut in extremo tertio scribis, ad veritatem est visa propensior. Sed quod
praetermissum est in illis libris, credo quia commodius arbitratus es separatim
id quaeri deque eo disseri, id est de divinatione, quae est earum rerum quae
fortuitae putantur praedictio atque praesensio, id si placet videamus quam
habeat vim et quale sit. ego enim sic existimo, si sint ea genera divinandi vera
de quibus accepimus quaeque colimus, esse deos, vicissimque si di sint, esse
qui divinent." 10 "Arcem tu quidem Stoicorum" inquam "Quinte defendis,
siquidem ista sic reciprocantur, ut et si divinatio sit, di sint, et si di sint, sit
divinatio. quorum neutrum tam facile quam tu arbitraris conceditur. nam et
natura significari futura sine deo possunt, et ut sint di, potest fieri ut nulla ab
iis divinatio generi humano tributa sit." Atque ille "mihi vero" inquit "satis
est argumenti et esse deos et eos consulere rebus humanis, quod esse clara et
perspicua divinationis genera iudico. de quibus quid ipse sentiam si placet
exponam, ita tamen si vacas animo neque habes aliquid quod huic sermoni
praevertendum putes." 11 "Ego vero" inquam "philosophiae Quinte semper
vaco; hoc autem tempore cum sit nihil aliud quod lubenter agere possim,
multo magis aveo audire de divinatione quid sentias."

"Nihil" inquit "equidem novi nec quod praeter ceteros ipse sentiam;
nam cum antiquissimam sententiam tum omnium populorum et gentium
consensu conprobatam sequor. duo sunt enim divinandi genera, quorum
alterum artis est alterum naturae. 12 quae est autem gens aut quae civitas,
quae non aut extispicum aut monstra aut fulgora interpretantium aut
augurum aut astrologorum aut sortium (ea enim fere artis sunt) aut
somniorum aut vaticinationum (haec enim duo naturalia putantur)
praedictione moveatur? Quarum quidem rerum eventa magis arbitror quam

causas quaeri oportere. est enim vis et natura quaedam, quae tum observatis longo tempore significationibus tum aliquo instinctu inflatuque divino futura praenuntiat. quare omittat urguere Carneades, quod faciebat etiam Panaetius, requirens Iuppiterne cornicem a laeva corvum ab dextera canere iussisset. observata sunt haec tempore inmenso et in significatione eventus animadversa et notata. nihil est autem quod non longinquitas temporum excipiente memoria prodendisque monumentis efficere atque adsequi possit. **13** Mirari licet quae sint animadversa a medicis herbarum genera, quae radicum ad morsus bestiarum ad oculorum morbos ad vulnera, quorum vim atque naturam ratio numquam explicavit, utilitate et ars est et inventor probatus. age ea quae quamquam ex alio genere sunt tamen divinationi sunt similiora videamus:

> atque etiam ventos praemonstrat saepe futuros
> inflatum mare, cum subito penitusque tumescit
> saxaque cana salis niveo spumat a liquore
> tristificas certant Neptuno reddere voces
> aut densus stridor cum celso e vertice montis
> ortus adaugescit scopulorum saepe repulsus.

atque his rerum praesensionibus prognostica tua referta sunt. quis igitur elicere causas praesensionum potest? etsi video Boëthum Stoicum esse conatum, qui hactenus aliquid egit, ut earum rationem rerum explicaret quae in mari caelove fierent. **14** illa vero cur eveniant quis probabiliter dixerit:

> cana fulix itidem fugiens e gurgite ponti
> nuntiat horribilis clamans instare procellas
> haud modicos tremulo fundens e guttere cantus.
> saepe etiam pertriste canit de pectore carmen
> et matutinis acredula vocibus instat,
> vocibus instat et adsiduas iacit ore querellas,
> cum primum gelidos rores aurora remittit.
> fuscaque non numquam cursans per litora cornix
> demersit caput et fluctum cervice recepit.

15 videmus haec signa numquam fere mentientia nec tamen cur ita fiat videmus.

> vos quoque signa videtis, aquai dulcis alumnae,
> cum clamore paratis inanis fundere voces
> absurdoque sono fontis et stagna cietis.

quis est, qui ranunculos hoc videre suspicari possit? sed inest in ranunculis vis
et natura quaedam significans aliquid per se ipsa satis certa, cognitioni autem
hominum obscurior.

> mollipedesque boves spectantes lumina caeli
> naribus umiferum duxere ex aere sucum.

non quaero cur, quoniam quid eveniat intellego.

> iam vero semper viridis semperque gravata
> lentiscus triplici solita grandescere fetu
> ter fruges fundens tria tempora monstrat arandi.

16 ne hoc quidem quaero, cur haec arbor una ter floreat aut cur arandi
maturitatem ad signum floris accommodet; hoc sum contentus, quod etiamsi
cur quidque fiat ignorem, quid fiat intellego. Pro omni igitur divinatione idem
quod pro rebus iis quas commemoravi respondebo. quid scammoneae radix
ad purgandum, quid aristolochia ad morsus serpentium possit, quae nomen
ex inventore repperit, rem ipsam inventor ex somnio,—posse video, quod
satis est; cur possit nescio. sic ventorum et imbrium signa quae dixi rationem
quam habeant non satis perspicio; vim et eventum agnosco scio adprobo.
similiter quid fissum in extis quid fibra valeat accipio; quae causa sit nescio.
atque horum quidem plena vita est; extis enim omnes fere utuntur. Quid, de
fulgurum vi dubitare num possumus? nonne cum multa alia mirabilia tum
illud in primis: cum Summanus in fastigio Iovis optumi maxumi, qui tum
erat fictilis, e caelo ictus esset nec usquam eius simulacri caput inveniretur,
haruspices in Tiberim id depulsum esse dixerunt, idque inventum est eo loco
qui est ab haruspicibus demonstratus. **17** Sed quo potius utar aut auctore aut
teste quam te, cuius edidici etiam versus et lubenter quidem, quos in secundo
consulatu⟨s⟩ Urania Musa pronuntiat:

> principio aetherio flammatus Iuppiter igni
> vertitur et totum conlustrat lumine mundum
> menteque divina caelum terrasque petessit,
> quae penitus sensus hominum vitasque retentat
> aetheris aeterni saepta atque inclusa cavernis.
> et si stellarum motus cursusque vagantis
> nosse velis, quae sint signorum in sede locatae,
> quae verbo et falsis Graiorum vocibus errant
> re vera certo lapsu spatioque feruntur,
> omnia iam cernes divina mente notata.

18 nam primum astrorum volucris te consule motus
concursusque gravis stellarum ardore micantis
tu quoque, cum tumulos Albano in monte nivalis
lustrasti et laeto mactasti lacte Latinas,
vidisti et claro tremulos ardore cometas
multaque misceri nocturna strage putasti,
quod ferme dirum in tempus cecidere Latinae,
cum claram speciem concreto lumine luna
abdidit et subito stellanti nocte perempta est.
quid vero Phoebi fax tristis nuntia belli
quae magnum ad columen flammato ardore volabat
praecipitis caeli partis obitusque petessens;
aut cum terribili perculsus fulmine civis
luce serenanti vitalia lumina liquit;
aut cum se gravido tremefecit corpore tellus.
iam vero variae nocturno tempore visae
terribiles formae bellum motusque monebant
multaque per terras vates oracla furenti
pectore fundebant tristis minitantia casus
19 atque ea, quae lapsu tandem cecidere vetusto,
haec fore perpetuis signis clarisque frequentans
ipse deum genitor caelo terrisque canebat.
nunc ea, Torquato quae quondam et consule Cotta
Lydius ediderat Tyrrhenae gentis haruspex,
omnia fixa tuus glomerans determinat annus.
nam pater altitonans stellanti nixus Olympo
ipse suos quondam tumulos ac templa petivit
et Capitolinis iniecit sedibus ignis.
tum species ex aere vetus venerataque Nattae
concidit elapsaeque vetusto numine leges
et divom simulacra peremit fulminis ardor.
20 hic silvestris erat Romani nominis altrix
Martia, quae parvos Mavortis semine natos
uberibus gravidis vitali rore rigabat;
quae tum cum pueris flammato fulminis ictu
concidit atque avolsa pedum vestigia liquit.
tum quis non artis scripta ac monumenta volutans
voces tristificas chartis promebat Etruscis?
omnes civilem generosa a stirpe profectam
volvier in gentem cladem pestemque monebant.
tum legum exitium constanti voce ferebant

templa deumque adeo flammis urbemque iubebant
eripere et stragem horribilem caedemque vereri;
atque haec fixa gravi fato ac fundata teneri,
ni prius excelsum ad columen formata decore
sancta Iovis species claros spectaret in ortus.
tum fore ut occultos populus sanctusque senatus
cernere conatus posset, si solis ad ortum
convorsa inde patrum sedes populique videret.
21 haec tardata diu species multumque morata
consule te tandem celsa est in sede locata
atque una fixi ac signati temporis hora
Iuppiter excelsa clarabat sceptra columna
et clades patriae flamma ferroque parata
vocibus Allobrogum patribus populoque patebat.
rite igitur veteres quorum monumenta tenetis
qui populos urbisque modo ac virtute regebant,
rite etiam vestri quorum pietasque fidesque
praestitit et longe vicit sapientia cunctos,
praecipue coluere vigenti numine divos.
haec adeo penitus cura videre sagaci,
otia qui studiis laeti tenuere decoris,
22 inque Academia umbrifera nitidoque Lyceo
fuderunt claras fecundi pectoris artis.
e quibus ereptum primo iam a flore iuventae
te patria in media virtutum mole locavit.
tu tamen anxiferas curas requiete relaxans
quod patriae vacat his studiis nobisque sacrasti.

tu igitur animum poteris inducere contra ea, quae a me disputantur de divinatione, dicere, qui et gesseris ea quae gessisti, et ea quae pronuntiavi accuratissume scripseris? 23 quid, quaeris, Carneades, cur haec ita fiant aut qua arte perspici possint? nescire me fateor, evenire autem te ipsum dico videre. 'casu' inquis. itane vero, quidquam potest casu esse factum, quod omnes habet in se numeros veritatis? quattuor tali iacti casu Venerium efficiunt: num etiam centum Venerios, si quadringentos talos ieceris, casu futuros putas? aspersa temere pigmenta in tabula oris liniamenta efficere possunt: num etiam Veneris Coae pulchritudinem effici posse aspersione fortuita putas? sus rostro si humi A litteram inpresserit, num propterea suspicari poteris Andromacham Enni ab ea posse describi? fingebat Carneades in Chiorum lapicidinis saxo diffisso caput extitisse Panisci: credo aliquam non dissimilem figuram, sed certe non talem ut eam factam a Scopa diceres. sic enim se profecto res habet, ut numquam perfecte veritatem casus imitetur.

24 'At non numquam ea quae praedicta sunt minus eveniunt.' quae tandem id ars non habet, earum dico artium, quae coniectura continentur et sunt opinabiles. an medicina ars non putanda est? quam tamen multa fallunt. quid, gubernatores nonne falluntur? an Achivorum exercitus et tot navium rectores non ita profecti sunt ab Ilio, ut 'profectione laeti piscium lasciviam intuerentur,' ut ait Pacuvius, 'nec tuendi satietas capere posset?

> interea prope iam occidente sole inhorrescit mare,
> tenebrae conduplicantur noctisque et nimbum occaecat nigror.'

num igitur tot clarissimorum ducum regumque naufragium sustulit artem gubernandi? aut num imperatorum scientia nihil est, quia summus imperator nuper fugit amisso exercitu? aut num propterea nulla est rei publicae gerendae ratio atque prudentia, quia multa Cn. Pompeium quaedam M. Catonem non nulla etiam te ipsum fefellerunt? similis est haruspicum responsio omnisque opinabilis divinatio; coniectura enim nititur, ultra quam progredi non potest. 25 ea fallit fortasse non numquam, sed tamen ad veritatem saepissime dirigit; est enim ab omni aeternitate repetita, in qua cum paene innumerabiliter res eodem modo evenirent isdem signis antegressis, ars est effecta eadem saepe animadvertendo ac notando.

Auspicia vero vestra quam constant, quae quidem nunc a Romanis auguribus ignorantur (bona hoc tua venia dixerim), a Cilicibus Pamphyliis Pisidis Lyciis tenentur. 26 nam quid ego hospitem nostrum clarissumum atque optumum virum Deiotarum regem commemorem, qui nihil umquam nisi auspicato gerit. qui cum ex itinere quodam proposito et constituto revertisset aquilae admonitus volatu, conclave illud, ubi erat mansurus si ire perrexisset, proxima nocte corruit. 27 itaque, ut ex ipso audiebam, persaepe revertit ex itinere, cum iam progressus esset multorum dierum viam. cuius quidem hoc praeclarissimum est, quod posteaquam a Caesare tetrarchia et regno pecuniaque multatus est, negat se tamen eorum auspiciorum quae sibi ad Pompeium proficiscenti secunda evenerint paenitere; senatus enim auctoritatem et populi Romani libertatem atque imperii dignitatem suis armis esse defensam, sibique eas aves quibus auctoribus officium et fidem secutus esset bene consuluisse; antiquiorem enim sibi fuisse possessionibus suis gloriam. ille mihi videtur igitur vere augurari. nam nostri quidem magistratus auspiciis utuntur coactis: necesse est enim offa obiecta cadere frustum ex pulli ore cum pascitur; 28 quod autem scriptum habetis * aut tripudium fieri, si ex ea quid in solidum ceciderit, hoc quoque quod dixi coactum tripudium solistimum dicitis. itaque multa auguria multa auspicia, quod Cato ille sapiens queritur, neglegentia collegii amissa plane et deserta sunt.

Nihil fere quondam maioris rei nisi auspicato ne privatim quidem gerebatur, quod etiam nunc nuptiarum auspices declarant, qui re omissa nomen tantum tenent. nam ut nunc extis, quamquam id ipsum aliquanto minus quam olim, sic tum avibus magnae res inpetriri solebant. itaque sinistra dum non exquirimus, in dira et in vitiosa incurrimus. **29** ut P. Claudius Appi Caeci filius eiusque collega L. Iunius classis maxumas perdiderunt, cum vitio navigassent. quod eodem modo evenit Agamemnoni, qui, cum Achivi coepissent

> inter se strepere aperteque artem obterere extispicum,
> solvere imperat secundo rumore adversaque avi.

sed quid vetera? M. Crasso quid acciderit, videmus, dirarum obnuntiatione neglecta. in quo Appius collega tuus bonus augur, ut ex te audire soleo, non satis scienter virum bonum et civem egregium censor C. Ateium notavit, quod ementitum auspicia subscriberet. esto, fuerit hoc censoris, si iudicabat ementitum; at illud minime auguris, quod adscripsit ob eam causam populum Romanum calamitatem maximam cepisse. si enim ea causa calamitatis fuit, non in eo est culpa qui obnuntiavit, sed in eo qui non paruit. veram enim fuisse obnuntiationem, ut ait idem augur et censor, exitus adprobavit; quae si falsa fuisset, nullam adferre potuisset causam calamitatis. etenim dirae, sicut cetera auspicia ut omina ut signa, non causas adferunt cur quid eveniat, sed nuntiant eventura nisi provideris. **30** non igitur obnuntiatio Atei causam finxit calamitatis, sed signo obiecto monuit Crassum quid eventurum esset nisi cavisset. ita aut illa obnuntiatio nihil valuit, aut si, ut Appius iudicat, valuit, id valuit ut peccatum haereat non in eo qui monuerit, sed in eo qui non obtemperarit.

Quid, lituus iste vester, quod clarissumum est insigne auguratus, unde vobis est traditus? nempe eo Romulus regiones direxit tum cum urbem condidit. qui quidem Romuli lituus [id est incurvum et leviter a summo inflexum bacillum, quod ab eius litui quo canitur similitudine nomen invenit], cum situs esset in curia Saliorum quae est in Palatio eaque deflagravisset, inventus est integer. **31** quid, multis annis post Romulum Prisco regnante Tarquinio quis veterum scriptorum non loquitur, quae sit ab Atto Navio per lituum regionum facta discriptio. qui cum propter paupertatem sues puer pasceret, una ex iis amissa vovisse dicitur, si recuperasset, uvam se deo daturum quae maxima esset in vinea; itaque sue inventa ad meridiem spectans in vinea media dicitur constitisse cumque in quattuor partes vineam divisisset trisque partis aves abdixissent, quarta parte quae erat reliqua in regiones distributa mirabili magnitudine uvam, ut scriptum videmus, invenit. qua re celebrata cum vicini omnes ad eum de rebus suis referrent, erat in magno nomine et gloria. 32 ex quo factum est ut eum ad se rex Priscus arcesseret. cuius cum temptaret scientiam auguratus, dixit ei cogitare se quiddam; id possetne fieri consuluit. ille augurio acto posse respondit. Tarquinius autem dixit se cogitasse cotem novacula posse praecidi. tum Attum iussisse experiri. ita cotem in comitium allatam inspectante et rege et populo novacula esse discissam. ex eo evenit ut et Tarquinius augure Atto Navio uteretur et populus de suis rebus ad eum referret. 33 cotem autem illam et novaculam defossam in comitio supraque inpositum puteal accepimus.

Negemus omnia, comburamus annales, ficta haec esse dicamus, quidvis denique potius quam deos res humanas curare fateamur; quid, quod scriptum apud te est de Tiberio Graccho nonne et augurum et haruspicum conprobat disciplinam? qui cum tabernaculum vitio cepisset inprudens, quod inauspicato pomerium transgressus esset, comitia consulibus rogandis habuit. nota res est et a te ipso mandata monumentis. sed et ipse augur Tiberius Gracchus auspiciorum auctoritatem confessione errati sui conprobavit et haruspicum disciplinae magna accessit auctoritas, qui recentibus comitiis in senatum introducti negaverunt iustum comitiorum rogatorem fuisse.

34 Iis igitur adsentior qui duo genera divinationum esse dixerunt, unum quod particeps esset artis, alterum quod arte careret. Est enim ars in iis qui novas res coniectura persequuntur, veteres observatione didicerunt. Carent autem arte ii qui non ratione aut coniectura observatis ac notatis signis sed concitatione quadam animi aut soluto liberoque motu futura praesentiunt, quod et somniantibus saepe contigit et non numquam vaticinantibus per furorem, ut Bacis Boeotius ut Epimenides Cres ut Sibylla Erythraea. cuius generis oracla etiam habenda sunt, non ea quae aequatis sortibus ducuntur, sed illa quae instinctu divino adflatuque funduntur; etsi ipsa sors contemnenda non est, si et auctoritatem habet vetustatis, ut eae sunt sortes quas e terra editas accepimus; quae tamen ductae ut in rem apte cadant, fieri credo posse divinitus. quorum omnium interpretes, ut grammatici poetarum, proxume ad eorum quos interpretantur divinationem videntur accedere. 35 Quae est igitur ista calliditas res vetustate robustas calumniando velle pervertere? 'Non reperio causam.' latet fortasse obscuritate involuta naturae; non enim me deus ista scire sed his tantum modo uti voluit. utar igitur nec adducar aut in extis totam Etruriam delirare aut eandem gentem in fulgoribus errare aut fallaciter portenta interpretari, cum terrae saepe fremitus saepe mugitus saepe motus multa nostrae rei publicae, multa ceteris civitatibus gravia et vera praedixerint. 36 quid, qui inridetur partus hic mulae nonne, quia fetus extitit in sterilitate naturae, praedictus est ab haruspicibus

incredibilis partus malorum? quid, Tib. Gracchus P. filius qui bis consul
et censor fuit idemque et summus augur et vir sapiens civisque praestans,
nonne, ut C. Gracchus filius eius scriptum reliquit, duobus anguibus domi
conprehensis haruspices convocavit? qui cum respondissent, si marem
emisisset, uxori brevi tempore esse moriendum, si feminam, ipsi, aequius esse
censuit se maturam oppetere mortem quam P. Africani filiam adulescentem:
feminam emisit, ipse paucis post diebus est mortuus. Inrideamus haruspices,
vanos futtiles esse dicamus, quorumque disciplinam et sapientissimus vir et
eventus ac res conprobavit, contemnamus, ⟨condemnemus⟩ etiam Babylonem
et eos qui e Caucaso caeli signa servantes numeris [et motibus] stellarum
cursus persequuntur, condemnemus inquam hos aut stultitiae aut vanitatis
aut inpudentiae qui quadringenta septuaginta milia annorum ut ipsi dicunt
monumentis conprehensa continent, et mentiri iudicemus nec saeculorum
reliquorum iudicium quod de ipsis futurum sit pertimescere. **37** age barbari
vani atque fallaces; num etiam Graiorum historia mentita est? quae Croeso
Pythius Apollo, ut de naturali divinatione dicam, quae Atheniensibus quae
Lacedaemoniis quae Tegeatis quae Argivis quae Corinthiis responderit quis
ignorat? collegit innumerabilia oracula Chrysippus nec ullum sine locuplete
auctore atque teste; quae quia nota tibi sunt relinquo, defendo unum hoc:
numquam illud oraclum Delphis tam celebre et tam clarum fuisset neque
tantis donis refertum omnium populorum atque regum, nisi omnis aetas
oraclorum illorum veritatem esset experta. 'Idem iam diu non facit.' **38** Ut
igitur nunc minore gloria est, quia minus oraculorum veritas excellit, sic
tum nisi summa veritate in tanta gloria non fuisset. potest autem vis illa
terrae quae mentem Pythiae divino adflatu concitabat evanuisse vetustate,
ut quosdam evanuisse et exaruisse amnes aut in alium cursum contortos
et deflexos videmus. sed, ut vis, acciderit, magna enim quaestio est; modo
maneat id quod negari non potest nisi omnem historiam perverterimus,
multis saeclis verax fuisse id oraculum.

39 Sed omittamus oracula, veniamus ad somnia. de quibus disputans
Chrysippus multis et minutis somniis colligendis facit idem quod Antipater ea
conquirens, quae Antiphontis interpretatione explicata declarant illa quidem
acumen interpretis, sed exemplis grandioribus decuit uti. Dionysi mater eius
qui Syracosiorum tyrannus fuit, ut scriptum apud Philistum est et doctum
hominem et diligentem et aequalem temporum illorum, cum praegnans
hunc ipsum Dionysium alvo contineret, somniavit se peperisse satyriscum.
huic interpretes portentorum, qui galeotae tum in Sicilia nominabantur,
responderunt, ut ait Philistus, eum quem illa peperisset clarissimum Graeciae
diuturna cum fortuna fore. **40** Num te ad fabulas revoco vel nostrorum vel
Graecorum poetarum? narrat enim et apud Ennium Vestalis illa:

Et cita cum tremulis anus attulit artubus lumen.
talia tum memorat lacrimans exterrita somno:
'Eurydica prognata, pater quam noster amavit,
vires vitaque corpus meum nunc deserit omne.
nam me visus homo pulcher per amoena salicta
et ripas raptare locosque novos; ita sola
postilla, germana soror, errare videbar
tardaque vestigare et quaerere te neque posse
corde capessere; semita nulla pedem stabilibat.
41 exim compellare pater me voce videtur
his verbis: "O gnata, tibi sunt ante gerendae
aerumnae, post ex fluvio fortuna resistet."
haec ecfatus pater, germana, repente recessit
nec sese dedit in conspectum corde cupitus,
quamquam multa manus ad caeli caerula templa
tendebam lacrumans et blanda voce vocabam.
vix aegro cum corde meo me somnus reliquit.'

42 haec etiamsi ficta sunt a poeta, non absunt tamen a consuetudine somniorum. sit sane etiam illud commenticium quo Priamus est conturbatus, quia

. . . mater gravida parere ⟨ex⟩ se ardentem facem
visa est in somnis Hecuba; quo facto pater
rex ipse Priamus somnio mentis metu
perculsus curis sumptus suspirantibus
exsacrificabat hostiis balantibus.
tum coniecturam postulat pacem petens,
ut se edoceret obsecrans Apollinem
quo sese vertant tantae sortes somnium.
ibi ex oraclo voce divina edidit
Apollo puerum primus Priamo qui foret
postilla natus temperaret tollere:
eum esse exitium Troiae, pestem Pergamo.

43 sint haec ut dixi somnia fabularum, hisque adiungatur etiam Aeneae somnium, quod in nostri Fabi Pictoris Graecis annalibus eius modi est ut omnia quae ab Aenea gesta sunt quaeque illi acciderunt ea fuerint quae ei secundum quietem visa sunt.

Sed propiora videamus. cuiusnam modi est Superbi Tarquini somnium, de quo in Bruto Acci loquitur ipse?

44 quoniam quieti corpus nocturno inpetu
dedi sopore placans artus languidos,
visust in somnis pastor ad me appellere
pecus lanigerum eximia pulchritudine;
duos consanguineos arietes inde eligi
praeclarioremque alterum immolare me;
deinde eius germanum cornibus conitier
in me arietare eoque ictu me ad casum dari;
exin prostratum terra, graviter saucium,
resupinum in caelo contueri maximum ac
mirificum facinus: dextrorsum orbem flammeum
radiatum solis linquier cursu novo.

45 eius igitur somnii a coniectoribus quae sit interpretatio facta, videamus:

rex, quae in vita usurpant homines cogitant curant vident
quaeque agunt vigilantes agitantque, ea si cui in somno accidunt,
minus mirandum est; sed in re tanta haut temere inproviso offerunt.
proin vide ne quem tu esse hebetem deputes aeque ac pecus
is sapientia munitum pectus egregium gerat
teque regno expellat; nam id quod de sole ostentum est tibi,
populo commutationem rerum portendit fore
perpropinquam. haec bene verruncent populo. nam quod ad dexteram
cepit cursum ab laeva signum praepotens, pulcherrume
auguratum est rem Romanam publicam summam fore.

46 Age nunc ad externa redeamus. matrem Phalaridis scribit Ponticus
Heraclides doctus vir auditor et discipulus Platonis visam esse videre in
somnis simulacra deorum quae ipsa domi consecravisset; ex is Mercurium
e patera quam dextera manu teneret sanguinem visum esse fundere, qui
cum terram attigisset refervescere videretur sic ut tota domus sanguine
redundaret. quod matris somnium inmanis filii crudelitas conprobavit. quid
ego quae magi Cyro illi principi interpretati sint ex Dinonis Persicis libris
proferam? nam cum dormienti ei sol ad pedes visus esset, ter eum scribit
frustra adpetivisse manibus, cum se convolvens sol elaberetur et abiret; ei
magos dixisse, quod genus sapientium et doctorum habebatur in Persis, ex
triplici adpetitione solis XXX annos Cyrum regnaturum esse portendi. quod
ita contigit, nam ad septuagesimum pervenit, cum quadraginta natus annos
regnare coepisset.
47 Est profecto quiddam etiam in barbaris gentibus praesentiens atque
divinans, siquidem ad mortem proficiscens Callanus Indus cum inscenderet

in rogum ardentem 'o praeclarum discessum' inquit 'e vita, cum, ut Herculi contigit, mortali corpore cremato in lucem animus excesserit'; cumque Alexander eum rogaret si quid vellet ut diceret, 'optume,' inquit 'propediem te videbo.' quod ita contigit, nam Babylone paucis post diebus Alexander est mortuus. (discedo parumper a somniis, ad quae mox revertar.) qua nocte templum Ephesiae Dianae deflagravit, eadem constat ex Olympiade natum esse Alexandrum, atque ubi lucere coepisset clamitasse magos pestem ac perniciem Asiae proxuma nocte natam. Haec de Indis et magis. redeamus ad somnia.

48 Hannibalem Coelius scribit, cum columnam auream, quae esset in fano Iunonis Laciniae, auferre vellet dubitaretque utrum ea solida esset an extrinsecus inaurata, perterebravisse cumque solidam invenisset statuisse tollere; ei secundum quietem visam esse Iunonem praedicere ne id faceret, minarique si fecisset se curaturam ut eum quoque oculum quo bene videret amitteret, idque ab homine acuto non esse neglectum, itaque ex eo auro quod exterebratum esset buculam curasse faciendam et eam in summa columna conlocavisse. **49** hoc item in Sileni, quem Coelius sequitur, Graeca historia est (is autem diligentissume res Hannibalis persecutus est): Hannibalem, cum cepisset Saguntum, visum esse in somnis a Iove in deorum concilium vocari; quo cum venisset, Iovem imperavisse ut Italiae bellum inferret, ducemque ei unum e concilio datum, quo illum utentem cum exercitu progredi coepisse; tum ei ducem illum praecepisse ne respiceret; illum autem id diutius facere non potuisse elatumque cupiditate respexisse; tum visam beluam vastam et immanem circumplicatam serpentibus quacumque incederet omnia arbusta virgulta tecta pervertere; et eum admiratum quaesisse de deo quodnam illud esset tale monstrum; et deum respondisse vastitatem esse Italiae praecepisseque ut pergeret protinus, quid retro atque a tergo fieret ne laboraret. **50** Apud Agathoclem scriptum in historia est Hamilcarem Carthaginiensem, cum oppugnaret Syracusas, visum esse audire vocem se postridie cenaturum Syracusis; cum autem is dies inluxisset, magnam seditionem in castris eius inter Poenos et Siculos milites esse factam; quod cum sensissent Syracusani, inproviso eos in castra inrupisse Hamilcaremque ab iis vivum esse sublatum. ita res somnium conprobavit. (Plena exemplorum est historia, tum referta vita communis.) **51** At vero P. Decius ille Quinti f., qui primus e Deciis consul fuit, cum esset tribunus militum M. Valerio A. Cornelio cos. a Samnitibusque premeretur noster exercitus, cum pericula proeliorum iniret audacius monereturque ut cautior esset, dixit, quod extat in annalibus, ⟨se⟩ sibi in somnis visum esse, cum in mediis hostibus versaretur, occidere cum maxuma gloria. et tum quidem incolumis exercitum obsidione liberavit; post triennium autem cum consul esset devovit se et in aciem

Latinorum inrupit armatus. quo eius facto superati sunt et deleti Latini. cuius mors ita gloriosa fuit, ut eandem concupisceret filius.

52 Sed veniamus nunc, si placet, ad somnia philosophorum. Est apud Platonem Socrates, cum esset in custodia publica, dicens Critoni suo familiari sibi post tertium diem esse moriendum; vidisse se in somnis pulchritudine eximia feminam, quae se nomine appellans diceret Homericum quendam eius modi versum:

Tertia te Phthiae tempestas laeta locabit.

quod ut est dictum sic scribitur contigisse. Xenophon Socraticus, qui vir et quantus, in ea militia, qua cum Cyro minore perfunctus est, sua scribit somnia quorum eventus mirabiles extiterunt. 53 mentiri Xenophontem an delirare dicemus? Quid, singulari vir ingenio Aristoteles et paene divino ipsene errat an alios vult errare, cum scribit Eudemum Cyprium familiarem suum iter in Macedoniam facientem Pheras venisse, quae erat urbs in Thessalia tum admodum nobilis, ab Alexandro autem tyranno crudeli dominatu tenebatur; in eo igitur oppido ita graviter aegrum Eudemum fuisse, ut omnes medici diffiderent; ei visum in quiete egregia facie iuvenem dicere fore ut perbrevi convalesceret, paucisque diebus interiturum Alexandrum tyrannum, ipsum autem Eudemum quinquennio post domum esse rediturum. atque illa quidem prima statim scribit Aristoteles consecuta et convaluisse Eudemum et ab uxoris fratribus interfectum tyrannum; quinto autem anno exeunte, cum esset spes ex illo somnio in Cyprum illum ex Sicilia esse rediturum, proeliantem eum ad Syracusas occidisse; ex quo ita illud somnium esse interpretatum, ut cum animus Eudemi e corpore excesserit tum domum revertisse videatur.

54 Adiungamus philosophis doctissimum hominem, poetam quidem divinum Sophoclem; qui, cum ex aede Herculis patera aurea gravis subrepta esset, in somnis vidit ipsum deum dicentem qui id fecisset. quod semel ille iterumque neglexit. ubi idem saepius, ascendit in Arium pagum detulit rem; Areopagitae conprehendi iubent eum qui a Sophocle erat nominatus; is quaestione adhibita confessus est pateramque rettulit. quo facto fanum illud Indicis Herculis nominatum est.

55 Sed quid ego Graecorum: nescio quo modo me magis nostra delectant. Omnes hoc historici, Fabii Gellii sed proxume Coelius: cum bello Latino ludi votivi maxumi primum fierent, civitas ad arma repente est excitata itaque ludis intermissis instaurativi constituti sunt. qui ante quam fierent, cumque iam populus consedisset, servus per circum, cum virgis caederetur, furcam ferens ductus est. exin cuidam rustico Romano dormienti visus est venire qui diceret praesulem sibi non placuisse ludis, idque ab eodem iussum esse eum

senatui nuntiare; illum non esse ausum. iterum esse idem iussum et monitum
ne vim suam experiri vellet; ne tum quidem esse ausum. exin filium eius esse
mortuum, eandem in somnis admonitionem fuisse tertiam. tum illum etiam
debilem factum rem ad amicos detulisse, quorum de sententia lecticula in
curiam esse delatum, cumque senatui somnium enarravisset, pedibus suis
salvum domum revertisse. itaque somnio comprobato a senatu ludos illos
iterum instauratos memoriae proditum est. **56** Gaius vero Gracchus multis
dixit, ut scriptum apud eundem Coelium est, sibi in somnis quaesturam
petenti Ti. fratrem visum esse dicere, quam vellet cunctaretur, tamen eodem
sibi leto quo ipse interisset esse pereundum. hoc ante quam tribunus plebi
C. Gracchus factus esset et se audisse scribit Coelius et dixisse multis. quo
somnio quid inveniri potest certius?

Quid, illa duo somnia, quae creberrume commemorantur a Stoicis, quis
tandem potest contemnere: unum de Simonide, qui cum ignotum quendam
proiectum mortuum vidisset eumque humavisset haberetque in animo
navem conscendere, moneri visus est, ne id faceret, ab eo quem sepultura
adfecerat; si navigavisset, eum naufragio esse periturum; itaque Simonidem
redisse, perisse ceteros qui tum navigassent. **57** Alterum ita traditum clarum
admodum somnium: cum duo quidam Arcades familiares iter una facerent
et Megaram venissent, alteram ad coponem devertisse, ad hospitem alterum.
qui ut cenati quiescerent, concubia nocte visum esse in somnis ei, qui erat
in hospitio, illum alterum orare ut subveniret, quod sibi a copone interitus
pararetur; eum primo perterritum somnio surrexisse, dein cum se conlegisset
idque visum pro nihilo habendum esse duxisset recubuisse; tum ei dormienti
eundem illum visum esse rogare ut, quoniam sibi vivo non subvenisset,
mortem suam ne inultam esse pateretur; se interfectum in plaustrum a
copone esse coniectum et supra stercus iniectum; petere ut mane ad portam
adesset prius quam plaustrum ex oppido exiret. hoc vero eum somnio
commotum mane bubulco praesto ad portam fuisse, quaesisse ex eo quid
esset in plaustro; illum perterritum fugisse, mortuum erutum esse, cauponem
re patefacta poenas dedisse. quid hoc somnio dici potest divinius?

58 Sed quid aut plura aut vetera quaerimus: saepe tibi meum narravi,
saepe ex te audivi tuum somnium: me, cum Asiae pro cos. praeessem, vidisse
in quiete, cum tu equo advectus ad quandam magni fluminis ripam provectus
subito atque delapsus in flumen nusquam apparuisses, me contremuisse
timore perterritum; tum te repente laetum extitisse eodemque equo adversam
ascendisse ripam nosque inter nos esse conplexos. facilis coniectura huius
somnii, mihique a peritis in Asia praedictum est fore eos eventus rerum qui
acciderunt. **59** Venio nunc ad tuum. audivi equidem ex te ipso, sed mihi
saepius noster Sallustius narravit, cum in illa fuga nobis gloriosa patriae
calamitosa in villa quadam campi Atinatis maneres magnamque partem

noctis vigilasses, ad lucem denique arte et graviter dormire te coepisse; itaque quamquam iter instaret tamen silentium fieri iussisse ⟨se⟩ neque esse passum te excitari; cum autem experrectus esses hora secunda fere, te sibi somnium narravisse: visum tibi esse, cum in locis solis maestus errares, C. Marium cum fascibus laureatis quaerere ex te quid tristis esses, cumque tu te patria vi pulsum esse dixisses, prehendisse eum dextram tuam et bono animo te iussisse esse lictorique proxumo tradidisse, ut te in monumentum suum deduceret, et dixisse in eo tibi salutem fore. tum et se exclamasse Sallustius narrat reditum tibi celerem et gloriosum paratum et te ipsum visum somnio delectari. nam illud mihi ipsi celeriter nuntiatum est, ut audivisses in monumento Marii de tuo reditu magnificentissumum illud senatus consultum esse factum referente optumo et clarissimo viro consule idque frequentissimo theatro incredibili clamore et plausu comprobatum, dixisse te nihil illo Atinati somnio fieri posse divinius.

60 'At multa falsa.' immo obscura fortasse nobis. sed sint falsa quaedam; contra vera quid dicimus? quae quidem multo plura evenirent, si ad quietem integri iremus. nunc onusti cibo et vino perturbata et confusa cernimus. vide quid Socrates in Platonis politia loquatur. dicit enim 'cum dormientibus ea pars animi quae mentis et rationis sit particeps sopita langueat, illa autem in qua feritas quaedam sit atque agrestis inmanitas, cum sit inmoderato obstupefacta potu atque pastu, exsultare eam in somno inmoderateque iactari. itaque huic omnia visa obiciuntur a mente ac ratione vacua, ut aut cum matre corpus miscere videatur aut cum quovis alio vel homine vel deo saepe belua atque etiam trucidare aliquem et impie cruentari multaque facere inpure atque taetre cum temeritate et inpudentia. 61 at qui salubri et moderato cultu atque victu quieti se tradiderit ea parte animi quae mentis et consilii est agitata et erecta saturataque bonarum cogitationum epulis, eaque parte animi quae voluptate alitur nec inopia enecta nec satietate afluenti (quorum utrumque praestringere aciem mentis solet, sive deest naturae quippiam sive abundat atque affluit), illa etiam tertia parte animi, in qua irarum existit ardor, sedata atque restincta, tum eveniet duabus animi temerariis partibus compressis ut illa tertia pars rationis et mentis eluceat et se vegetam ad somniandum acremque praebeat: tum ei visa quietis occurrent tranquilla atque veracia.' haec verba ipsa Platonis expressi. 62 Epicurum igitur audiemus potius? namque Carneades concertationis studio modo ait hoc modo illud: at ille, quod sentit; sentit autem nihil umquam elegans, nihil decorum. hunc ergo antepones Platoni et Socrati? qui ut rationem non redderent, auctoritate tamen hos minutos philosophos vincerent. iubet igitur Plato sic ad somnum proficisci corporibus adfectis, ut nihil sit quod errorem animis perturbationemque adferat. ex quo etiam Pythagoricis interdictum putatur ne faba vescerentur, quod habet inflationem magnam is cibus tranquillitati

mentis quaerenti vera contrariam. **63** cum ergo est somno sevocatus animus
a societate et a contagione corporis, tum meminit praeteritorum praesentia
cernit futura providet; iacet enim corpus dormientis ut mortui, viget autem
et vivit animus. quod multo magis faciet post mortem, cum omnino corpore
excesserit. itaque adpropinquante morte multo est divinior. nam et id
ipsum vident qui sunt morbo gravi et mortifero adfecti, instare mortem;
itaque is occurrunt plerumque imagines mortuorum tumque vel maxume
laudi student eosque qui secus quam decuit vixerunt peccatorum suorum
tum maxume paenitet. **64** divinare autem morientes illo etiam exemplo
confirmat Posidonius, quod adfert, Rhodium quendam morientem sex
aequales nominasse et dixisse qui primus eorum qui secundus qui deinde
deinceps moriturus esset. Sed tribus modis censet deorum adpulsu homines
somniare, uno quod provideat animus ipse per sese, quippe qui deorum
cognatione teneatur, altero quod plenus aer sit inmortalium animorum,
in quibus tamquam insignitae notae veritatis appareant, tertio quod ipsi
di cum dormientibus conloquantur. idque, ut modo dixi, facilius evenit
adpropinquante morte, ut animi futura augurentur. **65** ex quo et illud est
Callani, de quo ante dixi, et Homerici Hectoris, qui moriens propinquam
Achilli mortem denuntiat. neque enim illud verbum temere consuetudo
adprobavisset, si ea res nulla esset omnino:

> praesagibat animus frustra me ire, cum exirem domo.

sagire enim sentire acute est; ex quo sagae anus, quia multa scire volunt,
et sagaces dicti canes. is igitur qui ante sagit quam oblata res est, dicitur
praesagire id est futura ante sentire.

66 Inest igitur in animis praesagitio extrinsecus iniecta atque inclusa
divinitus. ea si exarsit acrius, furor appellatur, cum a corpore animus
abstractus divino instinctu concitatur.

> 'Sed quid oculis rapere visa est derepente ardentibus?
> ubi illa paulo ante sapiens virginali modestia?'
> 'Mater, optumatum multo mulier melior mulierum,
> missa sum superstitiosis hariolationibus;
> neque me Apollo fatis fandis dementem invitam ciet.
> virgines vereor aequalis, patris mei meum factum pudet,
> optumi viri; mea mater, tui me miseret, mei piget.
> optumam progeniem Priamo peperisti extra me; hoc dolet.
> men obesse, illos prodesse, me obstare, illos obsequi!'

o poema tenerum et moratum atque molle. Sed hoc minus ad rem; **67** illud
quod volumus expressum est, ut vaticinari furor vera soleat.

> adest, adest fax obvoluta sanguine atque incendio.
> multos annos latuit; cives, ferte opem et restinguite.

deus inclusus corpore humano iam, non Cassandra loquitur.

> iamque mari magno classis cita
> texitur; exitium examen rapit;
> adveniet, fera velivolantibus
> navibus complebit manus litora.

tragoedias loqui videor et fabulas. **68** At ex te ipso non commenticiam
rem sed factam eiusdem generis audivi: C. Coponium ad te venisse
Dyrrhachium, cum praetorio imperio classi Rhodiae praeesset, cum primo
hominem prudentem atque doctum, eumque dixisse remigem quendam e
quinqueremi Rhodiorum vaticinatum madefactum iri minus XXX diebus
Graeciam sanguine, rapinas Dyrrhachii et conscensionem in naves cum fuga
fugientibusque miserabilem respectum incendiorum fore, sed Rhodiorum
classi propinquum reditum ac domum itionem dari; tum neque te ipsum
non esse commotum Marcumque Varronem et M. Catonem qui tum ibi
erant doctos homines vehementer esse perterritos; paucis sane post diebus ex
Pharsalia fuga venisse Labienum; qui cum interitum exercitus nuntiavisset,
reliqua vaticinationis brevi esse confecta. **69** Nam et ex horreis direptum
effusumque frumentum vias omnis angiportusque constraverat, et naves
subito perterriti metu conscendistis et noctu ad oppidum respicientes
flagrantis onerarias, quas incenderant milites quia sequi noluerant, videbatis;
postremo a Rhodia classe deserti verum vatem fuisse sensistis.

    70 Exposui quam brevissime potui somnii et furoris oracla, quae carere
arte dixeram. quorum amborum generum una ratio est, qua Cratippus
noster uti solet, animos hominum quadam ex parte extrinsecus esse tractos
et haustos (ex quo intellegitur esse extra divinum animum humanus unde
ducatur), humani autem animi eam partem, quae sensum quae motum
quae adpetitum habeat, non esse ab actione corporis seiugatam; quae autem
pars animi rationis atque intellegentiae sit particeps, eam tum maxume
vigere, cum plurimum absit a corpore. **71** itaque expositis exemplis verarum
vaticinationum et somniorum Cratippus solet rationem concludere hoc
modo: 'si sine oculis non potest extare officium et munus oculorum, possunt
autem aliquando oculi non fungi suo munere, qui vel semel ita est usus oculis

ut vera cerneret, is habet sensum oculorum vera cernentium. item igitur si
sine divinatione non potest officium et munus divinationis extare, potest
autem quis cum divinationem habeat errare aliquando nec vera cernere, satis
est ad confirmandam divinationem semel aliquid esse ita divinatum ut nihil
fortuito cecidisse videatur. sunt autem eius generis innumerabilia; esse igitur
divinationem confitendum est.'

72 Quae vero aut coniectura explicantur aut eventis animadversa ac
notata sunt, ea genera divinandi, ut supra dixi, non naturalia sed artificiosa
dicuntur; in quo haruspices augures coniectoresque numerantur. haec
inprobantur a Peripateticis, a Stoicis defenduntur. quorum alia sunt posita
in monumentis et disciplina, quod Etruscorum declarant et haruspicini et
fulgurales et rituales libri, vestri etiam augurales, alia autem subito ex tempore
coniectura explicantur, ut apud Homerum Calchas qui ex passerum numero
belli Troiani annos auguratus est, et ut in Sullae scriptum historia videmus,
quod te inspectante factum est, ut cum ille in agro Nolano inmolaret ante
praetorium, ab infima ara subito anguis emergeret, cum quidem C. Postumius
haruspex oraret illum ut in expeditionem exercitum educeret; id cum Sulla
fecisset, tum ante oppidum Nolam florentissuma Samnitium castra cepit. 73
Facta coniectura etiam in Dionysio est paulo ante quam regnare coepit; qui
cum per agrum Leontinum iter faciens equum ipse demisisset in flumen,
submersus equus voraginibus non extitit; quem cum maxima contentione
non potuisset extrahere, discessit, ut ait Philistus, aegre ferens; cum autem
aliquantum progressus esset, subito exaudivit hinnitum respexitque et
equum alacrem laetus aspexit, cuius in iuba examen apium consederat. quod
ostentum habuit hanc vim, ut Dionysius paucis post diebus regnare coeperit.
74 Quid, Lacedaemoniis paulo ante Leuctricam calamitatem quae significatio
facta est, cum in Herculis fano arma sonuerunt Herculisque simulacrum
multo sudore manavit. at eodem tempore Thebis, ut ait Callisthenes, in templo
Herculis valvae clausae repagulis subito se ipsae aperuerunt, armaque quae
fixa in parietibus fuerant ea sunt humi inventa. cumque eodem tempore
apud Lebadiam Trophonio res divina fieret, gallos gallinaceos in eo loco sic
adsidue canere coepisse ut nihil intermitterent; tum augures dixisse Boeotios
Thebanorum esse victoriam, propterea quod avis illa victa silere soleret,
canere si vicisset. 75 eademque tempestate multis signis Lacedaemoniis
Leuctricae pugnae calamitas denuntiabatur. namque et in Lysandri, qui
Lacedaemoniorum clarissimus fuerat, statua, quae Delphis stabat, in capite
corona subito extitit ex asperis herbis et agrestibus, stellaeque aureae, quae
Delphis erant a Lacedaemoniis positae post navalem illam victoriam Lysandri
qua Athenienses conciderunt,—qua in pugna quia Castor et Pollux cum
Lacedaemoniorum classe visi esse dicebantur, eorum insignia deorum, stellae
aureae quas dixi Delphis positae paulo ante Leuctricam pugnam deciderunt

neque repertae sunt. **76** maximum vero illud is portentum isdem Spartiatis
fuit, quod cum oraclum ab Iove Dodonaeo petivissent de victoria sciscitantes
legatique ⟨vas⟩ illud, in quo inerant sortes, collocavissent, simia, quam rex
Molossorum in deliciis habebat, et sortes ipsas et cetera quae erant ad sortem
parata disturbavit et aliud alio dissupavit. Tum ea quae praeposita erat
oraclo sacerdos dixisse dicitur de salute Lacedaemoniis esse non de victoria
cogitandum. **77** Quid, bello Punico secundo nonne C. Flaminius cons. iterum
neglexit signa rerum futurarum magna cum clade rei publicae? qui exercitu
lustrato cum Arretium versus castra movisset et contra Hannibalem legiones
duceret, et ipse et equus eius ante signum Iovis Statoris sine causa repente
concidit nec eam rem habuit religioni obiecto signo, ut peritis videbatur,
ne committeret proelium. idem cum tripudio auspicaretur, pullarius diem
proelii committendi differebat. tum Flaminius ex eo quaesivit si ne postea
quidem pulli pascerentur quid faciendum censeret. cum ille quiescendum
respondisset, Flaminius: 'praeclara vero auspicia, si esurientibus pullis res
geri poterit, saturis nihil geretur'; itaque signa convelli et se sequi iussit.
quo tempore cum signifer primi hastati signum non posset movere loco
nec quicquam proficeretur plures cum accederent, Flaminius re nuntiata
suo more neglexit. itaque tribus his horis concisus exercitus atque ipse
interfectus est. **78** magnum illud etiam, quod addidit Coelius, eo tempore
ipso cum hoc calamitosum proelium fieret tantos terrae motus in Liguribus
Gallia compluribusque insulis totaque in Italia factos esse, ut multa oppida
conruerint, multis locis labes factae sint terraeque desiderint fluminaque in
contrarias partes fluxerint atque in amnes mare influxerit.

Fiunt certae divinationum coniecturae a peritis. Midae illi Phrygi cum
puer esset dormienti formicae in os tritici grana congesserunt. divitissumum
fore praedictum est; quod evenit. at Platoni cum in cunis parvulo dormienti
apes in labellis consedissent, responsum est singulari illum suavitate orationis
fore. ita futura eloquentia provisa in infante est. **79** quid, amores ac deliciae
tuae Roscius num aut ipse aut pro eo Lanuvium totum mentiebatur? qui cum
esset in cunabulis educareturque in Solonio, [qui est campus agri Lanuvini,]
noctu lumine apposito experrecta nutrix animadvertit puerum dormientem
circumplicatum serpentis amplexu. quo aspectu exterrita clamorem sustulit.
pater autem Roscii ad haruspices rettulit, qui responderunt nihil illo puero
clarius nihil nobilius fore. atque hanc speciem Pasiteles caelavit argento et
noster expressit Archias versibus.

Quid igitur expectamus? an dum in foro nobiscum di inmortales, dum
in viis versentur dum domi? qui quidem ipsi se nobis non offerunt, vim
autem suam longe lateque diffundunt, quam tum terrae cavernis includunt
tum hominum naturis implicant. nam terrae vis Pythiam Delphis incitabat,
naturae Sibyllam. quid enim, non videmus, quam sint varia terrarum genera?

ex quibus et mortifera quaedam pars est, ut et Ampsancti in Hirpinis et in
Asia Plutonia quae vidimus, et sunt partes agrorum aliae pestilentes aliae
salubres aliae quae acuta ingenia gignant aliae quae retusa; quae omnia
fiunt et ex caeli varietate et ex disparili adspiratione terrarum. 80 Fit etiam
saepe specie quadam saepe vocum gravitate et cantibus ut pellantur animi
vehementius, saepe etiam cura et timore, qualis est illa

> flexanima tamquam lymphata aut Bacchi sacris
> commota in tumulis Teucrum commemorans suum.

atque etiam illa concitatio declarat vim in animis esse divinam. negat enim
sine furore Democritus quemquam poetam magnum esse posse, quod idem
dicit Plato. quem si placet appellet furorem, dum modo is furor ita laudetur ut
in Phaedro Platonis laudatus est. quid, vestra oratio in causis, quid, ipsa actio
potest esse vehemens et gravis et copiosa, nisi est animus ipse commotior?
equidem etiam in te saepe vidi et, ut ad leviora veniamus, in Aesopo familiari
tuo tantum ardorem vultuum atque motuum, ut eum vis quaedam abstraxisse
a sensu mentis videretur.

81 Obiciuntur etiam saepe formae, quae reapse nullae sunt, speciem
autem offerunt. quod contigisse Brenno dicitur eiusque Gallicis copiis, cum
fano Apollinis Delphici nefarium bellum intulisset. tum enim ferunt ex oraclo
ecfatam esse Pythiam:

> ego providebo rem istam et albae virgines.

ex quo factum ut et viderentur virgines ferre arma contra et nive Gallorum
obrueretur exercitus.

Aristoteles quidem eos etiam qui valetudinis vitio furerent et melancholici
dicerentur censebat habere aliquid in animis praesagiens atque divinum. ego
autem haut scio an nec cardiacis hoc tribuendum sit nec phreneticis; animi
enim integri, non vitiosi est corporis divinatio.

82 Quam quidem esse re vera hac Stoicorum ratione concluditur: 'si sunt
di neque ante declarant hominibus quae futura sint, aut non diligunt homines,
aut quid eventurum sit ignorant, aut existumant nihil interesse hominum
scire quid sit futurum, aut non censent esse suae maiestatis praesignificare
hominibus quae sunt futura, aut ea ne ipsi quidem di significare possunt. at
neque non diligunt nos: sunt enim benefici generique hominum amici; neque
ignorant ea quae ab ipsis constituta et designata sunt; neque nostra nihil
interest scire ea quae eventura sint: erimus enim cautiores si sciemus; neque
hoc alienum ducunt maiestate sua: nihil est enim beneficentia praestantius;
neque non possunt futura praenoscere. 83 non igitur sunt di nec significant

futura. sunt autem di; significant ergo. et non, si significant, nullas vias dant
nobis ad significationis scientiam: frustra enim significarent. nec, si dant
vias, non est divinatio. est igitur divinatio.' **84** Hac ratione et Chrysippus et
Diogenes et Antipater utitur.

Quid est igitur cur dubitandum sit, quin sint ea quae disputavi verissima,
si ratio mecum facit si eventa si populi si nationes si Graeci si barbari si
maiores etiam nostri si denique hoc semper ita putatum est, si summi
philosophi si poetae si sapientissimi viri qui res publicas constituerunt
qui urbes condiderunt. an dum bestiae loquantur expectamus, hominum
consentiente auctoritate contenti non sumus? **85** Nec vero quicquam aliud
adfertur, cur ea quae dico divinandi genera nulla sint, nisi quod difficile dictu
videtur quae cuiusque divinationis ratio quae causa sit. 'quid enim habet
haruspex cur pulmo incisus etiam in bonis extis dirimat tempus et proferat
diem; quid augur cur a dextra corvus a sinistra cornix faciat ratum; quid
astrologus cur stella Iovis aut Veneris coniuncta cum luna ad ortus puerorum
salutaris sit, Saturni Martisve contraria'; cur autem deus dormientes nos
moneat, vigilantes neglegat; quid deinde causae sit cur Cassandra furens
futura prospiciat, Priamus sapiens hoc idem facere non queat: **86** cur fiat
quidque, quaeris; recte omnino, sed non nunc id agitur: fiat necne fiat, id
quaeritur. ut, si magnetem lapidem esse dicam qui ferrum ad se adliciat et
trahat, rationem cur id fiat adferre nequeam, fieri omnino neges. quod idem
facis in divinatione, quam et cernimus ipsi et audimus et legimus et a patribus
accepimus. Neque ante philosophiam patefactam, quae nuper inventa est, hac
de re communis vita dubitavit, et posteaquam philosophia processit, nemo
aliter philosophus sensit in quo modo esset auctoritas. **87** dixi de Pythagora
de Democrito de Socrate, excepi de antiquis praeter Xenophanem neminem,
adiunxi veterem Academiam Peripateticos Stoicos; unus dissentit Epicurus.
quid vero hoc turpius, quam quod idem nullam censet gratuitam esse
virtutem?

Quis est autem quem non moveat clarissumis monumentis testata
consignataque antiquitas? Calchantem augurem scribit Homerus longe
optumum, eumque ducem classium fuisse ad Ilium, auspiciorum credo
scientia non locorum. **88** Amphilochus et Mopsus Argivorum reges fuerunt
sed iidem augures, iique urbis in ora maritima Ciliciae Graecas condiderunt.
atque etiam ante hos Amphiaraus et Tiresias non humiles et obscuri neque
eorum similes, ut apud Ennium est,

> qui sui quaestus causa fictas suscitant sententias,

sed clari et praestantes viri, qui avibus et signis admoniti futura dicebant;
quorum de altero etiam apud inferos Homerus ait 'solum sapere, ceteros

umbrarum vagari modo'; Amphiaraum autem sic honoravit fama Graeciae, deus ut haberetur atque ut ab eius solo in quo est humatus oracla peterentur. **89** quid, Asiae rex Priamus nonne et Helenum filium et Cassandram filiam divinantes habebat, alterum auguriis alteram mentis incitatione et permotione divina? quo in genere Marcios quosdam fratres nobili loco natos apud maiores nostros fuisse scriptum videmus. quid, Polyidum Corinthium nonne Homerus et aliis multa et filio ad Troiam proficiscenti mortem praedixisse commemorat? Omnino apud veteres qui rerum potiebantur iidem auguria tenebant; ut enim sapere, sic divinare regale ducebant. testis est nostra civitas, in qua et reges augures et postea privati eodem sacerdotio praediti rem publicam religionum auctoritate rexerunt.

　　90 Eaque divinationum ratio ne in barbaris quidem gentibus neglecta est, siquidem et in Gallia Druidae sunt, e quibus ipse Divitiacum Haeduum hospitem tuum laudatoremque cognovi, qui et naturae rationem, quam φυσιολογίαν Graeci appellant, notam esse sibi profitebatur et partim auguriis partim coniectura quae essent futura dicebat, et in Persis augurantur et divinant magi, qui congregantur in fano commentandi causa atque inter se conloquendi, quod etiam idem vos quondam facere Nonis solebatis; **91** nec quisquam rex Persarum potest esse qui non ante magorum disciplinam scientiamque perceperit. Licet autem videre et genera quaedam et nationes huic scientiae deditas. Telmesus in Caria est, qua in urbe excellit haruspicum disciplina; itemque Elis in Peloponneso familias duas certas habet, Iamidarum unam, alteram Clutidarum, haruspicinae nobilitate praestantes. in Syria Chaldaei cognitione astrorum sollertiaque ingeniorum antecellunt. **92** Etruria autem de caelo tacta scientissume animadvertit eademque interpretatur quid quibusque ostendatur monstris atque portentis. quocirca bene apud maiores nostros senatus tum cum florebat imperium decrevit ut de principum filiis x ex singulis Etruriae populis in disciplinam traderentur, ne ars tanta propter tenuitatem hominum a religionis auctoritate abduceretur ad mercedem atque quaestum. Phryges autem et Pisidae et Cilices et Arabum natio avium significationibus plurimum obtemperant, quod idem factitatum in Umbria accepimus.

　　93 Ac mihi quidem videntur e locis quoque ipsis, qui a quibusque incolebantur, divinationum oportunitates esse ductae. etenim Aegyptii, ut Babylonii in camporum patentium aequoribus habitantes, cum ex terra nihil emineret quod contemplationi caeli officere posset, omnem curam in siderum cognitione posuerunt—Etrusci autem, quod religione inbuti studiosius et crebrius hostias immolabant, extorum cognitioni se maxume dediderunt, quodque propter aëris crassitudinem de caelo apud eos multa fiebant, et quod ob eandem causam multa invisitata partim e caelo alia ex terra oriebantur quaedam etiam ex hominum pecudumve conceptu et satu, ostentorum exercitatissimi interpretes extiterunt. quorum quidem vim, ut tu soles dicere, verba ipsa prudenter a maioribus posita declarant. quia enim ostendunt portendunt monstrant praedicunt, ostenta portenta monstra prodigia dicuntur. 94 Arabes autem et Phryges et Cilices, quod pastu pecudum maxume utuntur campos et montes hieme et aestate peragrantes, propterea facilius cantus avium et volatus notaverunt; eademque et Pisidiae causa fuit et huic nostrae Umbriae. tum Caria tota praecipueque Telmeses, quos ante dixi, quod agros uberrumos maximeque fertiles incolunt, in quibus multa propter fecunditatem fingi gignique possunt, in ostentis animadvertendis diligentes fuerunt.

95 Quis vero non videt in optuma quaque re publica plurimum auspicia et reliqua divinandi genera valuisse? quis rex umquam fuit, quis populus, qui non uteretur praedictione divina? neque solum in pace sed in bello multo etiam magis, quo maius erat certamen et discrimen salutis. omitto nostros, qui nihil in bello sine extis agunt nihil sine auspiciis [dum habent auspicia]: externa videamus. namque et Athenienses omnibus semper publicis consiliis divinos quosdam sacerdotes, quos μάντεις vocant, adhibuerunt, et Lacedaemonii regibus suis augurem adsessorem dederunt, itemque senibus (sic enim consilium publicum appellant) augurem interesse voluerunt, iidemque de rebus maioribus semper aut Delphis oraclum aut ab Hammone aut a Dodona petebant. 96 Lycurgus quidem, qui Lacedaemoniorum rem publicam temperavit, leges suas auctoritate Apollinis Delphici confirmavit; quas cum vellet Lysander commutare, eadem est prohibitus religione. atque etiam qui praeerant Lacedaemoniis non contenti vigilantibus curis in Pasiphaae fano, quod est in agro propter urbem, somniandi causa excubabant, quia vera quietis oracla ducebant. 97 Ad nostra iam redeo. quotiens senatus decemviros ad libros ire iussit; ⟨quantis in rebus quamque saepe responsis haruspicum paruit!⟩ Nam et cum duo visi soles essent et cum tres lunae et cum faces, et cum sol nocte visus esset, et cum e caelo fremitus auditus, et cum caelum discessisse visum esset atque in eo animadversi globi, delata etiam ad senatum labes agri Privernatis, cum ad infinitam altitudinem terra desidisset Apuliaque maximis terrae motibus conquassata esset— quibus portentis magna populo Romano bella perniciosaeque seditiones denuntiabantur, inque his omnibus responsa haruspicum cum Sibyllae versibus congruebant. 98 quid, cum Cumis Apollo sudavit Capuae Victoria, quid, ortus androgyni nonne fatale quoddam monstrum fuit, quid, quod fluvius Atratus sanguine fluxit, quid, cum saepe lapidum, sanguinis non numquam, terrae interdum, quondam etiam lactis imber defluxit, quid, cum in Capitolio ictus Centaurus e caelo est, in Aventino portae et homines, Tusculi aedes Castoris et Pollucis Romaeque Pietatis: nonne et haruspices ea responderunt quae evenerunt, et in Sibyllae libris eaedem repertae

praedictiones sunt? [quotiens senatus decemviros ad libros ire iussit; quantis in rebus quamque saepe responsis haruspicum paruit.]

99 Caeciliae Q. f. somnio modo Marsico bello templum est a senatu Iunoni Sospitae restitutum. quod quidem somnium Sisenna cum disputavisset mirifice ad verbum cum re convenisse, tum insolenter, credo ab Epicureo aliquo inductus, disputat somniis credi non oportere. idem contra ostenta nihil disputat exponitque initio belli Marsici et deorum simulacra sudavisse et sanguinem fluxisse et discessisse caelum et ex occulto auditas esse voces, quae pericula belli nuntiarent, et Lanuvii clipeos, quod haruspicibus tristissumum visum esset, a muribus esse derosos. **100** quid quod in annalibus habemus Veienti bello, cum lacus Albanus praeter modum crevisset, Veientem quendam ad nos hominem nobilem perfugisse, eumque dixisse ex fatis, quae Veientes scripta haberent, Veios capi non posse, dum lacus is redundaret, et si lacus emissus lapsu et cursu suo ad mare profluxisset, perniciosum populo Romano; sin autem ita esset eductus, ut ad mare pervenire non posset, tum salutare nostris fore. ex quo illa mirabilis a maioribus Albanae aquae facta deductio est. cum autem Veientes bello fessi legatos ad senatum misissent, tum ex iis quidam dixisse dicitur non omnia illum transfugam ausum esse senatui dicere; in isdem enim fatis scriptum Veientes habere fore ut brevi a Gallis Roma caperetur, quod quidem sexennio post Veios captos factum esse videmus.

101 Saepe etiam et in proeliis Fauni auditi et in rebus turbidis veridicae voces ex occulto missae esse dicuntur; cuius generis duo sint ex multis exempla, sed maxuma: nam non multo ante urbem captam exaudita vox est a luco Vestae, qui a Palatii radice in novam viam devexus est, ut muri et portae reficerentur; futurum esse, nisi provisum esset, ut Roma caperetur. quod neglectum tum ⟨cum⟩ caveri poterat post acceptam illam maximam cladem expiatum est; ara enim Aio Loquenti quam saeptam videmus exadversus eum locum consecrata est. atque etiam scriptum a multis est, cum terrae motus factus esset, ut sue plena procuratio fieret, vocem ab aede Iunonis ex arce extitisse; quocirca Iunonem illam appellatam Monetam. haec igitur et a dis significata et a nostris maioribus iudicata contemnimus?

102 Neque solum deorum voces Pythagorei observitaverunt sed etiam hominum, quae vocant omina. quae maiores nostri quia valere censebant idcirco omnibus rebus agendis 'quod bonum, faustum, felix fortunatumque esset' praefabantur, rebusque divinis, quae publice fierent, ut 'faverent linguis' imperabatur inque feriis imperandis ut 'litibus et iurgiis se abstinerent.' itemque in lustranda colonia ab eo qui eam deduceret et cum imperator exercitum, censor populum lustraret, bonis nominibus qui hostias ducerent eligebantur. quod idem in dilectu consules observant, ut primus miles fiat bono nomine. **103** quae quidem a te scis et consule et imperatore summa cum religione esse servata. praerogativam etiam maiores omen iustorum comitiorum esse voluerunt. Atque ego exempla ominum nota proferam. L. Paulus consul iterum, cum ei bellum ut cum rege Perse gereret obtigisset, ut ea ipsa die domum ad vesperum rediit, filiolam suam Tertiam, quae tum erat admodum parva, osculans animum advertit tristiculam. 'quid est'inquit 'mea Tertia, quid tristis es?' 'mi pater' inquit 'Persa periit.' tum ille artius puellam conplexus 'Accipio' inquit 'mea filia omen.' erat autem mortuus catellus eo nomine. **104** L. Flaccum flaminem Martialem ego audivi cum diceret Caeciliam Metelli, cum vellet sororis suae filiam in matrimonium conlocare, exisse in quoddam sacellum ominis capiendi causa, quod fieri more veterum solebat. cum virgo staret et Caecilia in sella sederet neque diu ulla vox extitisset, puellam defatigatam petisse a matertera, ut sibi concederet paulisper ut in eius sella requiesceret; illam autem dixisse: 'vero mea puella tibi concedo meas sedes.' quod omen res consecuta est; ipsa enim brevi mortua est, virgo autem nupsit cui Caecilia nupta fuerat. Haec posse contemni vel etiam rideri praeclare intellego, sed id ipsum est deos non putare, quae ab iis significantur contemnere.

105 Quid de auguribus loquar? tuae partes sunt, tuum inquam auspiciorum patrocinium debet esse. tibi Ap. Claudius augur consuli nuntiavit addubitato salutis augurio bellum domesticum triste ac turbulentum fore; quod paucis post mensibus exortum paucioribus a te est diebus oppressum. cui quidem auguri vehementer adsentior; solus enim multorum annorum memoria non decantandi augurii sed divinandi tenuit disciplinam. quem inridebant collegae tui eumque tum Pisidam tum Soranum augurem esse dicebant; quibus nulla videbatur in auguriis aut praesensio aut scientia veritatis futurae: sapienter, aiebant, ad opinionem imperitorum esse fictas religiones. quod longe secus est; neque enim in pastoribus illis quibus Romulus praefuit nec in ipso Romulo haec calliditas esse potuit ut ad errorem multitudinis religionis simulacra fingerent. sed difficultas laborque discendi disertam neglegentiam reddidit; malunt enim disserere nihil esse in auspiciis quam quid sit ediscere. **106** Quid est illo auspicio divinius, quod apud te in Mario est, ut utar potissumum auctore te:

> hic Iovis altisoni subito pinnata satelles
> arboris e trunco serpentis saucia morsu
> subrigit ipsa feris transfigens unguibus anguem
> semanimum et varia graviter cervice micantem.
> quem se intorquentem lanians rostroque cruentans
> iam satiata animos, iam duros ulta dolores
> abiecit ecflantem et laceratum adfligit in unda
> seque obitu a solis nitidos convertit ad ortus.

hanc ubi praepetibus pinnis lapsuque volantem
conspexit Marius divini numinis augur
faustaque signa suae laudis reditusque notavit,
partibus intonuit caeli pater ipse sinistris.
sic aquilae clarum firmavit Iuppiter omen.

107 atque ille Romuli auguratus pastoralis non urbanus fuit nec fictus ad opiniones inperitorum sed a certis acceptus et posteris traditus. itaque Romulus augur, ut apud Ennium est, cum fratre item augure

curantes magna cum cura tum cupientes
regni dant operam simul auspicio augurioque.

in monte

Remus auspicio se devovet atque secundam
solus avem servat. at Romulus pulcher in alto
quaerit Aventino, servat genus altivolantum.
certabant urbem Romam Remoramne vocarent.
omnibus cura viris, uter esset induperator.
exspectant, veluti consul cum mittere signum
volt, omnes avidi spectant ad carceris oras,
108 quam mox emittat pictis e faucibus currus,
sic expectabat populus atque ore timebat
rebus, utri magni victoria sit data regni.
interea sol albus recessit in infera noctis.
exin candida se radiis dedit icta foras lux,
et simul ex alto longe pulcherruma praepes
laeva volavit avis. simul aureus exoritur sol,
cedunt de caelo ter quattuor corpora sancta
avium, praepetibus sese pulchrisque locis dant.
conspicit inde sibi data Romulus esse priora,
auspicio regni stabilita scamna solumque.

109 Sed ut unde huc digressa est eodem redeat oratio: si nihil queam disputare quam ob rem quicque fiat, et tantum modo fieri ea quae commemoravi doceam, parumne Epicuro Carneadive respondeam? Quid, si etiam ratio exstat artificiosae praesensionis facilis, divinae autem paulo obscurior? quae enim extis quae fulgoribus quae portentis quae astris praesentiuntur. haec notata sunt observatione diuturna. adfert autem vetustas

omnibus in rebus longinqua observatione incredibilem scientiam; quae potest
esse etiam sine motu atque inpulsu deorum, cum quid ex quoque eveniat et
quid quamque rem significet crebra animadversione perspectum est. 110
Altera divinatio est naturalis, ut ante dixi; quae physica disputandi subtilitate
referenda est ad naturam deorum, a qua, ut doctissimis sapientissimisque
placuit, haustos animos et libatos habemus; cumque omnia completa et
referta sint aeterno sensu et mente divina, necesse est cognatione divinorum
animorum animos humanos commoveri. sed vigilantes animi vitae
necessitatibus serviunt diiunguntque se a societate divina vinclis corporis
inpediti. 111 rarum est quoddam genus eorum qui se a corpore avocent et
ad divinarum rerum cognitionem cura omni studioque rapiantur: horum
sunt auguria non divini impetus sed rationis humanae; nam et natura futura
praesentiunt, ut aquarum eluviones et deflagrationem futuram aliquando caeli
atque terrarum; alii autem in re publica exercitati, ut de Atheniensi Solone
accepimus, orientem tyrannidem multo ante prospiciunt; quos prudentes
possumus dicere id est providentes, divinos nullo modo possumus, non plus
quam Milesium Thalem, qui ut obiurgatores suos convinceret ostenderetque
etiam philosophum si ei commodum esset pecuniam facere posse, omnem
oleam ante quam florere coepisset in agro Milesio coemisse dicitur: 112
animadverterat fortasse quadam scientia olearum ubertatem fore, et quidem
idem primus defectionem solis, quae Astyage regnante facta est, praedixisse
fertur. multa medici multa gubernatores agricolae etiam multa praesentiunt,
sed nullam eorum divinationem voco, ne illam quidem qua ab Anaximandro
physico moniti Lacedaemonii sunt ut urbem et tecta linquerent armatique in
agro excubarent, quod terrae motus instaret, tum cum et urbs tota corruit et
monte Taygeto extrema montis quasi puppis avulsa est. ne Pherecydes quidem
ille Pythagorae magister potius divinus habebitur quam physicus, quod cum
vidisset haustam aquam de iugi puteo, terrae motus dixit instare.

113 Nec vero umquam animus hominis naturaliter divinat nisi cum
ita solutus est et vacuus ut ei plane nihil sit cum corpore. quod aut vatibus
contingit aut dormientibus; itaque ea duo genera a Dicaearcho probantur
et ut dixi a Cratippo nostro; si propterea quod ea proficiscuntur a natura,
sint summa sane, modo ne sola; sin autem nihil esse in observatione putant,
multa tollunt quibus vitae ratio continetur. sed quoniam dant aliquid idque
non parvum, [vaticinationes cum somniis] nihil est quod cum his magnopere
pugnemus, praesertim cum sint qui omnino nullam divinationem probent.

114 Ergo et ii, quorum animi spretis corporibus evolant atque excurrunt
foras, ardore aliquo inflammati atque incitati cernunt illa profecto quae
vaticinantes pronuntiant, multisque rebus inflammantur tales animi qui
corporibus non inhaerent, ut ii qui sono quodam vocum et Phrygiis cantibus

incitantur. multos nemora silvaeque multos amnes aut maria commovent; quorum furibunda mens videt ante multo quae sint futura. quo de genere illa sunt:

> eheu videte,
> iudicavit inclitum iudicium inter deas tris aliquis,
> quo iudicio Lacedaemonia mulier, Furiarum una, adveniet.

eodem enim modo multa a vaticinantibus saepe praedicta sunt, neque solum verbis sed etiam

> versibus quos olim Fauni vatesque canebant.

115 similiter Marcius et Publicius vates cecinisse dicuntur; quo de genere Apollinis operta prolata sunt. credo etiam anhelitus quosdam fuisse terrarum quibus inflatae mentes oracla funderent.

   Atque haec quidem vatium ratio est, nec dissimilis sane somniorum. nam quae vigilantibus accidunt vatibus, eadem nobis dormientibus. viget enim animus in somnis liber ab sensibus omnique inpeditione curarum iacente et mortuo paene corpore. qui quia vixit ab omni aeternitate versatusque est cum innumerabilibus animis, omnia quae in natura rerum sunt videt, si modo temperatis escis modicisque potionibus ita est adfectus ut sopito corpore ipse vigilet. haec somniantis est divinatio. **116** Hic magna quaedam exoritur neque ea naturalis sed artificiosa somniorum interpretatio eodemque modo et oraculorum et vaticinationum, sunt enim explanatores, ut grammatici poetarum. nam ut aurum et argentum aes ferrum frustra natura divina genuisset, nisi eadem docuisset quem ad modum ad eorum venas perveniretur, nec fruges terrae bacasve arborum cum utilitate ulla generi humano dedisset, nisi earum cultus et conditiones tradidisset, materiave quid iuvaret, nisi confectionis eius fabricam haberemus—sic cum omni utilitate quam di hominibus dederunt ars aliqua coniuncta est per quam illa utilitas percipi possit. item igitur somniis vaticinationibus oraclis, quod erant multa obscura multa ambigua, explanationes adhibitae sunt interpretum.

   117 Quo modo autem aut vates aut somniantes ea videant quae nusquam etiam tunc sint magna quaestio est. sed explorata si sint ea quae ante quaeri debeant, sint haec quae quaerimus faciliora. continet enim totam hanc quaestionem ea ratio quae est de natura deorum, quae a te secundo libro est explicata dilucide. quam si obtinemus, stabit illud, quod hunc locum continet de quo agimus, esse deos et eorum providentia mundum administrari eosdemque consulere rebus humanis nec solum universis

verum etiam singulis. haec si tenemus, quae mihi quidem non videntur
posse convelli, profecto hominibus a dis futura significari necesse est. **118**
Sed distinguendum videtur quonam modo. nam non placet Stoicis singulis
iecorum fissis aut avium cantibus interesse deum: neque enim decorum est
nec dis dignum nec fieri ullo pacto potest; sed ita a principio inchoatum esse
mundum ut certis rebus certa signa praecurrerent, alia in extis alia in avibus
alia in fulgoribus alia in ostentis alia in stellis alia in somniantium visis alia in
furentium vocibus. ea quibus bene percepta sunt ii non saepe falluntur; male
coniecta maleque interpretata falsa sunt non rerum vitio sed interpretum
inscientia. hoc autem posito atque concesso, esse quandam vim divinam
hominum vitam continentem, non difficile est quae fieri certe videmus ea
qua ratione fiant suspicari. nam et ad hostiam deligendam potest dux esse vis
quaedam sentiens, quae est toto confusa mundo, et tum ipsum cum immolare
velis extorum fieri mutatio potest, ut aut absit aliquid aut supersit; parvis
enim momentis multa natura aut adfingit aut mutat aut detrahit. **119** quod ne
dubitare possimus maximo est argumento quod paulo ante interitum Caesaris
contigit. qui cum immolaret illo die quo primum in sella aurea sedit et cum
purpurea veste processit, in extis bovis opimi cor non fuit. Num igitur censes
ullum animal quod sanguinem habeat sine corde esse posse? qua † ille rei
novitate perculsus cum Spurinna diceret timendum esse ne et consilium et
vita deficeret; earum enim rerum utramque a corde proficisci, **. postero die
caput in iecore non fuit. quae quidem illi portendebantur a dis immortalibus,
ut videret interitum non ut caveret. cum igitur eae partes in extis non
reperiuntur sine quibus victuma illa vivere nequisset, intellegendum est in
ipso immolationis tempore eas partes quae absint interisse. **120** eademque
efficit in avibus divina mens, ut tum huc tum illuc volent alites, tum in hac
tum in illa parte se occultent, tum a dextra tum a sinistra parte canant oscines.
Nam si animal omne ut vult ita utitur motu sui corporis prono obliquo
supino, membraque quocumque vult flectit contorquet porrigit contrahit,
eaque ante efficit paene quam cogitat, quanto id deo est facilius, cuius numini
parent omnia. **121** Idemque mittit et signa nobis eius generis, qualia permulta
historia tradidit, quale scriptum illud videmus: si luna paulo ante solis ortum
defecisset in signo Leonis, fore ut armis Dareus et Persae ab Alexandra et
Macedonibus [proelio] vincerentur Dareusque moreretur, et si puella nata
biceps esset, seditionem in populo fore, corruptelam et adulterium domi; et
si mulier leonem peperisse visa esset, fore ut ab exteris gentibus vinceretur ea
res publica in qua id contigisset. eiusdem generis etiam illud est, quod scribit
Herodotus, Croesi filium cum esset infans locutum; quo ostento regnum
patris et domum funditus concidisse. caput arsisse Servio Tullio dormienti
quae historia non prodidit? Ut igitur qui se tradidit quieti praeparato animo

cum bonis cogitationibus tum rebus ad tranquillitatem adcommodatis, certa et vera cernit in somnis, sic castus animus purusque vigilantis et ad astrorum et ad avium reliquorumque signorum et ad extorum veritatem est paratior.

122 Hoc nimirum est illud quod de Socrate accepimus quodque ab ipso in libris Socraticorum saepe dicitur, esse divinum quiddam, quod δαιμόνιον appellat, cui semper ipse paruerit numquam impellenti, saepe revocanti. et Socrates quidem, quo quem auctorem meliorem quaerimus, Xenophonti consulenti sequereturne Cyrum, posteaquam exposuit quae ipsi videbantur, 'et nostrum quidem' inquit 'humanum est consilium, sed de rebus et obscuris et incertis ad Apollinem censeo referendum,' ad quem etiam Athenienses publice de maioribus rebus semper rettulerunt. 123 scriptum est item, cum Critonis sui familiaris oculum alligatum vidisset, quaesivisse quid esset; cum autem ille respondisset in agro ambulanti ramulum adductum ut remissus esset in oculum suum recidisse, tum Socrates: 'non enim paruisti mihi revocanti, cum uterer qua soleo praesagatione divina.' idem etiam Socrates, cum apud Delium male pugnatum esset Lachete praetore fugeretque cum ipso Lachete, ut ventum est in trivium, eadem qua ceteri fugere noluit. quibus quaerentibus cur non eadem via pergeret deterreri se a deo dixit; cum quidem ii qui alia via fugerant in hostium equitatum inciderunt. Permulta conlecta sunt ab Antipatro quae mirabiliter a Socrate divinata sunt; quae praetermittam; tibi enim nota sunt, mihi ad commemorandum non necessaria. 124 Illud tamen eius philosophi magnificum ac paene divinum, quod cum impiis sententiis damnatus esset aequissimo animo se dixit mori; neque enim domo egredienti neque illud suggestum, in quo causam dixerat, ascendenti signum sibi ullum quod consuesset a deo quasi mali alicuius inpendentis datum.

Equidem sic arbitror, etiamsi multa fallant eos qui aut arte aut coniectura divinare videantur, esse tamen divinationem; homines autem ut in ceteris artibus sic in hac posse falli. potest accidere ut aliquod signum dubie datum pro certo sit acceptum, potest aliquod latuisse aut ipsum aut quod esset illi contrarium. Mihi autem ad hoc de quo disputo probandum satis est non modo plura sed etiam pauciora divine praesensa et praedicta reperiri. 125 Quin etiam hoc non dubitans dixerim, si unum aliquid ita sit praedictum praesensumque ut cum evenerit ita cadat ut praedictum sit neque in eo quicquam casu et fortuito factum esse appareat, esse certe divinationem, idque esse omnibus confitendum.

Quocirca primum mihi videtur, ut Posidonius facit, a deo, de quo satis dictum est, deinde a fato, deinde a natura vis omnis divinandi ratioque repetenda. Fieri igitur omnia fato ratio cogit fateri. fatum autem id appello quod Graeci εἱμαρμένην id est ordinem seriemque causarum, cum causae causa nexa rem ex se gignat. ea est ex omni aeternitate fluens veritas sempiterna. Quod cum ita sit, nihil est factum quod non futurum fuerit,

eodemque modo nihil est futurum cuius non causas id ipsum efficientes
natura contineat. **126** Ex quo intellegitur, ut fatum sit non id quod
superstitiose sed id quod physice dicitur, causa aeterna rerum, cur et ea quae
praeterierunt facta sint et quae instant fiant et quae secuntur futura sint. Ita
fit ut et observatione notari possit quae res quamque causam plerumque
consequatur, etiamsi non semper (nam id quidem adfirmare difficile est),
easdemque causas veri simile est rerum futurarum cerni ab iis, qui aut per
furorem eas aut in quiete videant.

    127 Praeterea cum fato omnia fiant, id quod alio loco ostendetur, si
quis mortalis possit esse qui conligationem causarum omnium perspiciat
animo, nihil eum profecto fallat. qui enim teneat causas rerum futurarum,
idem necesse est omnia teneat quae futura sint. quod cum nemo facere nisi
deus possit, relinquendum est homini ut signis quibusdam consequentia
declarantibus futura praesentiat. Non enim illa quae futura sunt subito
exsistunt, sed est quasi rudentis explicatio sic traductio temporis nihil
novi efficientis et primum quicque replicantis. quod et ii vident quibus
naturalis divinatio data est, et ii quibus cursus rerum observando notatus
est. qui etsi causas ipsas non cernunt, signa tamen causarum et notas
cernunt; ad quas adhibita memoria et diligentia et monumentis superiorum
efficitur ea divinatio quae artificiosa dicitur extorum fulgorum ostentorum
signorumque caelestium. **128** Non est igitur ut mirandum sit ea praesentiri
a divinantibus quae nusquam sint; sunt enim omnia, sed tempore absunt.
atque ut in seminibus vis inest earum rerum quae ex iis progignuntur, sic
in causis conditae sunt res futurae, quas esse futuras aut concitata mens aut
soluta somno cernit aut ratio aut coniectura praesentit. Atque ut ii, qui solis
et lunae reliquorumque siderum ortus obitus motusque cognorunt, quo
quidque tempore eorum futurum sit multo ante praedicunt, sic qui cursum
rerum eventorumque consequentiam diuturnitate pertractata notaverunt aut
semper aut, si id difficile est, plerumque, quodsi ne id quidem conceditur, non
numquam certe quid futurum sit intellegunt. Atque haec quidem et quaedam
eiusdem modi argumenta cur sit divinatio ducuntur a fato.

    129 A natura autem alia quaedam ratio est, quae docet quanta sit animi
vis seiuncta a corporis sensibus, quod maxime contingit aut dormientibus
aut mente permotis. Ut enim deorum animi sine oculis sine auribus sine
lingua sentiunt inter se quid quisque sentiat (ex quo fit ut homines etiam
cum taciti optent quid aut voveant non dubitent quin di illud exaudiant), sic
animi hominum, cum aut somno soluti vacant corpore aut mente permoti
per se ipsi liberi incitati moventur, cernunt ea quae permixti cum corpore
animi videre non possunt. **130** Atque hanc quidem rationem naturae difficile
est fortasse traducere ad id genus divinationis, quod ex arte profectum
dicimus, sed tamen id quoque rimatur quantum potest Posidonius. esse

censet in natura signa quaedam rerum futurarum. etenim Ceos accepimus
ortum Caniculae diligenter quotannis solere servare coniecturamque capere,
ut scribit Ponticus Heraclides, salubrisne an pestilens annus futurus sit:
nam si obscurior ⟨et⟩ quasi caliginosa stella extiterit, pingue et concretum
esse caelum ut eius aspiratio gravis et pestilens futura sit; sin inlustris et
perlucida stella apparuerit, significari caelum esse tenue purumque et
propterea salubre. **131** Democritus autem censet sapienter instituisse veteres
ut hostiarum immolatarum inspicerentur exta; quorum ex habitu atque ex
colore tum salubritatis tum pestilentiae signa percipi, non numquam etiam
quae sit vel sterilitas agrorum vel fertilitas futura. Quae si a natura profecta
observatio atque usus agnovit, multa adferre potuit dies quae animadvertendo
notarentur, ut ille Pacuvianus qui in Chryse physicus inducitur minime
naturam rerum cognosse videatur:

> nam isti qui linguam avium intellegunt
> plusque ex alieno iecore sapiunt quam ex suo,
> magis audiendum quam auscultandum censeo.

cur, quaeso, cum ipse paucis interpositis versibus dicas satis luculente:

> quidquid est hoc, omnia animat format alit auget creat,
> sepelit recipitque in sese omnia omniumque idemst pater,
> indidemque eadem aeque oriuntur de integro atque eodem occidunt.

quid est igitur cur, cum domus sit omnium una eaque communis cumque
animi hominum semper fuerint futurique sint, cur ii quid ex quoque eveniat
et quid quamque rem significet perspicere non possint?"
     132 "Haec habui" inquit "de divinatione quae dicerem. Nunc illa testabor,
non me sortilegos neque eos qui quaestus causa hariolentur, ne psychomantia
quidem, quibus Appius amicus tuus uti solebat, agnoscere; non habeo denique
nauci Marsum augurem, non vicanos haruspices, non de circo astrologos, non
Isiacos coniectores, non interpretes somniorum; non enim sunt hi aut scientia
aut arte divini sed

> superstitiosi vates inpudentesque harioli
> aut inertes aut insani aut quibus egestas imperat,
> qui sibi semitam non sapiunt alteri monstrant viam;
> quibus divitias pollicentur, ab iis drachumam ipsi petunt.
> de his divitiis sibi deducant drachumam, reddant cetera.

atque haec quidem Ennius, qui paucis ante versibus esse deos censet, 'sed eos non curare' opinatur 'quid agat humanum genus.' Ego autem, qui et curare arbitror et monere etiam ac multa praedicere, levitate vanitate malitia exclusa divinationem probo." Quae cum dixisset Quintus, "praeclare tu quidem" inquam paratus * * *

Commentary

The introduction to *Div.* is far more compact than the expansive preface to *N. D.* and most of C.'s other philosophical treatises. He does not dedicate *Div.* to a friend, nor does he defend his decision to write philosophy or his allegiance to the Academy, preferring to launch immediately into the topic at hand. Though *Div.* as a whole is more Roman in its focus and character than many of his philosophical works, C. emphasizes from its beginning that divination is a universal and ancient phenomenon in which Rome has had a share from its very founding. This opening section sounds two other themes that recur throughout the dialogue: divination, often a private matter, is also an official state activity at Rome that often shapes governmental decision making, and it plays a significant role in forming Roman society and in defining Rome among the nations of the world. In this opening section, C. treats belief in divination as a middle ground between inordinate refinement and brutishness; his attitude, expressed in propria persona, is one of cautious reservation and neutrality. This stands apart from M.'s rigorous and often hostile questioning of the argument in favor of divination in Book 2.

1 From C.'s skeptical position, the antiquity and widespread popularity of divination (both of which are evoked in the appeal to the mythical heroic age of Greece and Rome) lend support to its authority, but they cannot prove its validity (*opinio . . . firmata*; cf. Q.'s *sententiam . . . conprobatam* at 11). The people of Rome are united in their belief that divination exists, and they share this belief with all other nations (see 11n. *antiquissimam sententiam tum omnium populorum et gentium consensu conprobatam*). **versari . . . divinationem**: "there is in use among men a particular (kind of) divination." Passive forms of *versare* can have a middle sense, as here (*OLD*, s.v. 11; *G&L* 212 with 218). C. singles out one type of divination (*OLD*, s.v. *quidam*[1] 2). **quam . . . appellant**: fixes an equivalence between the general Latin term used for all forms of divination and the more narrowly defined μαντικήν, which refers to inspired prophecy (cf. *Leg.* 2.32; *N. D.* 1.55). The equivalence will not be maintained throughout: both Q. and M. will use *divinatio* with its more general meaning. For C.'s rendering of Greek philosophical terms, see Powell 1995.   **praesensionem et scientiam rerum futurarum**: "preperception and knowledge of things to come." Although Roman *divinatio*, especially in a public context, was frequently restricted to the more limited goal of simply determining whether the gods approved of a proposed course of action, the distinction between that and foretelling the future is frequently blurred or ignored by the Romans generally and by the interlocutors here. *Scientia* is the standard rendering of Greek ἐπιστήμη.   **si modo est ulla**: "if any such thing exists." This is the central question explored by the dialogue.   **possit**: subjunctive of characteristic.   **nos melius**: sc. *facimus* (*vel sim.*).   **a divis . . . a furore**: C. establishes a Latin etymological link (*divinatio* as a gift *a divis*) that he feels is superior to the connection drawn by Plato (*Phdr.* 244a–c) among the seer (μάντις), his art (μαντική), and the madness from which it stems (μανία, rendered by Latin *furor*). Such etymologies are not uncommon in Plato, Aristotle, and especially the Stoics (cf. *N. D.* 3.63; Allen 2005): words were thought to reflect the inherent characteristics of the things to which they are connected and, therefore, to reveal certain truths about their nature. C. often expresses his preference for a Roman approach and Latin terminology in his philosophical works (e.g., *Fin.* 3.35 [cf. *Tusc.* 3.7, 23], 39; *Tusc.* 1.1).

2 neque tam humanam atque doctam neque tam inmanem tamque barbaram: reinforces, rather than negates, the preceding *gentem . . . nullam.* The repetition of *tam* (anaphora) emphasizes the antithesis of the two pairs *humanus/doctus* and *inmanis/barbarus*, with the third *tam* providing a crescendo. *Barbarus* is often used in *Div.* more specifically to denote peoples that are neither Greek nor Roman (e.g., 1.37, 47, 84, 90; 2.82).   **quae . . . censeat**: result clause.   **principio Assyrii**: continues the emphasis on the antiquity of divination. The Assyrians (the name is used by many Greek and Roman authors as a blanket term for the many ethnic groups that lived in the region that once was the Assyrian Empire [Parpola 2004]) were thought by most ancients to have been the inventors of astrology, that is, divination from the observation of celestial phenomena. In fact, the oldest evidence for astrology comes from Mesopotamia, in a text of the early second millennium BCE. For a survey of the ancient material and discussion of the origins of astrology, see Barton 1994, 9–31.   **ab ultumis:** "from the most remote times"; reinforces *principio* and should not be seen to refer to geographical distance (*contra* Pease *ad loc.*).   **observitaverunt:** a rare word appearing primarily in the context of observation of natural phenomena for divinatory purposes (*OLD*, s.v.). The frequentative underlines both the repetitious and long-term nature of astrological observation (cf. *diuturna observatione* and *longinquitate temporum innumerabilibus paene saeculis* in the next two sentences).   **quid . . . significaretur**: Pease notes the similarity of this phrase to *quid cuique eventurum* a few lines later but points out that the emphasis here is on prediction rather than actual outcome. Near repetition of words and phrases is more common in this work than in C.'s more polished treatises, perhaps an indication of the speed with which he composed the text.   **memoriae prodiderunt**: "they made a record of"; a favorite turn of phrase appearing far more frequently in C. than in any other author. See *OLD*, s.v. *memoria* 8b.   **qua in natione Chaldaei non ex artis sed ex gentis vocabulo nominati**: The Chaldeans ruled Babylonia until it was conquered by Cyrus of Persia in 539. They were so strongly associated with astrology that divination by observation of stars and planets came to be called Χαλδαική and that the term "Chaldeans" came to be used by the Greeks and Romans to refer to astrologers generally, often with a pejorative tone. C.'s point here is that the Chaldeans are an ethnic group and do not derive their name from their art.   **siderum**: with *scientiam*.   **Cilicum . . . et Pisidarum gens et . . . Pamphylia**: The culture of these three areas in Asia minor was a mix of indigenous, Greek, and Roman elements in varying degrees. It is not known if the forms of ornithoscopy (divination from the behavior of birds) and other types of divination practiced by these populations were similar to one another, if those practices derived from one ethnic tradition more than another, or how heavily they were influenced by Egyptian and Assyrian traditions. The Cilicians, Pisidians, and Pamphylians are three more examples of the universality of divination. Q. deploys them rather differently at 25, where he contrasts their practice of ornithoscopy rather positively with the sorry state of Roman augury.   **praefuimus ipsi**: C. commanded these regions as governor of the province of Cilicia (51 BCE).

3 in Aeoliam Ioniam Asiam Siciliam Italiam: the most important areas of Greek colonization.   **Pythio . . . oraculo**: The oracles of Pythian Apollo at Delphi, of Zeus at Dodona in Epirus, and of the Egyptian god Ammon (who was often assimilated to Zeus) at Egyptian Thebes were the most important oracles of the Greek world. Aside from C.'s remark here, however, little is known about the involvement of the oracles of Zeus and Ammon in the foundation of colonies. There is ample evidence that Apollo at Delphi selected leaders for colonizing expeditions and designated locations for new settlements. See Malkin 1987, 17–91.   **quam**: adverbial with *multa*.   **auspicato**: "after the auspices had been taken"; an ablative absolute used adverbially (*G&L* 410 n. 4). Taking the auspices (on which see Intro. 000) was an essential step before founding a new city or colony (Gargola 1995,

72–82): it ensured that the gods gave their blessing to the new enterprise (cf. Liv. 5.52.2, 28.28.11).   **optumus augur**: C. sometimes uses technical terms (e.g., *haruspex, augurare*) in a more general way. Here he praises Romulus's skill in augury but is not attributing to him any official position within the augural college, the group of public priests charged with practicing augury at Rome. He elsewhere describes the Greeks Pythagoras (5) and Calchas (87) as *augures*. Although Romulus is sometimes identified as the founder of the augural college (e.g., *Rep.* 2.15–16), he was never a member of it. His association with augury is most prominent in the story of his argument with Remus over the right to name and to rule their new city (Liv. 1.6.4–7.3). To settle the dispute, each brother established himself on a hilltop (Remus on the Aventine, Romulus on the Palatine) to watch the sky for a sign from Jupiter. Remus received a sign of six vultures first, but Romulus then reported seeing twice as many (called, from Ennius onward, the *augurium augustum*; see 107n. *apud Ennium*. For Ennius, see 23n. *Andromacham Enni*). A heated disagreement broke out between the brothers and their followers as to whether priority or the greater number took precedence. A fight broke out, and Remus was killed, leaving Romulus in charge. Romulus also followed proper augural procedure when he established the temple of Jupiter Feretrius (Liv. 1.10.5–7). See Gargola 1995, 28–29.   **auguribus**: ablative with *usi* (*sunt*).   **exactis regibus**: ablative absolute in place of a temporal clause.   **nec domi nec militiae**: "neither at home nor abroad"; an uncommon variation of *domi militiaeque*, the standard expression of the totality of Roman political activity: domestic affairs and foreign relations. *nec . . . nec* reinforces the preceding *nihil*. Cf. 2n. *neque . . . neque*.   **et inpetriendis . . . procurandis**: "in both seeking out and observing signs about the state of affairs and interpreting and expiating unnatural occurrences"; technical augural terms, all ablatives of respect. Though one might expect these to be datives of the gerundive, that construction is rare in Latin prose earlier than Livy (*G&L* 429.2). This chiastic phrase (*abba*) comprises the main division of signs within augural law: *signa impetrativa et oblativa*, on which see Intro. p. 7.   **haruspicum disciplina**: also known as *haruspicina*. It seems that the *haruspices* were originally specialists only in a particular type of extispicy (the inspection of animal entrails, esp. the liver, but see 16n. *quid fissum in extis, quid fibra valeat*). Their expertise expanded over time, and by the period of the late republic, they were responsible for all the types of prognostication that fell under the *Etrusca disciplina*, the name properly given to the whole body of Etruscan religious knowledge. In C.'s time, the *haruspices* dealt primarily with extispicy but were also consulted by the Roman Senate on some meteorological phenomena (mainly lightning) and the expiation of *portenta*, unusual events including monstrous births, bizarre animal behavior,

and inexplicable sounds. No detailed written records for Etruscan extispicy
survive, though several model organs thought to be teaching tools are
preserved, most famously a bronze liver from Piacenza. For excellent pictures
of the liver and artistic representations of *haruspices* divining, see Torelli 2001,
276–80; Jannot 2005, 19, fig. 2.1. Literary sources preserve more information
about Etruscan brontoscopy, the interpretation of lightning and thunder
(*fulgura*). Pliny the Elder records many details (*Nat.* 2.138–40), and Ioannes
Lydus's *De Ostentis* includes a Greek translation of an Etruscan divinatory
calendar published in Latin by C.'s contemporary P. Nigidius Figulus. We do
not know how the Etruscans determined the proper expiation for *portenta*.
For general discussion of Etruscan religion, including its divinatory practices,
see Haynes 2000, 268–86; Jannot 2005; de Grummond and Simon 2006,
which includes an English translation of Nigidius Figulus's brontoscopic
calendar. Haruspicy was so strongly identified with Etruria that the Romans
always considered it foreign, even though it became part of the civic religion
of Rome at a very early period. The Senate even issued a decree (of uncertain
date) requiring that sons of aristocratic Etruscan families be trained in the
practice (on which see 92n. *de principum filiis x . . . traderentur*) so that the
discipline might be preserved.

4 et cum duobus modis animi . . . incitarentur: Having sketched the main
forms of technical (or artificial) divination (see 11 for the distinction), C.
moves to natural divination, that is, prophecy through divine inspiration
and dreams.   **ratione et scientia**: "reason and knowledge."   **motu
ipsi suo soluto et libero**: that is, unhampered by the senses and bodily
necessities. *Ipsi* goes back to *animi*. Its unusual position here (it is rarely so
far delayed) emphasizes that the intervening phrase describes a distinctive
property of souls (*NLS* 37; *G&L* 311).   **furente . . . furoris**: emphasizes
the connection of waking prophecy to madness (note *furibundas* in the
next sentence).   **furoris divinationem . . . contineri arbitrati**: explains
decem interpretes delectos . . . esse voluerunt. Inspired prophecy was rarely
used for public purposes by the Romans, who preferred technical divination
that provided results that could be tested and verified. The only significant
exception is the Sibylline books (on which see Intro. pp. 7–8). Wariness of
inspired prophecy extended even to this august collection, and the Romans
tempered the *furor* behind the verses by requiring that they be subjected to
interpretation by the Board of Ten Men for Performing Rites, the *decemviri
sacris faciundis* (expanded to *quindecimviri* under Sulla). During the
republic, the books were kept originally in the temple of Jupiter Optimus
Maximus and later moved to the temple of Palatine Apollo. They could be
consulted only by the *decemviri* when they had been ordered to do so by the

Senate.   **Sibyllinis maxume versibus**: the most important and best-known
collection of prophecies used by the Romans. There were other collections:
the prophecies of Marcius (see 89n. *Marcios quosdam fratres nobili loco natos*)
and of the Etruscan nymph Vegoia were also kept by public officials in the
temple of Palatine Apollo (Serv., *A.* 6.72).   **ex quo genere**: sc. *furoris
divinatio*.   **saepe hariolorum etiam et vatum**: The distinction between
these two types of diviners, both often disparaged by Roman authors as being
low-class and driven by a desire for profit, cannot be recovered. *Saepe* is an
exaggeration: inspired prophecy played only an occasional role at Rome. It
was far more popular among the Greeks.   **ut Octaviano bello**: the conflict
between L. Cornelius Cinna, ally of Marius and consul of 87 BCE, and his
colleague Cn. Octavius, whose reliance on astrologers and other disreputable
diviners is recorded by Plutarch (*Mar.* 42.7).   **Culleoli**: sc. *praedictiones.*
Cornelius Culleolus is otherwise unknown. His cognomen is unusual
and suggests that he may have been from a senatorial family (Wiseman
1994, 59); his elevated social status would have increased his prestige as a
prophet.   **somnia graviora**: To the example given in the next sentence
can be added only the dream that caused the repetition of the *ludi maximi* in
either 491 (recounted at 55; see Liv. 2.36.1–8 with Ogilvie 1965, *ad loc.*) or 279
(Macr., *Sat.* 1.11.3–5).   **summo consilio**: sc. the Senate; not a technical
term.   **quin . . . nostra**: "Why, even within living memory." While C. is at
pains to demonstrate the antiquity of divination, he also stresses that it is not
confined to the past.   **templum . . . somnio**: The identity of the consuls
dates this episode to 90 BCE, during the Social War fought between Rome and
many of its former Italian allies. The restoration of Juno Sospita's temple is the
only historical instance of the republic responding to an individual's dream:
the dream reported at 55 is of such an early date that its historicity is suspect.
Caecilia Metella was a member of one of the most prominent political families
in Rome, daughter of the consul of 123. C. emphasizes the public nature of the
restoration of Juno's temple by observing that it was a consul who undertook
the project *de senatus sententia* (cf. 99). The timing of Caecilia's dream (details
of which are provided by Obs. 55) and the nature of Juno Sospita, a goddess of
martial appearance (cf. *N. D.* 1.82) whose association with Rome was a result
of Roman victory in the Latin War in 338 BCE, suggest that the dream was
understood to relate to the present conflict (see Schultz 2006).

5–7 *Doxography*

The value of C.'s enterprise is supported by the importance and the number of
philosophers, representing all the major schools, who have weighed in on the

subject; the lack of agreement among them provides a context for and perhaps justification of (cf. *N. D.* 1.1) C.'s own uncertainty (*Div.* 1.7). After laying out the basic positions of the most important followers of each philosophical school, C. explains that he will follow the Academic method of investigation he used in *N. D.* For the relationship between that earlier dialogue and *Div.*, see Intro. pp. 10–11.

5 Atque haec . . . probaverunt: C. only goes so far as to say that the empirical argument for divination has been more persuasive through the ages than any theoretical explanation (*ratione*).   **exquisita**: "precise."   **argumenta**: introduces the indirect question that follows. Cf. 128; *N. D.* 1.62, 3.10.   **Xenophanes unus . . . funditus sustulit, reliqui vero omnes praeter Epicurum**: Xenophanes of Colophon (fl. mid-sixth century) is singled out as the only major philosopher who believed in the gods but did not accept the validity of divination. Epicurus (341–270 BCE) was often, and unfairly, accused of atheism by C. (e.g., *Div.* 2.40; *N. D.* 1.85, 121–24) and many others (Obbink 1989); Q.'s disparaging remarks at 62 and 87 suggest that he shares C.'s uncharitable opinion. In truth, however, Epicurus agreed with Xenophanes that the existence of the gods did not entail the existence of divination. Though there are significant differences between them, both Xenophanes and Epicurus saw the gods as removed from human affairs and concerns, and both developed cosmologies that provided naturalistic explanations of phenomena taken by others to be portents. The fragments of the pre-Socratic philosophers are collected in Diels and Kranz 1967. English translations are available in Kirk, Raven, and Schofield 1983 and Waterfield 2009. The fragments of Epicurus and testimonia of later authors are collected in Arrighetti 1973.   **qui . . . diceret**: relative clause of concession.   **funditus sustulit**: "utterly did away with."   **balbutientem**: "blathering"; a rare word used primarily for animals, tedious individuals, and rival philosophers (e.g., *Ac.* 2.137; *Tusc.* 5.75).   **cum Socrates . . . cumque**: introduces a series of concessive clauses ending with *Democritus . . . conprobaret*. As he is portrayed by his students Plato and Xenophon, Socrates (469–399 BCE), who left posterity no writings of his own, accepted both natural and artificial divination, with a preference for the former (e.g., Pl., *Apol.* 33c; Pl., *Phdr.* 244a–d; Pl., *Leg.* 738b–d; Xen., *Mem.* 1.1.1–9). Indeed, Q. cites him as a believer in prophetic dreams and prophecy (52, 61, 87) and as capable of prophecy himself (see 123n. *qua soleo*). C. regarded the philosophy of Socrates and Plato as supreme (e.g., *De Orat.* 3.59; *Ac.* 1.15; *Scaur.* 4; *Opt. Gen.* 17).   **omnes Socratici**: The definition of this group is somewhat hazy given the variety of philosophical schools that claimed descent from Socrates (*De Orat.* 3.61–2). C. enumerates the positions of the most important of these schools (Academic, Peripatetic, and Stoic). For most of the Socratic schools, including the Cynics, who are not discussed here, there is little direct evidence for their position on divination (see Pease *ad loc.*). Testimonia are now collected in Giannantoni 1990. **Zenoque et ii qui ab eo essent profecti**: "Zeno and his successors." *Essent profecti* is attracted into the subjunctive because the relative clause is contained in the concessive clause *cum . . . manerent* (*G&L* 629). Zeno (335–263 BCE) of Citium on Cyprus founded Stoicism several generations after Plato (c. 429–347) established the Academy. He is given pride of place here because the Stoics were the most forceful defenders of divination; Q will argue the Stoic position. In the Stoic system, the validity of divination is inextricably intertwined with the arguments for the existence of the gods (9–10, 81–82; *N. D.* 2.163). Zeno himself accepted many forms of divination (D. L. 7.149; see 6 below). Fragments of the Stoics are gathered in von Arnim 1905–24. **manerent in . . . sententia**: "abided by the opinion." **vetere Academia et Peripateticis consentientibus**: ablative absolute. Both groups accepted some forms of divination, particularly natural divination. *Vetere Academia* refers to the Academic school under the leadership of Plato and his earliest successors until about 267, when Arcesilaus (see 7n. *etenim . . . comparemus*) took the helm. The Old Academy adhered closely to Socrates's teachings as laid out by Plato. For a more detailed discussion of the central tenets Plato established for his followers, see Dillon 2003, 1–29. Academics rigorously applied the dialectical method of investigation: questioning the views of philosophical rivals (esp. the Stoics) with the goal of exposing weaknesses and contradictions in their arguments. In the absence of knowable truth, Academics sought what seemed *simillimum veri* (see 9n. *ad veritatem . . . propensior*). The classic formulation is *Tusc.* 5.11. The Old Academy enjoyed fresh relevance in late republican Rome through the efforts of one of C.'s teachers, Antiochus of Ascalon, whose revival of its doctrines found adherents among politically prominent Romans, most notably Brutus (see Sedley 1997). **Peripateticis**: Aristotle (384–322), founder of the Peripatetic school, cautiously accepted divination through dreams (*Div. Somn.* 462b12). Wardle notes in his comment on this passage that Aristotle also discusses oracles in neutral terms in his historical works. Later Peripatetics followed their founder's opinions. C. cites Aristotle's followers Dicaearchus and Cratippus here as defenders of both major forms of natural divination. Cf. 70–72, 81, 113. **Pythagoras**: c. 570–c. 490 BCE; emigrated at about age forty from the Greek island of Samos to Croton in Italy, where his philosophical school flourished. He is most famous for his belief in the transmigration of souls (metempsychosis), though it is difficult to determine his beliefs in any detail. Pythagoras wrote nothing. In later sources, he becomes an almost divine figure capable of prophecy (Aristotle ap. Apollon., *Mir.* 6 = 191 Rose). See Huffman 1999; Pease *ad loc.* The tradition that Numa, the second king of Rome, was a student of Pythagoras was vigorously denied by C. (*Tusc.* 4.3) and Livy (1.18.2).   **qui etiam ipse augur vellet esse**: a causal relative clause.   **Democritus**: born c. 460 BCE; he and his teacher Leucippus were the first to establish an atomic theory of the universe. Although atomism is associated with the denial of divine providence (see Taylor 1999, 188–95, 211–16) and although M. cites Democritus in his argument against divination (2.57, 120), Democritus advocated the practice of extispicy (131), divination from the shape and color of animal entrails (*exta*). Furthermore, D. L. (9.34) records a tradition that Democritus learned the arts of astrology and theology from magi (on whom see 46n. *magi*) and Chaldeans. C. most often cites him as a natural philosopher, though he also pairs him and Plato as exemplary eloquent speakers (e.g., *De Orat.* 1.49; *Orat.* 67).   **praesensionem**: See 1n. *praesensionem . . . futurarum.* For a more limited understanding of Democritus's notion of preperception as only the perception of another's intention to act, see Bicknell 1969.   **Dicaearchus**: Dicaearchus of Messana (fl. c. 320–300 BCE) was a student of Aristotle and the author of works on many subjects, including on the oracle of Trophonius at Lebadea in Boeotia (on which see 74n. *Trophonio res divina fieret*) and on divine inspiration. He also wrote a *magnus liber* arguing that it is better not to know the future (*Div.* 2.105). The little of his work that survives has been collected by Mirhady 2001. On Dicaearchus in C., see Sharples 2001, 163–73.   **Cratippusque familiaris noster**: Cratippus of Pergamum was a prominent Peripatetic philosopher whose early career had been spent as a student of the Academic Antiochus of Ascalon (on whom see 5n. *vetere Academia et Peripateticis consentientibus*). He was a very close friend of the Tullii (cf. 70, 113, 2.107; *Brut.* 250); of Pompey, whom he tried to comfort in the aftermath of the battle of Pharsalus (Plu., *Pomp.* 75.4); and of M. Brutus (Plu., *Brut.* 24.1). After the Civil War, he was granted citizenship by Caesar through C.'s efforts (Plu., *Cic.* 24.7) and took on C.'s praenomen and nomen, which he passed on to his descendents: an inscription from Pergamum, now lost, records the existence of the family of M. Tullius Cratippus *sacerdos Romae et Salutis* (*CIL* 3.399; see O'Brien-Moore 1942 with Habicht's comments in *IPerg.* 3.164–65), who was probably the son or grandson of the philosopher. C. held Cratippus in such high regard that he entrusted his son's education to him (*Off.* 1.1 with Dyck 1996, *ad loc.*). Indeed, the younger Marcus was with Cratippus in Athens at the time C. was writing *Div.* (see *Fam.* 12.16.2, 16.21.3 = *SBF* 328.2, 337.3). Nothing is known of Cratippus's views on divination except what is preserved here and at 70–71.

6 sed cum Stoici omnia fere illa defenderent: The Stoics did not accept
all forms of divination. Q. excludes certain diviners who worked only for
payment (132), and there is evidence that some Stoics took a limited view of
astrology. They were willing to accept that astrology could foretell general
things, such as what sort of personality a baby born on a certain day might
have, but they did not think that it could be used to predict specific events
in the life of an individual. See Hankinson 1988.   **quod et Zeno in suis
commentariis quasi semina quaedam sparsisset et ea Cleanthes paulo
uberiora fecisset, accessit . . . Chrysippus**: The subjunctives attibute the
explanation to the Stoics. **commentariis**: an informal work such as a fairly
unpolished narrative or even just a collection of notes, often intended for
expansion and enhancement later on. Both C. and Atticus had composed
commentarii on C.'s consulship (*Att.* 1.19.10, 2.1.1–2 = *SBA* 19.10, 21.1–
2). Atticus's version was published (Nep., *Att.* 18.6), but C.'s efforts to get
Posidonius (on whom see 6n. *noster Posidonius*) to turn his into something
ornatius were unsuccessful. The most famous ancient *commentarii, those of*
Caesar, are unusual in that they are already well polished and adorned with
direct discourse, dramatizations, and the like that are the stuff of *historia*.
It is not clear to which of Zeno's works C. refers. The extant fragments of
Zeno and his successors are collected in von Arnim 1905–24. **Cleanthes . . .
Chrysippus**: Zeno's first two successors. Cleanthes died in 232; Chrysippus
died around 206. **uberiora fecisset**: "he had developed them more copiously."
Uberiora, primarily an agricultural term, continues the image in *semina . . .
sparsisset*. In a rhetorical context, *uber* describes a richness and complexity
not just of sentence structure but also in the use of examples, details, allusions,
and other devices that make an argument clear and interesting. Cleanthes
need not have done much to add noticeably to Zeno: C. elsewhere criticizes
the Stoics generally for an excessively terse style (*Brut.* 120). A thorough
discussion is found in Hays 1987. **accessit**: "joined in." The verb is similarly
used at *Att.* 4.18.3 = *SBA* 92.3.   **Diogenes**: Diogenes of Babylon (c. 240–
152 BCE) was the fifth scholarch (leader) of the Stoa at Athens, where he
taught Panaetius and Carneades among others.   **Antipater**: Antipater of
Tarsus succeeded Diogenes as scholarch. He is most famous for his written
rebuttal of Carneades (*Ac.* 2.17, 28, 109, 143; Plu., *Garr.* 23 = *Mor.* 514C–
D). The work mentioned here included numerous anecdotes of Socrates's
prophetic powers (see 123).   **noster Posidonius**: so described also at 2.47,
N. D. 1.123 and 2.88, *Fin.* 1.6, and *Tusc.* 2.61. During C.'s tour of Greece in
79–77, he studied Stoicism with Posidonius, whose school in Rhodes was a
popular stopping place for prominent Romans abroad (Pompey among them).
Posidonius had long had access to the highest circles of Rome's political class:
he visited with Marius while in Rome as an ambassador in 87 (Plu., *Mar.*

45.7). His interest in determining the causes of natural phenomena (including prophetic dreams; see 64) set him apart from earlier Stoic leaders. Though usually respectful of and affectionate toward his former teacher, C. does not shy away from holding his positions up to thorough critique (e.g., 2.35; *Fat.* 5–7).   **a Stoicis vel princeps eius disciplinae . . . degeneravit Panaetius**: "even the foremost of their school, Panaetius, broke with the Stoics." Cf. 2.97; *Luc.* 107 (*princeps . . . Stoicorum*). Sometime after 146, Panaetius (c. 185–109) came to Rome, where he became part of the group of intellectuals, Greek and Roman, associated with P. Cornelius Scipio Aemilianus. He left Rome in 129 to assume the leadership of the Stoa after the death of Antipater. Panaetius revised or refined several traditional Stoic positions, including that on divination. See Morford 2002, 23–28.   **Quod illi in aliqua re invitissumis Stoicis Stoico facere licuit**: The relative clause precedes its antecedent *id*. **invitissumis Stoicis:** ablative absolute. **illi . . . Stoico:** "to him, a Stoic." **Stoicis Stoico**: The polyptoton, repetition of a word or its cognates in different forms or cases, emphasizes the dissension among the Stoics, a group often mocked for demanding that its members rigidly adhere to basic tenets.   **ut**: delayed to highlight *id nos*, heightening the contrast between the clauses introduced by *Quod illi* and *id nos*.   **a Stoicis non concedetur?**: C. asks that the Stoics grant him generally (*in reliquis rebus*) the same indulgence they granted to Panaetius on the issue of divination (*in aliqua re*), namely, the right to refuse to commit wholly to any position.   **liquet**: from *liquere* (to be evident), impersonal.   **reliquis eiusdem disciplinae**: the other Stoics.

7 haec . . . laus: "this virtue" (*OLD*, s.v. 3); points forward to the next sentence, where C. offers a clear statement of the Academic approach (*verentibusque ne temere vel falsae rei vel non satis cognitae adsentiamur*) and method (*argumenta cum argumentis comparemus*).   **etenim . . . comparemus**: Cf. *Ac.* 2.7; *N. D.* 1.1, 11. The rigorous skepticism of the Middle, or Second, Academy, headed by Arcesilaus, dictated the impossibility of knowledge. In its place, the Academy advocated the suspension of belief with regard to unverifiable impressions. Carneades, whose assumption of the leadership in the early second century BCE marks the period of the New, or Third, Academy, modified this rigid position. He accepted opinions that were founded on an assessment of probable truthfulness: one could support a position that seemed likely to be true. Carneades made quite an impression in Rome during a visit to the city in 155 BCE as a member of an Athenian diplomatic embassy (which also included Diogenes and Critolaus, the heads of the Stoic and Peripatetic schools), when he delivered public lectures for and against justice on consecutive days (C., *Rep.* 3.11 = Lact., *Div. Inst.* 5.14.3–5).   **nobismet ipsis quaerentibus . . . verentibusque**: depends on

videtur. The emphatic *nobismet ipsis* marks the transition from the review
of past philosophers to the opinions of C. himself and establishes him next
in the succession.   **acute et copiose**: desirable oratorical qualities that C.
associates particularly with Carneades (*Tusc.* 5.11; cf. Quint., *Inst.* 8.3.49). Like
Socrates and Arcesilaus, Carneades did not write down his teachings, leaving
that task to his students. His most important disciple was Clitomachus, who
eventually succeeded him as leader of the Academy. Clitomachus's works
were known to C. (e.g., 2.87) but are no longer extant.   **temeritas . . .**
errorque: picks up *temere . . . cognitae* in the previous sentence. In addition to
rashness and inaccuracy, these words connote randomness and the absence
of any guiding principle (cf. *Div.* 2.85; *N. D.* 2.56), which is antithetical
to the Carneadean position (*Ac.* 2.108).   **auspiciis rebusque divinis**
religionique: "auspices, divine rites, and religious feeling." The phrase is
difficult to render into English, since *res divina* and *religio* are highly elastic
terms. The precise difference between *res divina* and *religio* is not clear but
seems to be one of action and emotion/thought. *Res divina* can be used to
mean sacrifice in specific, a cultic pattern of activity at a particular shrine,
or even something as large and vague as "divine affairs." Despite the obvious
relationship of *religio* to "religion," there is no evidence for a Roman concept
that matches the modern idea of religion as something that embraces rituals,
beliefs, laws, ethics, a body of sacred writings, and congregations populated
by initiated members, until many centuries later (see Nongbri 2013, 15–64).
C., Lucretius, and other writers of the late Roman Republic and the Roman
Empire usually use *religio* to refer to a feeling of reverence or scruples, though
the term can refer also to a set of ritual practices (cf. *Dom.* 32). At *N. D.* 3.5,
C. has the pontifex Cotta offer a tripartite division of *omnis populi Romani*
religio into *sacra, auspicia,* and pronouncements of the *haruspices* and the
decemviri sacris faciundis (cf. *Leg.* 2.20, 2.30; *Har. Resp.* 18; Aug., *Civ. D.* 6.3).
The apparent clarity of this definition is obfuscated, however, by two things.
First, Cotta goes on to refer to these three components as *religiones* themselves
(that *religio* can be plural further complicates any attempt to render it into
English with a single word). Second, Cotta's subdivision of *sacra* is as hard
to pin down as a *religio*, since *sacer* can refer to anything that belongs to the
gods (Macr., *Sat.* 3.3.2), including an individual, a sanctuary, a festival, a rite,
or the sum total of all of these: an entire cult.   **neglectis iis . . . susceptis**:
ablative absolutes with a conditional force.   **impia fraude**: Religious views
outside the mainstream and disregard for regular forms of worship often
provoked accusations of *impietas* (Grk. ἀσέβεια) or atheism. See Obbink 1989,
189–90.   **anili superstitione**: Old women are frequently portrayed as
unduly credulous and excessively devoted to worship. Their marginal status in
Roman society is reflected in the fact that they are commonly associated with

practices and beliefs at the fringes of Roman religious life—activities we might
now call magic or superstition. See Margel 2006. *Superstitio* is the antithesis
of *religio* (*N. D.* 2.71–72 with Pease *ad loc.*; Fest. 366L; Sen., *Cl.* 2.5.1): it is
less respectable, less rational, and outside the *mos maiorum*. Belittling his
opponents' religious beliefs is one of C.'s preferred rhetorical tactics (cf. 2.19,
125; *N. D.* 2.5, 2.7, 2.70, 3.12, 3.92; *Dom.* 105; *Tusc.* 1.48).

8–11 Setting the Scene

Here C. establishes the setting for the debate and the positions to be argued
by the interlocutors. The author fades into the background as the characters
Q. and M. begin their conversation. It is as intimate, private, and personal as
possible, conducted without an audience as the brothers stroll the grounds of
C.'s favorite country estate. The preliminary interchange between M. and Q.
closely links *Div.* and Book 2 of *N. D.*

8 et alias saepe et paulo accuratius nuper: "often on other occasions and
recently in a somewhat more thorough way."   **Q. fratre**: C.'s brother,
younger by several years, with whom he had a close and affectionate, if
sometimes rocky, relationship (see *SBQ*, pp. 3–6 with Shackleton Bailey 1971,
67–69, 179–85). Q.'s crowning political achievement was the praetorship
of 62 BCE and the governorship of Asia for the three years following. The
young Q. traveled with C. to Greece in the early seventies and shared in his
studies there. Though his character here is given the task of arguing the Stoic
point of view, Q.'s philosophical leanings were closer to the Peripatetic school
(2.100; *Fin.* 5.96).   **Tusculano**: Romans often refer to a country estate
(*praedium*) by the adjectival form of its location. The proximity of Tusculum
to Rome made it a popular location for country homes of the Roman elite.
C.'s villa, also the setting for *Tusc.*, had once belonged to the dictator Sulla
(Plin., *Nat.* 22.12). Other Romans who had property in Tusculum in the
early first century include L. Licinius Crassus (cos. of 95; see *De Orat.* 1.24)
and L. Licinius Lucullus (cos. of 74; see *Fin.* 3.7–8), one of the wealthiest
men in Rome.   **cum ambulandi causa in Lyceum venissemus (id enim
superiori gymnasio nomen est)**: A *gymnasium* was originally a place for
the athletic and military training of young Greek men, but by the Hellenistic
period, *gymnasia* housed libraries (as did the one mentioned here [2.8]) and
had become centers of education and philosophical debate. Private libraries
of considerable size were a common feature of Roman aristocratic life in
the first century BCE (see Casson 2001, 61–79). C. named his library after
the Lyceum, the Athenian *gymnasium* that housed the Peripatetic school

founded in 335 BCE by Aristotle, whom C. ranked second only to Plato.
The Peripatetics took their name from a *peripatos*, a covered walkway at the
Lyceum; *ambulandi causa* suggests that the Tusculan Lyceum imitated this
feature of the original. Our interlocutors do not sit down until the beginning
of Book 2 (2.8). As C. implies by the phrase *superiori gymnasio*, his Lyceum
was just one of two libraries at his Tusculan estate. The other was named
after the Academy (*Tusc.* 2.9, 3.7), Plato's school; it, too, was furnished with
walkways.   **tertium**: sc. *librum*. Much of the third book of *N. D.* is lost.
It contained the Academic rebuttal, presented by the figure of C. Aurelius
Cotta (cos. of 75 and pontifex maximus), of the Stoic argument on the nature
of the gods and their providential governance of the universe, put forward
by Q. Lucilius Balbus in Book 2 of the work.   **ipse Cotta sic disputat ut
Stoicorum magis argumenta confutet quam hominum deleat religionem**:
Cotta's argument draws largely on Carneades's critiques of the Stoics (see
Pease *N. D.*, pp. 48–49), highlighting difficulties in the Stoic position rather
than putting forward a counterargument that the gods do not exist. On
the Academic use of the dialectical method, see 5n. *vetere Academia et
Peripateticis consentientibus*.   **istud**: "the point you just made"; refers
to the *ut* clause in the previous sentence.   **saepius**: Cotta is at pains to
make his position clear, repeating it at *N. D.* 3.1, 4, and 93.   **communia
iura migrare**: "to do away with the laws common among men." The phrase
commune ius almost always appears in the singular, frequently modified by a
genitive (e.g., *civitatis, gentium*). The plural here subsumes the rights common
to all societies, whether a small group or entire nations. For the negative
reception of theological beliefs outside the mainstream, see 7n. *impia fraude*.

9 eius orationi non sane desidero quid respondeam: This is a departure
from the normal word order (anastrophe): *quid respondeam eius orationi non
sane desidero*. The effect is to emphasize that Q.'s argument will respond to
Cotta's. **desidero**: "I am not lacking, not at a loss for." **in extremo tertio**:
"at the very end of the third book." **ad veritatem est visa propensior**: Q.
makes M. sound more Stoic than he is at *N. D.* 3.95. In that passage, M. says
that Balbus's Stoic argument about the nature of the gods seemed *ad veritatis
similitudinem . . . propensior*, as close to an assertion of truthfulness as M.
could make given his allegiance to the Academy. Whereas Stoics believed
that the truth could be known, at least by the sage, the Academics denied this
possibility. In the absence of a knowable truth, then, Academics sought to
determine what seemed most likely to be true (cf. 2.150). See 7n. *etenim . . .
comparemus*. It is unclear whether the criterion for a determination of *veritatis
similitudinem* in an argument is logical consistency or accordance with the
reality of everyday existence (Glucker 1995). **Sed quod praetermissum**

est in illis libris . . . id est de divinatione . . . videamus quam habeat vim et quale sit: The *quod* clause, explained by *id est de divinatione*, is the subject of the two indirect questions dependent on *videamus*. The logical link among these three core parts of the sentence is interrupted by two intervening clauses, an explanatory phrase (*credo quia . . . disseri*) and a definition of divination (*quae est . . . praesensio*). This loose organization makes the sentence unwieldy, but it reflects the way people often speak, giving the passage a conversational rhythm. Q. here echoes Balbus's complaint at *N. D.* 3.19. As Wynne (2008, 140–45) points out, however, divination is an issue in Balbus's Stoic argument in Book 2, where it plays a prominent role in the argument for the existence of the gods (4–12) and their interest in human affairs (162–66). Yet Balbus's treatment of divination itself is limited. Q. supplements Balbus's argument by taking up two topics it left unexplored: proof of the reality of divination and some description of the mechanisms by which divination operates.   **id quaeri deque eo disseri**: "that this be investigated and discussed" (*OLD*, s.v. *dissero*[2] 2b). *Id* and *eo* go back to *quod praetermissum est*. *Quaerere et disserere* is C.'s preferred rendering of Greek λογική (cf. *Fin.* 1.22).   **quae est earum rerum quae fortuitae putantur praedictio atque praesensio**: Q. offers his own definition of divination, similar to that offered by C. at 1 except that Q. adds the critical element of ostensible randomness (*quae fortuitae putantur*). In his lengthy rejection of this definition at 2.13–21, M. misquotes Q., turning apparent chance into actual chance (*quae essent fortuitae* [13]). Pease (p. 68) attributes the misquotation to the author's changing sources between books, but it is more likely an instance (not unique; see also the paraphrase of 38 at 2.117 and of 118 at 2.35) of M. not playing fairly, by turning a defensible position (that things that appear to happen without a cause can, in fact, have a cause) into an impossible one (that things that happen randomly, i.e., without a cause, can be predicted).   **id si placet**: parenthetical; another conversational touch. Q. repeats *si placet* in 10.

10 siquidem: a strong conditional ("if it is really possible that").   **ut et si divinatio sit, di sint, et si di sint, sit divinatio**: The two present general conditions are attracted into the subjunctive by the result clause that contains them; the result clause is itself within the protasis of a present general condition. This phrase articulates an important Stoic tenet, the mutual entailment of the existence of gods and the validity of divination, which is maintained by Balbus in *N. D.* 2.7–12 and elaborated on by Q. at 82–83 and 117. The argument is not as circular as M. makes it out to be (2.41–42), because neither premise rests exclusively on the other; that is, there are other avenues of proof for each claim. The Stoics demonstrated the existence of

the gods largely by appeal to common conception (κοιναὶ ἔννοιαι, not to
be confused with the *consensus omnium*, on which see 11n. *antiquissimam
sententiam tum omnium populorum et gentium consensu conprobatam*), that
is, a general intuition, drawn from nature and shared by all rational humans,
that the gods exist. Benevolent gods, defined by the Stoics as wanting to assist
mankind, must have a method to communicate their assistance to us: if there
are gods, there is divination. Divination can be proved by demonstrating
a link between *signa* and *eventa* (as Q. will do for most of his speech). It is
thus further evidence for the existence of gods who desire to send us that
information: if there is divination, there are gods. See Wynne 2008, 140–
43; Brittain 2005.   **natura**: "by the natural order of things." M. posits a
physical world that operates without any divine guidance, which Q. dismisses
below. In 13–16, Q. points to predictive signs in the natural world as evidence
that long observation has been able to establish links between otherwise
seemingly unconnected phenomena.   **ut sint di**: *Ut* is concessive ("granted
that . . .", *G&L* 608).   **clara et perspicua**: "unambiguous and clear." Pease
(*ad loc.*) notes that *perspicua* is a stronger term than *clara*. The theme of the
ease or difficulty of understanding signs sent by the gods, frequently cast, as
here, in visual terms (clear/obscure, light/dark), runs through the dialogue.
An important element of Q.'s defense is that the meanings of some signs are
incontrovertible, so that their relationship to the *eventa* that follow them
cannot be lightly dismissed.   **si vacas animo**: "if you have nothing on your
mind." Philosophy is proper only for a Roman gentleman's *otium*, hence C.'s
dialogues are often set on holidays (e.g., *De Orat.* 1.24; *Fin.* 3.8; *N. D.* 1.15)
or, as here, in times of imposed inactivity.   **putes**: subjunctive in a relative
clause of characteristic.

11 sit nihil aliud quod lubenter agere possim: This is the closest C. comes
in this dialogue to acknowledging his withdrawal from politics after Caesar's
victory in the Civil War with Pompey. In *N. D.*, he addresses the issue at
greater length (1.5–9).

11–16 Quintus Begins

Q. begins with a *partitio*; that is, he lays out the organizing principles of his
argument and the most important categories of evidence he will use. It is clear
that his argument is shaped by and builds on Balbus's defense of the Stoic
position on the nature of the gods in *N. D.* 2 and, more important, Cotta's
critique in *N. D.* 3. One significant exception is that Q. largely dismisses the
need to offer any explanation of the mechanisms by which divination works

(demanded by Cotta of Balbus at *N. D.* 3.13), since there is *vis et natura quaedam, quae . . . futura praenuntiat* (12). Q. has almost immediate recourse to C.'s poetry, namely, his *Prognostica,* the final section of his *Aratea* (on which see Intro. pp. 5–6). In his philosophical works, C. quotes Greek poetry only in translation, so the choice to use his own, well received translation of Aratus here is not exceptional. Q.'s citation of the *Prognostica* tightens the connection between his argument and that of Balbus, who deploys sections of the poem in his argument for divine providence (2.104–15). Q.'s heavy use of C.'s earlier writings, especially his poetry, might be dismissed as shameless self-promotion by the author. The strategy, however, also ties the author much more closely to Q.'s argument for divination than he might otherwise be. His choice of material also allows Q. to compromise M.'s counterargument with his own words.

11 Nihil . . . novi nec quod praeter ceteros ipse sentiam: "I shall put forward nothing new and nothing that departs from what others have said." Cf. *OLD,* s.vv. *sentio* 6 and *praeter* 3b. **sentiam**: polyptoton with preceding *sentias* and *sententiam* below.   **antiquissimam sententiam tum omnium populorum et gentium consensu conprobatam**: Q.'s expression of the *consensus omnium* in civic terms (*omnium populorum et gentium consensu*) continues the focus on divination as a national practice from the introduction. Note, however, that Q. is more sanguine about the value of the *consensus omnium* than C.'s cautious statement (*vetus opinio . . . et populi Romani et omnium gentium firmata consensu*). The argument from *consensus omnium,* that something believed by everyone must be true, was deployed by several Hellenistic philosophical schools (including the Epicureans and the Stoics) to support basic principles that cannot be verified empirically, such as the existence of fate or, as here, of the gods. The argument is rhetorically satisfying—it lends a great deal of popular authority—but logically weak. How can a person ascertain that, in fact, *everyone* agrees? A single example to the contrary suffices to demolish the universal appeal. See Obbink 1992. In Latin authors, the authority of the *consensus omnium* is not limited to philosophical discussion but appears frequently (esp. in the works of C. and Livy) in a political context.   **duo . . . divinandi genera**: Q. articulates one of the organizing principles of his speech (natural vs. artificial divination) and introduces the main categories of evidence to be addressed (different types of divination). *Divinatio naturae* occurs when a divine message is sent directly through a dream or prophecy without any need for further, skilled interpretation. Its counterpart, *divinatio artis,* by definition requires the application of *ars,* that is, a developed system of interpretive principles. This distinction between natural and artificial divination goes back at least to Plato (*Phdr.* 244a–245a). It is important to bear in mind that some important ancient practices, such as the technical interpretation of dreams and the interpretation of the Sibylline books by Roman priests (see Intro. p. 8), lay somewhere between purely natural and purely artificial divination. C.'s taxonomy of divination is quite different from that provided by his contemporary M. Terentius Varro as it is preserved in Serv., *A.* 3.359. Varro seems to have concerned himself only with those forms of divination that would fall into C.'s category of artificial divination, dividing them according to medium (earth, air, water, or fire).

12 extispicum aut monstra aut fulgora interpretantium: *Extispex* is an old, rare word for a diviner who specialized in the inspection of *exta* (entrails). It appears another three times in *Div.* (in a quotation, probably of Pacuvius, at 1.29 and in M.'s response at 2.26 and 2.42), but only twice more in all of extant Latin, in one fragment each of Accius's *Medea* and Varro's *Menippean Satires*, both preserved in the entry for *extispices* in Non. 23L (cf. 88L). Nonius suggests that *extispex* is equivalent to *haruspex* (on which see 3n. *haruspicum disciplina*), but here *extispex* seems to be a more general term for those who predict the future from *exta*. Q. includes *haruspices* in this list through the periphrasis *monstra aut fulgora interpretantium* (cf. 2.26).   **aut sortium . . . aut somniorum aut vaticinationum**: Q. switches from practitioners to the media in which they work. Lots were the province of *sortilegi*, dreams of *coniectores*, and fortune-telling of *vates* and *harioli*.   **ea enim fere artis sunt**: "for in general these things require technical skill." *Fere* normally follows the word it modifies and implies exceptions to the rule. We have already seen that some forms of divination identified as natural can involve the methods used in technical interpretation (see, e.g., 4n. *furoris divinationem . . . contineri arbitrati*, on the consultation of the Sibylline books). Conversely, some instances of technical divination could be sufficiently complex that a diviner could not rely on his training alone: some diviners claimed to descend from famous families of seers and, as a corollary, to have inherited a heightened sensitivity to signs in the natural world (cf. 91n. *Elis . . . familias duas certas habet*).   **Quarum quidem rerum eventa magis arbitror quam causas quaeri oportere**: This is the second organizing principle of Q.'s argument: the importance of *eventa* (outcomes) over *causae* as proof of the validity of the *duo divinandi genera*. Though he occasionally comments on the explanatory theories (*rationes*) of other philosophers (e.g., Aristotle on the cause of prophetic power in the sick, at 81), not until 109 does Q. turn his full attention to any sort of explanation of the link between signs and the events they foretell.   **tum . . . tum**: "both . . . and."   **quare omittat urguere Carneades**: *Omittat* is a jussive subjunctive. Q. waves away Academic objections here but responds at 118–19.   **quod faciebat etiam Panaetius**:

For Panaetius's departure from the Stoic position on divination, see 6n. *a Stoicis vel princeps eius disciplinae . . . degeneravit Panaetius.* **Iuppiterne cornicem a laeva corvum ab dextera canere iussisset**: The enclitic *-ne* introduces an indirect question that expects a simple yes or no answer. *Canere* is the verb for both *cornicem a laeva* and *corvum ab dextra*: the conjunction *et* should be supplied between the two phrases. Carneades and Panaetius asked if Jupiter orders both the crow and raven to sing, not if he orders one or the other. Both are examples of positive *auspicia* (on which see Intro. p. 7; cf. 85). Augurs took the auspices only from certain species of birds (see 2.76 with Pease *ad loc.*; Sen., *Nat.* 2.32.5), and their *disciplina* determined the interpretation of the birds' call or flight. The augur's task was to ascertain that the bird had in fact behaved in a particular way or appeared in a particular quadrant of the sky. See Linderski 1986, 2226–29. **animadversa et notata**: For artificial divination, such as augury, the importance of the observation of phenomena is matched by the importance of the preservation, over long periods of time, of records of those observations. Cf. 25, 109, 131. The keeping of records facilitates the *interpretatio* of signs identical to those that have occurred previously and provides guidelines for the *coniectura* required for interpreting unprecedented events. **excipiente**: *Excipere* = "to seize upon." **monumentis**: written records of any form.

13 Mirari licet quae sint animadversa a medicis herbarum genera: The leap from augury to medicine is not a long one. Medicine and natural philosophy—that is, the study of nature and the physical universe (including divination and the workings of the human body)—were closely related (indeed, overlapping) fields of inquiry in the ancient world (Frede 1987, 225–60). There was debate among the various medical schools that sprang up, much like philosophical schools, throughout the Greek world in the Hellenistic period, about the importance of understanding the relationship between *causae* and *eventa*. For a good introduction, see Nutton 2004, 140–56. The Empiricist school staked out a position on medicine akin to the Stoic position on divination: they rejected investigation into the causes of disease, focusing instead on cures discovered through observation and experience. Their critics attacked the Empiricists for failing to provide an explanatory theory, just as M. will attack the Stoics about divination in Book 2. In the context of contemporary epistemological debates in other sciences, the Stoic arguments for the validity of divination are much more rational than they appear when evaluated in modern terms (Hankinson 1988, 141–42). **vim atque naturam**: Cf. 12. **age**: "Come now." This use of the imperative (also at 37 and 46) is much more common in spoken language than in formal prose. It is also characteristic of didactic poetry. **atque etiam ventos**

praemonstrat . . . : C. often quotes Greek authors directly in his letters, but in his philosophical works, he either translates them himself or draws on Latin versions by other authors (Jocelyn 1973, 65, 73–74). This fragment comes from the final section of C.'s *Aratea*, a translation into Latin hexameters of the *Phaenomena* of the Hellenistic Greek poet Aratus (see Intro. pp. 5–6). The first three lines from the next quotation, in 14, follow directly from this fragment, preserving nine consecutive lines (Soubiran 1972, 193–94, frag. III). From the extant portions of the translation, preserved both in manuscripts and as quotations by C. and other authors, C.'s *Aratea* appears to have been a faithful rendering, though not *verbum pro verbo*, of Aratus's poem. Though there are some modifications, expansions, and occasional misinterpretations, C. generally preserves the length and the tone of the original (Gee 2001; Soubiran 1972, 85–149). These six lines, rendering four of the original, are somewhat fuller, expanded by the addition of the phrase *cum . . . tumescit* (which C. has taken from a scholiast; see Pease *ad loc.*), the image of Neptune, and the rich use of descriptives such as *inflatum*, *cana*, and *niveo*. C. also uses sound patterning to reinforce the poetic image. Note the frequent repetition of *s* throughout the whole passage to imitate the sound of wind and surf, as well as the rhythm and the repetition of *t* and *p* in the first two lines to mimic the motion of sea swells.   **inflatum mare**: subject of *praemonstrat* and *tumescit*.   **salis**: genitive singular; metonymy for the sea.   **tristificas . . . voces**: an expansion of Aratus's βοώμεναι. C. uses the same phrase in the fragment of his *Consulatus Suus* quoted later (20). Compound adjectives are a hallmark of older, epic Latin poetry. C. uses one here to contribute to the weighty tone.   **scopulorum saepe**: "barrier of the rocks." *Saepe* = ablative here; contrast the adverb *saepe* five lines above.   **prognostica tua**: "your *Prognostica*." Aratus's *Phaenomena* was divided by later grammarians into parts: the first, which dealt with celestial phenomena, was called the Φαινόμενα, and the second, which addressed meteorological matters, the Διοσημεῖαι (rendered by C. as *Prognostica*). A passage in a letter to Atticus from the year 60 (2.1.11 = *SBA* 21.11) raises the question of whether C. retranslated the *Prognostica* later in life or perhaps simply recopied it. Current scholarly opinion (for neat summaries, see Kubiak 1990, 199–201; Courtney 2003, 149–50; Wardle *ad loc.*) tends toward the latter option.   **elicere**: often used to describe the coercion of reluctant divinities (e.g., C., *Vat.* 14; Hor., *Sat.* 1.8.29). The image of drawing the answers out from the heavens is appropriate for a discussion of signs of impending storms: the Romans turned to Jupiter Elicius to provide them with rain. See Liv. 1.20.7 and 31.8 with Ogilvie 1965, 101–2.   **Boëthum**: Boethus of Sidon, the second-century Stoic philosopher and student of Diogenes of Babylon (on whom see 6n. *Diogenes*), wrote a commentary on Aratus. He is to be distinguished from

the Peripatetic philosopher of the same name who was C.'s contemporary
and a commentator on Aristotle. See R. Goulet, "47. Boéthos de Sidon, *RE*
4," in *Dictionnaire des Philosophes Antiques*, 2.123–25 (Paris, 1994).   **qui
hactenus aliquid egit, ut . . . explicaret**: "who went so far as to lay out."

14 quis probabiliter dixerit: "who has explained convincingly?" The
subjunctive implies that Q. expects a negative response (*G&L* 259).   **cana
fulix itidem fugiens e gurgite ponti . . .** : The *fulix* (more commonly, *fulica*)
has been variously identified with the coot, the red-breasted merganser, and
the egret (see Wardle *ad loc.*). Aratus has ἐρωδιός (heron), = Latin *ardea*.
It is not clear why C. has changed the bird in Aratus's original. Q. brings
together lines from two separate passages. The first three lines of this fragment
correspond to Arat. 913–15 and the rest to Arat. 948–51 (Soubiran 1972,
194, frags. III–IV). By omitting the intervening lines, Q. groups together
three avian *exempla* (*fulix, acredula,* and *cornix*).   **fugiens . . . clamans . . .
fundens**: C.'s earlier poetry is far richer in present active participles than his
later works, perhaps in imitation of Ennius (on whom see 23n. *Andromacham
Enni*; von Albrecht 2003, 120).   **haud modicos tremulo fundens e
guttere cantus**: The frequent *o* and *u* sounds imitate the cry of the *fulix* (an
onomatopoetic effect repeated in *acredula . . . querellas*, two lines below). This
is a golden line, an artful chiastic arrangement (*abba*) of two adjectives and
two substantives with a verb in the middle. C.'s use of this pattern, popular
among Hellenistic Greek poets but generally absent from early Latin poetry,
reflects his early interest in Alexandrianism. See Kubiak 1990. Golden
lines and other forms of intricate wordplay became increasingly popular a
generation later with Catullus and his friends (Ross 1969, 132–37).   **saepe
etiam pertriste canit . . . gelidos rores aurora remittit**: an unusually
expansive rendering of a single line of Aratus (ἡ τρύζει ὀρθρινὸν ἐρημαίη
ὀλολυγών, 948). C. has added emotive language to give a tinge of unhappiness
(*pertriste . . . carmen . . . adsiduas . . . querellas*), and he makes the bird's call
more pointed and forceful (*canit . . . instat . . . iacit ore*). He also stresses the
frequency of the phenomenon (*saepe . . . adsiduas*), which seems to contrast
with Aratus's image of a solitary animal. **acredula**: "nightingale"; see Kubiak
1990, 210–11 with Wardle *ad loc.* **vocibus instat / vocibus instat**: Epanalepsis,
the repetition of words from the end of one line at the beginning of the
succeeding line, is frequent in Hellenistic poetry. This is its earliest appearance
in extant Latin poetry; it dramatizes *adsiduas querellas*. **rores aurora remittit**:
C. liberally uses alliteration, a stylistic device common in all early Latin epic
but less so in poetry of the late republic onward. There is consonance and
assonance in this phrase.   **demersit . . . recepit**: Both verbs are gnomic
(*G&L* 236).

15 fere: with *numquam*.   **cur ita fiat**: that is, why the signs are usually right.   **aquai dulcis alumnae**: that is, frogs (cf. Verg., *G.* 1.378). *Aquai dulcis* = fresh water. *Aquai* has an archaic genitive ending, scanned as two long syllables. The ability of frogs to foretell the weather is also noted by Pliny (*Nat.* 18.361, in connection with *fulicae*; cf. *fulix* in 14 above). In this passage, C. alters his model (Arat. 946–47) by addressing the frogs directly (Kubiak 1990, 204–9). He emphasizes the humorous character of frogs (*inanis . . . voces / absurdoque sono*, followed by the playful diminutives *ranunculos / ranunculis* after the quotation). For the comic career of frogs in ancient drama and literature, see C. Hünemörder, *BNP* 5.560–62, s.v. "Frog"; Dover 1993, 56– 57, esp. n. 2.   **fontis**: accusative plural.   **quis est**: introduces another negative example, parallel to *quis igitur elicere causas praesensionum potest* at 13.   **qui . . . possit**: relative clause of characteristic.   **mollipedesque . . . sucum**: These lines would have followed directly after *demersit caput et fluctum cervice recepit* (14) in the *Aratea*. The poetic compounds *mollipedes* (slow-footed) and *umiferum* (moisture-bearing) are *hapax legomena* (words that appear only once in extant Latin) and are C.'s embellishments of Arat. 954–55. Cf. 13n. *tristificas . . . voces*. C. may have found a model for *mollipedes* in Theocritus 15.103 (μαλακαὶ πόδας; see Kubiak 1990, 212–13), and *duxere . . . sucum* draws on a scholium (see Pease *ad loc.*).   **duxere**: For metrical reasons, poets often use this alternate form of the third plural perfect active indicative.   **aëre**: a dactyl.   **iam vero . . . arandi**: corresponds to Arat. 1051–53 (Soubiran 1972, 195, frag. V).   **triplici . . . ter . . . tria**: The repetition mimics the action of the mastic tree (*lentiscus*), as do the three mentions of the tree's fertility (*gravata, grandescere fetu, fruges fundens*). Note the alliteration of *t* and *f* in the second and third lines. On the custom of ploughing three times per year, see Wardle *ad loc.*

16 ne . . . quidem: emphasizes *hoc*, which precedes the two indirect questions to which it refers, marking this phenomenon as the extreme case.   **cur arandi maturitatem ad signum floris accommodet**: Though the general sense is clear, the text presents a difficulty in that it makes the *lentiscus* control the timing of the season for ploughing. Pease (*ad loc.*) follows Giese in arguing for a proleptic sense, making the sign of the event into its cause. It is worth noting, however, that Q. expressly denies this very position at 29. The problem may be resolved by either rearranging the word order to *ad arandi maturitatem* (cf. Freyburger and Scheid 2004, *ad loc.*) or assuming that a different subject of *accommodet* (*natura vel sim.*) has dropped out.   **scammoneae**: Scammony (*convolvulus scammonia*) is a type of bindweed, a vine (now invasive to North America) sometimes confused with morning glory because its flower is also shaped like a trumpet bell. Scammony is native to the eastern Mediterranean, no further west than Greece. Its medicinal properties were long known; scammony appears in medical writings from the fifth century BCE. For references, see André 1985, 228. Historically, the juice obtained from the living plant has been used as a purgative, but the resin produced from the dried root is more potent and more reliable.   **aristolochia**: The common name for *aristolochia* is birthwort; it is a creeping plant with heart-shaped dark green leaves. Several species were used in antiquity for various medicinal purposes (see André 1985, 25). Though its primary use was as an aide for childbirth (see 16n. *quae nomen ex inventore repperit, rem ipsam inventor ex somnio*), several species of aristolochia are still used in different parts of the world as treatment for snakebites. A recent study of the use of a species of aristolochia native to Venezuela found that the extract of the plant had some efficacy against snakebites in mice (Usubillaga et al. 2005). No such properties have been identified in *Aristolochia Longa*, the species referred to here. For the treatment of snakebites and other poisonings, Dioscorides recommends drinking aristolochia with wine or using it as a plaster (3.4.4). Aristolochic acid is toxic and can cause death.   **possit**: "is efficacious for" (*OLD*, s.v. 8b). Q. omits an implied *non quaero* that governs the indirect question, moving on to his next thought (*posse video, quod satis est*). Dropping a grammatical construction before it is completed (anacoluthon) is unusual in polished written prose but common in everyday speech. Its frequent use in Q.'s speech (cf. 34, 111, 131) contributes to the liveliness of his argument, giving it a feel of real conversation.   **quae nomen ex inventore repperit, rem ipsam inventor ex somnio**: This is a less popular etymology; more widespread is the story that the herb is so named from its being the best (ἀρίστη) for women in childbirth (λεχούσαις) (Plin., *Nat.* 25.95; Dioscorides 3.4.1; Isid., *Etym.* 17.9.52). Tales of cures discovered through direct communications from the divine are not unusual (see Pease and Wardle *ad loc.* for references). It was believed that the god Asclepius, worshipped throughout the Mediterranean, frequently appeared in dreams to worshippers seeking diagnoses and cures (therapeutic incubation); for Asclepius at Rome, see Renberg 2006–7. Thessalus of Tralles, the writer of an astrobotanical treatise of the first or second century CE, claims that the novel cures contained in his work were revealed to him in a waking vision of the god himself. The standard text of Thessalus's *De Virtutibus Herbarum* is that of H.-V. Friedrich (1968) in the series Beiträge zur Klassischen Philologie 28. A translation of the preface is available in Ogden 2002, 52–54; see also Moyer 2003.   **posse video**: I follow Ax and Timpanaro in retaining the manuscripts' *posse*, though many editors (including Pease, Schäublin, and Wardle) have deleted it to avoid an anacoluthon. Timpanaro rightly points out the parallels between *posse* here and the preceding *quid . . . possit* and succeeding *cur possit.*   **agnosco scio adprobo**: "I perceive, I am cognizant, I assent." This tricolon neatly sums up the major steps in the Stoic epistemological process: perception, apprehension, and assent. For a good introduction, see Long 1986, 123–31. *Scio* here does not refer to the sure knowledge of the Stoic sage but is used in a weaker, more general sense for the result of combining logic with perception (cf. 81), akin to *intellego* in 15 and 16. Note that *nescio* is used in a similarly weak way in *cur possit nescio* above and *quae causa sit nescio* below. Asyndeton, the deliberate omission of conjunctions in a series of related items, hastens the pace of the argument, making it more forceful (cf. *Cat.* 2.1) and allowing this bit of Q's argument to end in a satisfying cadence.   **quid fissum in extis quid fibra valeat**: Extispicy was a common form of divination among the Romans both privately and publicly. At the public level, it was frequently performed by *haruspices* (see 3n. *haruspicum disciplina*), though not exclusively so. After an animal (usually a sheep or a cow) had been sacrificed, the officiant, with or without the consultation of a *haruspex*, inspected its entrails—including the liver, heart, lungs, gallbladder, and peritoneum (the membrane lining the abdominal cavity)—to see if the organs were perfect in form. Deformities had various meanings and were interpreted differently in different places (cf. 2.28). The liver was by far the most important organ. Fictile representations of sheep's livers, presumably created for teaching purposes, have been discovered; the most famous is a bronze liver from Piacenza dating to the second century BCE (on which see 3n. *haruspicum disciplina*). The visceral side of the Piacenza liver is incised with lines dividing it into sixteen zones, each labeled with the name of an Etruscan god. Similarities between Etruscan and Mesopotamian divination have long been noted (see Wardle and Pease *ad loc.*), though no direct relationship can be established. Support for such a link, however, now comes from an unexpected source: recent genetic research—published in a series of articles in *American Journal of Human Genetics* 74 (2004), 75 (2004), and 80 (2007)—supports ancient claims that the Etruscans originated in the Near East (Herodot. 1.94). *Fissum* (cleft) is used almost exclusively in anatomical (but not necessarily divinatory) contexts, whereas *fibra* (here probably "striation") has a much broader range of uses.   **horum**: that is, instances of people accepting the messages conveyed through entrails, even though they cannot explain why the appearance of a liver or other organ should have any significance for future events.   **Quid**: accusative of exclamation, the object of an unexpressed question—along the lines of "What can you object to in this?"—that impeaches the validity of the counterargument. This interjection marks out the last *exemplum*, which receives more attention than the other *exempla* in the series. Cf. 24.   **nonne cum multa alia mirabilia tum illud in primis**: Something akin to *videmus* must be supplied.   **Summanus**:

Jupiter was responsible for thunder in daylight hours, Summanus at night. Pease's assertion (*ad loc.*) that Summanus is an epithet of Jupiter goes too far. Literary sources distinguish between the gods (Paul. ex Fest. 66L; Fest. 254L; Plin. *Nat.* 2.138), and a survey of *CIL* 6 (inscriptions from Rome) and *ILS* indicates that Summanus is not found as an epithet of Jupiter at Rome, although it is used in this way elsewhere. Late sources identify Summanus not with Jupiter, a celestial deity, but with the chthonic Dis Pater or Pluto (Arn. 5.37, 6.3; Mart. Cap. 2.161). The event referred to here occurred in 278 BCE (Liv., *Per.* 14); it was one of a number of portents signaling a renewed threat to the Romans from Pyrrhus, king of Epirus, who had come to Italy to assist Tarentum. M. later scoffs at the notion that divination played a role in this episode (2.45).   **in fastigio Iovis optumi maxumi**: "on the pediment [of the temple] of Jupiter Optimus Maximus." Representations of one deity often adorned the temple of another. The Capitoline temple of Jupiter was the most important sacred site in Roman religion and the largest structure atop the Capitoline hill, itself the religious center of the city. The temple had *cellae* for the other two members of the Capitoline triad, Juno and Minerva, and was the site of sacrifices by newly elected magistrates, by generals about to set off on campaign, and by victorious generals just returned from the field. Tradition and archaeology date the original foundation of the temple to the sixth century BCE. It burned to the ground in 83 BCE and was subsequently rebuilt. Although very little of it remains now, literary sources preserve a significant amount of information about the original decorative program. At the invitation of Tarquinius Superbus, the last king of Rome, the Etruscan sculptor Vulca produced a cult statue of the god, and other Etruscan coroplasts, specialists in terracotta, produced a quadriga (four-horse chariot) for Jupiter, which was located on the roof of the temple (see G. Tagliamonte, *LTUR* 3.144–48, s.v. "Iuppiter Optimus Maximus Captiolinus, Aedes, Templum (fino all'a. 83 a.c.)"; *NTDAR* 221–24, s.v. "Iuppiter Optimus Maximus (Capitolinus), Aedes"). The terracotta Summanus was perhaps the work of the same artisans. As Rome grew wealthier and as more expensive materials came into use, the terracotta quadriga was replaced with one of bronze in 269 BCE (Liv. 10.23.12). The phrase *qui tum erat fictilis* may imply that Summanus's statue was also replaced later by a metal version.   **e caelo**: that is, by lightning.

17–23 *From Consulatus Suus*

Q. takes another *exemplum* from C.'s poetry, this time from his *Consulatus Suus*, an original epic celebrating his consular year. This passage comprises a list of portents related to the Catilinarian conspiracy (see Intro. pp. 3–4) and corresponds to the previous anecdote at several key points: a threat to Rome is foretold by a lightning strike on Jupiter's property on the Capitoline hill, *inter alia*. The placement of this fragment immediately after the Summanus episode encourages the reader to associate C.'s suppression of the conspiracy in 63 BCE with a major military victory. Whereas other philosophical schools were hostile to poetry as a source of truth and wisdom, the Stoics often adduced poetic passages in their arguments (Jocelyn 1973, 67–71). Q. directly challenges M. to dismiss his own words as false, a challenge that M. sidesteps at 2.46. The frequent citation of C.'s poetry by Q. throughout Book 1 allows his Stoic argument to draw some authority from C. himself (though a very different view is presented by Krostenko 2000, 380–85), bringing C. closer to the argument that is opposed by the character M. in Book 2. The events related here are of types commonly interpreted by the Romans as harbingers of disaster (see Pease *ad loc.*). They are also recounted in *Cat.* 3.18–21, originally delivered on 3 December 63 but revised for publication around the time C. was working on this poem in the year 60 (*Att.* 2.1.1–3 = SBA 21.1–3). As is evident from the parallel citations in the notes below, the portents became a standard element of the events of 63 as retold by later authors. Their unambiguous nature is emphasized throughout this passage through the repetition of images of shining light.

17 consulatu⟨s⟩: Ancient sources (Non. 298L, 300L) knew the work as *Consulatus Suus*. Modern scholars often follow Manuzio's emendation of this passage to ⟨de⟩ *consulatu* and refer to the poem as *De Consulatu Suo*. C. appears to have been working on the poem in 60 BCE (*Att.* 1.19.10, 1.20.6, 2.3.4 = SBA 19.10, 20.6, 23.4), having decided to sing his own praises after an epic promised by the poet Archias (*Arch.* 28; *Att.* 1.16.15 = SBA 16.15) failed to materialize and just as the backlash against his handling of the Catilinarian conspirators began to gain momentum. On the poem's reception, see Intro. p. 6. This work should not be confused with a slightly later poem that is no longer extant, *De Temporibus Meis* (*Fam.* 1.9.23 = SBF 20.23). In quoting such an extensive passage, Q. follows a long-standing Stoic tradition of lengthy quotation of individual works (*Tusc.* 2.26; D. L. 7.180). These seventy-eight lines constitute the bulk of the surviving fragments from the original three books and are, in fact, the longest quotation of Latin poetry by any author (Courtney 2003, 162). **Urania**: patron of the study of astronomy. Her speech, addressed to C., falls into several sections: lines 1–10 describe Jupiter's role in ordering the heavens and establishing predictive signs, 11–65 recount the signs foretelling the civil strife (11–32 signs observed in 63 BCE, 33–65 signs observed two years earlier), 66–74 name authoritative groups who accept the validity of divination, and 75–78 praise C. for his study of astronomy and philosophy. This fragment is generally presented as a single continuous text, though some have argued that some verses of the original have been omitted (see 18n. *nam primum . . . perempta est*; Jocelyn 1984, 51–54).   **conlustrat lumine**: Repetition contributes to the elevated tone of this passage. Cf. *Arat.* 332; *Div.* 2.91; *N. D.* 2.92; *Rep.* 6.17.   **petessit**: "seeks out"; an old word appearing several times in Plautus but infrequently in later authors: only twice in Lucr. (3.648, 5.810), again later in this passage (line 22), and in *Tusc.* 2.62. Cf. Fest. 226L.   **quae**: sc. *mens divina.*   **aetheris aeterni saepta atque inclusa cavernis**: The words mimic the image: *saepta atque inclusa* describes the *mens divina* and is enclosed by *aetheris aeterni . . . cavernis.* The "vaults of the sky" appear also at *Arat.* 252, Lucr. 4.171 (see Bailey's commentary; cf. 6.252, 4.391, 5.467–70), and Var., *Men.* 270. There are numerous affinities between this passage and that of Lucretius, but a lack of firm chronology makes it impossible to determine the nature of the relationship between the poems. A common source for the image in both cannot be identified: the image does not appear in the extant fragments of earlier Latin poetry. Alliteration, consonance, and assonance (in *aetheris aeterni saepta*) are devices common in early Latin verse; C. uses them here to enhance his archaizing style (e.g., lines 14, 18, 37, 54, 65).   **quae sint signorum in sede locatae**: That is, they are situated in the zodiac. *Signa* = constellations.   **quae verbo et falsis Graiorum vocibus errant**: "which 'wander' literally in the false speech of the Greeks." The two ablatives are adverbial; the conjunction between them is unnecessary. C. objects to the term *planetae*, from Greek πλάνητες (wanderers), since the planets' movements are not random but are, in fact, predictable (cf. Pease *N. D.* 2.51). Plato, too, disapproved (*Leg.* 821b–822a).   **certo lapsu spatioque**: "in a set trajectory and track."   **notata**: "marked"; cf. *signati* in line 62 (Jocelyn 1984, 52; Courtney 2003, 163).

18 nam primum . . . perempta est: Anacoluthon results from the repetition of the subject of the ablative absolute *te consule* (line 11) as the nominative subject of the main clause (13). This long, meandering sentence refers to the sacrifice C. offered in 63 at the *feriae Latinae*, rites celebrated by the consuls each year at the sanctuary of Jupiter Latiaris on the Mons Albanus (modern Monte Cavo), about thirteen miles southeast of Rome. The *feriae*, which dated back to the archaic period when the Mons Albanus was a federal sanctuary for Rome and her Latin neighbors, included the sacrifice of a bull and offerings of sheep, cheese, and milk (Liv. 1.31.3–4; D. H. 4.49.1–3; Fest. 212–14L). The logical connection between this scene and what has preceded is not entirely clear, which is perhaps a sign that C. has omitted portions of his poem to adapt this quotation to Q.'s rhetorical needs. The precise dating of these celestial events is subject to debate (see Wardle *ad loc.*).   **concursusque gravis**: "and the ill-omened conjunctions," accusative plural.   **cum tumulos . . . lacte Latinas**: Note the heavy alliteration of *l* and *t*. Homoeoteleuton (in the syncopated forms *lustrasti . . . mactasti* with *vidisti* and *putasti*, the latter also syncopated, in lines 14–16) is common in early Latin sacred writings and in legal sources, but not elsewhere. **laeto mactasti lacte Latinas**: "you honored the Latin festival with rich milk." *Laeto* also carries the sense of "propitious." Cf. 52n. *Tertia te Phthiae tempestas laeta locabit*; 85n. *pulmo incisus etiam in bonis extis*. **Latinas**: sc. *ferias*. Milk is an unusual offering for Roman gods. It is generally associated by the Romans with antiquity and country living. Romulus was said to have offered the gods libations of milk rather than the wine preferred in later ages (Plin., *Nat.* 14.88). In the historical period, milk was still offered to rustic deities, including Priapus (Verg., *E.* 7.33), Pales (Tib. 1.1.36), and the *divae Ruminae* (Var., *R.* 2.11.5). The Bona Dea received libations of wine, but her worshippers were required to call it milk (Macr., *Sat.* 1.12.25). See Purcell 2003 on changes in eating habits as markers of historical change in Roman historiography.   **claro tremulos ardore cometas**: *Cometas* is masculine. The interlocking word order is a demonstration of C.'s technical skill.   **cecidere**: the alternative form, preferred for metrical reasons. Cf. 15n. *duxere*.   **concreto lumine**: "with clouded light." This is one of C.'s less successful images, not imitated by later poets. Cf. Jocelyn 1984, 47: "The reader, however, could not help thinking a humble thought about some congealing liquid."   **stellanti nocte**: ablative of separation.   **quid vero Phoebi fax . . . caeli partis obitusque petessens**: It is impossible to know what verb is missing, but something like *significat* is a reasonable choice. **Phoebi fax**: the sun. See Wardle *ad loc.*; Courtney 2003, 164–65. **praecipitis . . . petessens**: *Praecipitis* is accusative plural with *partes*. This line describes westward, sinking movement (*OLD*, s.v. *praeceps*[1] 1c).   **aut cum terribili . . . vitalia lumina liquit**: *Lumina* is a poetic plural. Note the shift from the interlocking order of *terribili perculsus fulmine civis* to the *aabb* order of the next line. There is consonance of *l* and *t* in *luce serenanti vitalia lumina liquit*. The poetic *lumina liquit* is probably taken from Greek λείπειν φάος, common in tragedy. It appears in early Latin (Enn., *Ann.* 137 Skutsch; Naev. 28 Ribbeck; Pl., *Cist.* 643), as well as in Catullus, Lucretius, and Vergil.   This episode is also mentioned in *Cat.* 3.18, Dio Cass. 37.25.2, and Plu., *Cic.* 14.4. Lightning strikes, especially in clear weather (*luce serenanti*), were always portentous; one that caused a death was even more so. Such instances regularly appear in prodigy lists (Hillard 1996, 142). Pliny (*Nat.* 2.137) identifies the *civis* as a Herennius from Pompeii. The *gens Herennia* is indeed amply attested epigraphically there. Obs. 61 incorrectly

identifies him as a Vargunteius, apparently confusing him with one of
Catiline's co-conspirators (*Sull.* 6, 67; Sall., *BC* 17.3). The interpretation of
signs among the Romans frequently linked the physical to the conceptual.
In this case, the elite status of the victim indicates the impending doom for
the upper classes: cf. the account of the death by lightning of a daughter of
an equestrian in 114 that led to the conviction of three Vestal Virgins (Obs.
37).   **aut cum se gravido tremefacit corpore tellus**: Obs. 61. Though
frequently seen as signs of impending doom by the Roman state (e.g., 78;
Har. Resp. 62; *Cat.* 3.18; Liv. 34.55.1, 41.28.2), earthquakes were treated as
explicable natural phenomena by some philosophers (see 112).   **terribiles
formae**: "apparitions."   **multaque . . . oracla**: *Oracla* is syncopated for
metrical reasons. Several prophecies were associated with the conspiracy,
most famously two preserved by C. himself (*Cat.* 3.9): (1) *ex fatis Sibyllinis
haruspicumque* that a third Cornelius (after Cinna and Sulla) would
rule Rome (which encouraged Catiline's ally P. Cornelius Lentulus) and
(2) another, of unknown provenance, that 63 was the year fated for the
destruction of the city. Elsewhere C. mentions predictions by the augur Ap.
Claudius (105) and by the *haruspices* (*Cat.* 3.19).

**19 ea, quae lapsu tandem cecidere vetusto . . . ipse deum genitor caelo
terrisque canebat**: "those events which finally happened after a long time . . .
the father of the gods himself proclaimed on earth and in the heavens." *Ea*
anticipates *haec* in the next line. **lapsu . . . vetusto**: The events occurred long
after they were predicted. **cecidere**: "happened," "occurred"; cf. line 17 of this
fragment.   **signis**: It is unlikely that this refers to the portents of the years
63 and 65 described in the preceding and following lines. A gap of no more
than two years is too short to be described as *lapsu . . . vetusto*. There is no
need for this to be a specific reference, though Pease (*ad loc.*) argues that the
whole sentence refers to 87 BCE, when some similar portents were reported
during the Bellum Octavianum (see 4n. *Culleoli*). He takes *ea* to refer to that
war, *lapsu cecidere* as "failed," and *vetusto* as "years ago." Courtney and Wardle
follow Pease, although Wardle dates the events to 83 and the aftermath of
the burning of the Capitoline temple of Jupiter Optimus Maximus. Courtney
(2003, 166) prefers to explain *ea quae* as "Roman loyalties and morals" and
posits a missing line immediately after *vetusto*.   **deum genitor**: a poetic
epithet of Jupiter (but see Enn., *Ann.* 444 Skutsch, where *genitor* is applied
to Saturn) that is not attested epigraphically at Rome.   **Torquato . . . et
consule Cotta**: that is, 65 BCE. Urania's list moves in reverse chronological
order.   **Lydius ediderat Tyrrhenae gentis haruspex**: also mentioned at
Cat. 3.19. For the ancient belief that the Etruscans came from the Near East,
see 16n. *quid fissum in extis quid fibra valeat*. Note the chiastic arrangement

of the adjectives and substantives in this line.   **tuus . . . annus**: that is,
63 BCE, the year of C.'s consulship.   **altitonans**: "high-thundering";
an archaic epic compound used by Ennius, who also applies it to Jupiter
(*contremuit templum magnum Iovis altitonantis, Ann.* 554 Skutsch). Lucretius
uses it to describe the river Volturnus (5.745).   **nixus**: "having rested";
from *nitor*.   **suos quondam tumulos ac templa petivit**: "attacked his
own heights and temples at times"; also mentioned at *Cat.* 3.19. The two
summits of the Capitoline (*suos tumulos*) were home to numerous sacred
sites in addition to the temple of Jupiter Optimus Maximus. See Coarelli
2007, 28–41.   **species ex aere vetus venerataque Nattae**: "an old and
revered bronze figure of Natta." It is not clear whose image this was, though
M. identifies him at 2.47 as belonging to the *gens Pinaria*, an ancient patrician
family at Rome with ties to the cult of Hercules at the Ara Maxima. After
enjoying prominence in the fifth century with two consulships held by
brothers from another branch of the family (Pinarius Mamercinus), the
Pinarii went into significant decline. The Pinarii Nattae first appear in our
sources with the *magister equitum* of 363 (*MRR*, 1.117, s.a.), who perhaps
also served as praetor in 349. After him, no other Pinarius Natta held
political office until two moneyers, perhaps brothers, in the mid-second
century BCE (*RRC* 1.246 [#200], 252 [#208]). The pontifex L. Pinarius Natta
officiated at the consecration of C.'s property on the Palatine hill as a shrine
to Libertas in 58 BCE (*Dom.* 118 and 134–37 with *Mur.* 73; Babcock 1965,
6–8).   **elapsaeque vetusto numine leges**: "and laws of ancient sanctity
melted away"; also reported at *Cat.* 3.19, Dio Cass. 37.9.2, and Obs. 61. The
Romans required that laws be inscribed, most frequently on bronze, and
displayed publicly *unde de plano legi possit*. See Crawford 1996, 1.1–38,
esp. 25–26. At least by the imperial period, the Capitoline was full of such
documents (Suet., *Vesp.* 8.5).   **divom**: archaic genitive plural, = *divorum*.
Like Ennius and other poets before him, C. uses both this form and *deum* (for
deorum), as in *deum genitor* at 32.

20 hic silvestris erat Romani nominis altrix / Martia: The adverbial *hic*,
"in this place," makes clear that this is a statue group of the wolf and twins
on the Capitoline, not (as Pease argues) the bronze wolf and twins erected
by Q. and Cn. Ogulnius as aediles in 269 BCE (depicted on Rome's earliest
silver coinage [*RRC* 1.137 (#20)]). As Wardle rightly points out, the Ogulnian
statue group was set up at the *ficus Ruminalis* (Liv. 10.23.11–12; D. H. 1.79.8)
in the Lupercal, below the southwest slope of the Palatine. This line does not
refer to the famous Capitoline Wolf, a bronze statue now on display (with a
Renaissance addition of suckling twins) in the Capitoline museum in Rome.
The Capitoline Wolf shows no sign of the gilding reported to have been on

the statue group struck in 65 (*Cat.* 3.19 with Dio Cass. 37.9.1; Obs. 61) and
has now been dated incontrovertibly to the medieval period (see A. La Regina
in *La Repubblica*, 9 July 2008). **altrix**: "foster mother," sc. *lupa*. *Altrix* is a
poetic alternative for *alma mater*, which is unusable in dactylic hexameter.
The wolf is *Martia* because she is sacred to Mars. **Mavortis**: *Mavors* is an old
Latin variant of *Mars*, attested epigraphically (from Rome, *ILLRP* 217 = *CIL*
1^2.991 = *CIL* 6.473 = *ILS* 3144; from Tusculum, *ILLRP* 221 = *CIL* 1^2.49 = *CIL*
14.2578 = *ILS* 3142) and common in poetry. Cf. Liv. 22.1.11–12.   **artis
scripta ac monumenta volutans**: "rolling out the written records of the art."
Artis = haruspicy. *Scripta ac monumenta* is hendiadys (the expression by two
substantives of a concept that is often best translated into one substantive and
a modifier), "written records" rather than "writings and records." Records on
clay, stone, or metal cannot be unrolled: C. is thinking of texts on papyrus or,
more likely, linen. The longest extant Etruscan text is a portion of a sacred
liber linteus that came to be used as wrappings on an Egyptian mummy,
known as the Zagreb mummy after the city in Croatia where it is housed.
Representations of linen books appear on the lids of some Etruscan ash urns,
where they are represented as folded like blankets rather than rolled into
scrolls (e.g., Haynes 2000, 272, fig. 219). For further discussion and some
illustrations, see the various contributions to de Grummond and Simon
2006. *Monumenta* need not be restricted to written records maintained by
the *haruspices*. Several other collections of sacred written texts were linked
to the Etruscans, among them the *Libri Rituales*, *Libri Fatales*, *Libri de
Fulguratura*, and *Libri Acheruntici* (on the underworld). It is not clear how
widely these texts circulated or how common forgeries were (though one
suspects they were not unusual).   **voces tristificas**: See 13n. *tristificas . . .
voces*.   **omnes**: Their exact identification is not clear, but comparison
with *Cat.* 3.19–21 suggests that they are the *haruspices*; the recipient of the
warning is the Roman people. Cf. Dio Cass. 37.9.2.   **civilem generosa a
stirpe profectam . . . cladem pestemque**: *Civilem* and *profectam* both modify
cladem pestemque. I have followed Pease in retaining Müller's correction of the
manuscripts' *generosam*. Ax prints *generosa* without the following preposition.
Although it can take an ablative of origin, *proficiscor* is accompanied most
frequently by a prepositional phrase, as at 5. Cf. Lucr. 4.1222. **generosa . . .
stirpe**: Catiline came from an impoverished and eclipsed patrician family
(Sall., *BC* 5.1); his most prominent supporters were of senatorial or equestrian
rank or members of the municipal aristocracy (*BC* 17.3–4).   **volvier**: "was
being spun out"; picks up the image of *volutans* three lines above. This form
of the present passive infinitve is common in early Latin and in poetry of all
periods. C. uses it sparingly in his later poetry: it appears only once more, in
a fragment of a translation of Homer preserved at 2.64.   **monebant . . .**

ferebant . . . iubebant . . . vereri . . . teneri: an unusually long run of rhyming line endings.   **adeo**: "in addition."   **iubebant**: governs two indirect commands (*templa . . . eripere et stragem . . . vereri*).   **atque haec fixa gravi fato ac fundata teneri**: the apodosis of a present general condition dependent on an implied *dicebant* (*G&L* 656–57).   **excelsum ad columen**: "on a high column"; cf. 18.   **sancta Iovis species**: Among the statues damaged in 65 was one of Jupiter. The *haruspices* declared that it should be replaced by a statue of the god that faced east, opposite to the direction of the original (*Cat.* 3.20).   **claros spectaret in ortus**: "looks toward the shining east." Cf. *solis ad ortum / convorsa* two lines below. Both the prose version in *Cat.* 3 and this poetic rendering are filled with images of light and revelation (see *solis ad ortum . . . clarabat . . . patebat* below) that are contrasted with the *occultos . . . conatus* of the conspirators. By facing eastward toward the Forum, Jupiter gazed on the source of the salvation of Rome: the people, the Senate, and the consul.   **tum fore ut**: the second indirect statement dependent on the implied *dicebant* and the apodosis of a future more vivid condition. When a future idea has to be expressed in *oratio obliqua*, the periphrasis *fore ut* + result clause is preferred. There is a rare elision in the second short syllable of a dactyl in *fore ut* (Soubiran 1972, 103 n. 2).   **populus sanctusque senatus**: a series of three end rhymes. The phrase *sanctus senatus* also appears in Enn., *Ann.* 272 Skutsch and Verg., *A.* 1.426.   **convorsa**: sc. *sancta Iovis species*.   **patrum sedes populique**: The Senate and the people appear as a unit three times in a relatively short space (again 2 and 8 lines below), recalling the setting of C.'s original oration and emphasizing the unity of the Roman state in its opposition to Catiline.

21 una fixi ac signati temporis hora: "at that one moment in time, fated and marked out." At 2.47, M. does not dispute the coincidence of his speech and the restoration of the statue but attributes it to chance rather than to *deorum numen*. Cf. *Cat.* 3.21; Dio Cass. 37.34.3–4. Vasaly (1993, 81) asserts that C. arranged for the statue to be set up on the morning of his speech, but there is no evidence to support this.   **clarabat sceptra**: "made his scepter plain to see." *Sceptra* is a poetic plural.   **vocibus Allobrogum**: Delegates from the Allobroges, a tribe from central Gaul that had been conquered by Rome in 121 BCE, were in Rome in the fall of 63 to protest the increasingly aggressive predations of Roman tax collectors (Sall., *BC* 40.1; cf. *Mur.* 42). They were recruited by Catiline's ally P. Umbrenus, a freedman who was already known to the Allobroges through business connections. On learning the details of the conspiracy, the Allobroges revealed all they knew to their patron, Q. Fabius Sanga, who, in turn, reported to C. This information led to the interception, at the Milvian bridge, of incriminating evidence, which C. presented, along with the Allobroges themselves, to the Roman Senate (*Cat.* 3.8–10).   **rite . . .**

rite: The repetition stresses the continuity of Roman ritual observance over the generations. This marks a new section of Urania's speech.   **veteres . . . vestri**: Both are subjects of *coluere*, a historical perfect; thus *vestri* must refer to ancient Romans, not the Romans of C.'s own day (*contra* Ewbank 1933, 120). *Veteres* is best understood as "ancient wise men" generally. Pease takes *veteres* to be the ancient Greeks; Timpanaro proposes that Etruscans might also be included.   **coluere**: alternative third plural perfect active indicative; see also *videre* and *tenuere* below.   **vigenti numine**: "of vital power"; ablative of description.   **haec**: The antecedent is not clear but is something like "the merits of proper reverence for the gods."   **otia qui studiis laeti tenuere decoris**: serves as the subject of *videre* in the previous line. *Qui* = philosophers.

22 inque Academia umbrifera nitidoque Lyceo: The penultimate syllable of *Academia* is long (as in Greek). See Ewbank 1933, 121 with a general discussion of C.'s hexameter at 40–71. Urania returns to the theme of light and dark, although with a different emphasis. The famous wooded grove of the Academy was cut down by Sulla (Plu., *Sulla* 12.4), but later references to its shade suggest that it was replanted (Hor., *Ep.* 2.2.45; Plin., *Nat.* 12.9). Pease and Courtney (2003, 170) take *nitido* to refer to the oil applied to the bodies of those exercising at the Lyceum (see 8n. *cum ambulandi causa in Lyceum venissemus (id enim superiori gymnasio nomen est)*). C. is probably also playing on *nitidus* as a term for an elegant and polished style (*OLD*, s.v. 7; cf. *De Orat.* 1.81: *Aliud enim mihi quoddam orationis genus esse videtur eorum hominum, de quibus paulo ante dixisti, quamvis illi ornate et graviter aut de natura rerum aut de humanis rebus loquantur: nitidum quoddam genus est verborum et laetum, et palaestrae magis et olei, quam huius civilis turbae ac fori*).   **iam a**: Ewbank (1933, 58) notes only nine examples of the elision of monosyllables in C.'s extant poetry, a slighly lower rate of frequency than in Ennius, Lucretius, and Vergil.   **in media virtutum mole**: "in the midst of a trial of your character" (*OLD*, s.v. *moles*[1] 7a). Cf. Liv. 7.29.5 (with Oakley's commentary), 32.11.   **anxiferas**: found in classical Latin only here and at *Tusc.* 2.21.   **quod patriae vacat**: "what time was not taken up with the state." *Vacare*, "to be free from," usually takes an ablative of separation but sometimes (as here) takes a dative for the same purpose. See *OLD*, s.v. 4b.   **animum . . . inducere contra . . . dicere**: "to bring yourself to speak against." In fact, M. will not take on this portion of Q.'s argument. He merely waves it away (see esp. 2.46).   **gesseris . . . scripseris**: subjunctives in a relative clause of characteristic. Q. appeals several times to C.'s own writings or personal experience as particularly convincing evidence (cf. 33, 58–59, 68, 106).

23 Carneades: With this apostrophe (cf. 12), Q. reminds us to whose challenge he ultimately responds, although it is through the intermediary of Cotta at *N. D.* 3.14–15. M. will take up the counterarguments of Carneades at 2.9.   **omnes . . . numeros veritatis**: "all the hallmarks of truth"; cf. *OLD*, s.v. *numerus* 12. There is almost certainly a pun (noted in Wynne 2008, 336 n. 289) on *numeros* as the term for the result of a throw of dice (*OLD*, s.v. 2e).   **Venerium**: Q. moves from one pair of examples pertaining to Jupiter to another pair pertaining to Venus. A *talus* (or *astragalos*) was a die made from the knucklebone of a sheep (or imitated in bronze or other material), with four flat sides and two rounded ends. Each side was assigned a number, either 1, 3, 4, or 6, arranged so that each pair of opposite sides totaled 7. The Venus throw consists of four dice, each of which has landed on a different number; it was considered the most desirable combination (see, e.g., Pl., *As.* 905). The ancients used dice not only for gambling but also for divinatory purposes (see Graf 2005). Wardle *ad loc.* discusses the limits of the ancient understanding of probability. Q. argues that given the way the world is, it is unreasonable to assume that if one got one hundred Venus throws in a row, it must be attributed to chance. He does not argue that one hundred Venus throws in a row (or any of the next three *exempla*) can never happen by chance. This particular argument may seem disconnected from what has preceded, but it is placed here for maximum strategic value. The lesson Q. takes from this *exemplum* is that exceptional events can be due not to chance alone but sometimes to divine intervention or inspiration. This reinforces the remarkable coincidence of the circumstances of C.'s third Catilinarian oration and the erection of the statue of Jupiter in the poetic passage that Q. has just quoted.   **Veneris Coae**: a famous painting by Apelles of Colophon (fl. second half of the fourth century), probably the painter most celebrated by ancient authors (e.g., C., *Fam.* 1.9.15 = *SBF* 20.15; C., *Off.* 3.10; Ov., *Ars* 3.401; Quint., *Inst.* 12.10.6). The painting was originally done for the temple of Asclepius at Cos but at some point came to Rome. Augustus dedicated it in the temple of Divus Iulius (Plin., *Nat.* 35.91).   **rostro**: "with his snout."   **Andromacham Enni**: The poet Ennius (239–169 BCE) came originally from the Calabrian region of Italy, where he grew up speaking Greek, Latin, and Oscan (Gel. 17.17.1). He settled in Rome at the end of the Second Carthaginian War and made his living teaching Latin and Greek as a *grammaticus* (Suet., *Gramm.* 1). He proudly proclaimed his Roman citizenship (*Ann.* 525 Skutsch with commentary; C., *Arch.* 22). Ennius is best known for his poem *Annales*, Rome's national epic for two centuries, until it was displaced by the *Aeneid* (see 40n. *apud Ennium*). He also composed works in other genres, including tragedy. Approximately twenty of his plays are known from fragments or titles; of his *Andromache*, only about thirty-

five lines survive, mostly through quotation by C. and Varro. On the day the
Senate decided to recall C. from exile in 57, the great tragic actor Aesopus
(mentioned by Q. at 80) received thunderous applause from his audience
when, during a performance of Accius's *Eurysaces*, he inserted a substantial
passage from the *Andromache* that was understood to allude to C.'s imminent
homecoming (see Intro. p. 4; *Sest.* 116–23 with commentary in Kaster 2006;
Jocelyn 1967, 238–41). This personal connection perhaps explains the
pointed reference to Ennius's version of the story rather than to any of the
numerous Greek treatments.   **in Chiorum lapicidinis saxo diffisso caput
extitisse Panisci**: This diminutive *Panisci* is not rare (cf. 2.48; *N. D.* 3.43;
Plin., *Nat.* 35.144; Suet., *Tib.* 43.2) and may refer to either a young Pan or to
the diminutive size of the head. The quarries on the island of Chios were well
known in antiquity for their variegated pink marble. Given that this head of
Pan was found in stone (rather than in the soil), it was most likely a fossil of
some variety: there are other accounts of the ancients finding "giants' bones"
on Chios (e.g., Ael., *N. A.* 16.39), and paleontologists are still making valuable
discoveries on the island (Mayor 2000, 136–38). A similar tale, perhaps a
variant of the same event, is told at Plin., *Nat.* 36.4: *sed in Pariorum mirabile
proditur, glaeba lapidis unius cuneis dividentium soluta, imaginem Sileni intus
extitisse*. An alternative explanation is that such stories belong to a tradition
of tales of workmen finding heads in the ground at various sites, most
famously the *Caput Oli* (Liv. 1.55.5 with Ogilvie's commentary), uncovered
during construction of the temple of Jupiter Optimus Maximus. Glinister
(2000) has proposed that discoveries like the *Caput Oli* happened when the
ancients uncovered sacred refuse (e.g., damaged architectural items and votive
offerings) that had been buried by earlier worshippers. Carneades would
have used this *exemplum* against the Stoics to demonstrate the possibility that
chance can approximate *veritas*.   **Scopa**: Scopas was a celebrated sculptor
of the mid-fourth century BCE who specialized in creating statues of the gods,
especially of deities who appear primarily as youths.

24–33 *Accuracy*

Q. continues to argue that it is unnecessary to search for an explicable causal
link between signs and the events they foretell. Here he counters the objection
that signs sometimes predict events inaccurately, with a two-part defense.
First (24–25), Q. concedes the point but sets divination alongside other fields
that also rely on the interpretation of signs and are also sometimes wrong.
In the second section (25–33), Q. argues that Roman auspices are more
accurate than M. will admit. He draws some of his supporting evidence for

this argument from mythology but focuses on recent political events at Rome, particularly errors in judgment by those opposed to Caesar (including C. himself), thus emphasizing the relevance of the debate to the current political scene.

24 At non numquam: "but sometimes." *At* introduces an anticipated objection (anticipated again at 60), which M. will indeed raise at 2.109. The two negatives cancel out one another, turning the statement into an indefinite affirmative.   **minus**: "not quite" (*OLD*, s.v. *minus*² 4a).   **quae coniectura continentur et sunt opinabiles**: *Opinabilis* (meaning "subject to individual interpretation") is very rare, appearing only a handful of times in Latin, always in a philosophical context. Q. has already established a similarity between the inexplicability of accurately predictive *signa* and that of the medical efficacy of certain herbs and the reliability of celestial and terrestrial phenomena in predicting weather and managing crops (13–16). Here Q. develops the analogy further: practitioners of medicine and other *artes* requiring subjective interpretation of signs are also sometimes misled by the signs they read. M. will take the opposite view, dissociating divination from navigation, farming, and so on, in 2.9–16 (cf. 2.122–23). Grouping divination with other technical fields, especially farming and medicine, is a commonplace of philosophical argument going back to Plato. For debate on the exact nature of the Stoic view of the relationship between divination and other *artes*, see Denyer 1985; Hankinson 1988.   **quam tamen multa fallunt**: "Yet many things lead it astray."   **quid, gubernatores nonne falluntur**: See 16n. *Quid*. Here Q. intends the standard meaning of *gubernator* as "helmsman." Following the quote from Pacuvius, however, Q. moves onto metaphorical *gubernatores*, that is, political leaders who were statesmen and commanders on the battlefield (*imperatores*). The dual meaning of *gubernator* is an extension of the metaphor of the ship of state, the oldest and perhaps the most ubiquitous analogy for the state in classical literature. The *gubernator* as statesman is common throughout C.'s speeches, letters, and philosophical writings (May 1980; Fantham 1972, 125–36). C. plays with the analogy between diviner and statesman elsewhere (e.g., *Att.* 10.8.6–8 = *SBA* 199.6–8).   **profectione laeti . . . intuerentur . . . capere posset**: C. has altered at least the original verb, whatever its form, to *intuerentur* to suit the result clause introduced by the preceding *ut. Achivorum exercitus et . . . rectores* are the subjects of *intuerentur* and are the antecedents of an implied *eos* that is the object of *capere posset*. The quotation, consisting of a partial first line (ending at *lasciviam*) followed by three trochaic septenarii, is thought to be from either the *Teucer* or the *Dulorestes* of Pacuvius (220–c. 130 BCE; D'Anna 1967, 155; Schierl 2006, 494–97), considered by C. to

be the greatest of the Roman tragedians (*Opt. Gen.* 2). It is possible that
the fragment quoted below at 29 comes from the same play. For C.'s use of
quotations from tragedy to establish common ground between himself and
his reader, see Goldberg 2000. The quotation here adds the vividness of an
image to the upcoming catalog of misled leaders and imbues the examples
that follow with a sense of heroism. It is clear from his letters that C. often
thought of the events of the forties in terms of Homer and the tragedians (see
Wiseman 1985, 10–13).   **inhorrescit mare, / tenebrae conduplicantur
noctisque et nimbum occaecat nigror**: Take *noctisque* with *nigror*. C.
quotes the same passage, plus an additional three-and-a-half lines, in *De
Orat.* 3.157.   **summus imperator nuper fugit**: Q. refers to Pompey, the
commander in chief of republican forces, and to Pompey's escape to Egypt
after his final loss to Caesar at Pharsalus in the summer of 48. Reports of
Pompey's disastrous defeat at Pharsalus were brought to C. and the other
Pompeians (including the younger Cato, descendant of Cato the Censor and
a devout Stoic who reached the praetorship in 54 [*MRR* 2.221–22, s.a. 54]) at
Dyrrachium, by survivors of the battle who had not surrendered to Caesar.
See 68n. *ex te ipso . . . audivi* and M.'s rebuttal at 2.114; Plu., *Cic.* 39.1–5; Plu.,
Cat. Min. 55.3–6. The theme of C.'s personal connection to the events of the
fifties and forties runs throughout the dialogue.   **prudentia**: closely related
etymologically to *providentia* and key to the comparison of statesmanship
and divination. For the importance of *civilis prudentia* for the wise leader, see
Rep. 1.45, 2.45.   **multa . . . quaedam . . . non nulla**: As above (24n. *At non
numquam*), the double negative becomes an indefinite affirmative, meaning
"some." Cf. 25. The theme of mistaken leadership in recent politics is first
sounded with this tricolon that highlights C.'s alignment with the opposition
to Caesar.   **coniectura**: ablative with *nititur*; picked up by *quam* in the next
phrase.

25 ea: sc. *divinatio*. The subject continues from the previous sentence.   **ab
omni aeternitate repetita**: "traced back from infinite time" (*OLD*, s.v. *repeto*
7b).   **in qua**: sc. *aeternitate*.   **Auspicia vero vestra quam constant**:
"Indeed, how truthful are your auspices!" *Vestra* refers to the college of augurs,
of which C. became a member in 53.   **quae quidem nunc a Romanis
auguribus ignorantur**: This echoes the statement made by Balbus, the Stoic
interlocutor in *N. D.* 2.9, that the *augurii disciplina* was no longer respected
(for further parallels, see Pease *N. D. ad loc.*). According to the argument of
Linderski (1986, 2152–53), the complaint is not about widespread disbelief
in the validity of augury but indicates, rather, that the priests charged with
protecting augural law from alteration and emendation were allowing
tradition to be bent to suit political needs. In Book 2, M. does not repeat

exactly Q.'s assertion that the *auspicia* are disregarded by his contemporaries, but he does distinguish between augury as it was observed in previous ages and current practice (2.70–75).   **bona hoc tua venia dixerim**: "I would say this with your indulgence" (*OLD*, s.v. *venia* 3). The subjunctive expresses a cautious assertion.   **Cilicibus Pamphyliis Pisidis Lyciis**: Asyndeton hastens the pace of the sentence and underlines Q.'s irritation with the state of Roman augury. Earlier (2), C. cited the first three nations as foreign peoples of great antiquity who practiced divination, and he noted his personal experience of them. Lycia did not become a part of the Roman Empire until it was made a province in 43 CE. For Q.'s belief that other peoples are more loyal to their nations' traditions of divination, see Krostenko 2000.

26 quid ego hospitem nostrum . . . Deiotarum regem commemorem: This rhetorical question introduces the next case in Q.'s argument, King Deiotarus of Galatia, an area just north of the region of the peoples named in the previous sentence, in what is now central Turkey. He is the best known of the eastern client kings of the late republic, owing to the preservation of C.'s speech on his behalf (*Deiot.*) delivered before Julius Caesar as judge in November 45, in which C. responded to charges brought by Deiotarus's grandson that the old king had attempted to murder Caesar while the two traveled together after the battle of Zela in 47. Before Pompey's reorganization of the East in 63, Deiotarus held only the title of tetrarch of the Tolistobogii, one of three tribes in Galatia. Pompey confirmed Deiotarus as sole tetrarch of his tribe and bestowed on him the title *rex* and control of a good deal of territory along the south coast of the Black Sea (*Har. Resp.* 29). For Deiotarus's friendship with the Tullii, see *Fam.* 15.4.4–5 = *SBF* 110.4–5; *Att.* 5.17.3, 5.18.1–4 = *SBA* 110.3, 111.1–4.   **auspicato**: Cf. 3n. *auspicato*.   **aquilae admonitus volatu**: The eagle was thought to be the messenger of Jupiter and was closely associated with supreme rulers (e.g., Liv. 1.34.8 [cf. Ogilvie 1965, *ad loc.* with references]; Suet., *Aug.* 94.7; Suet., *Vesp.* 5.7). The story of Deiotarus's abortive trip is addressed by M. at 2.20 and is repeated at Val. Max. 1.4 ext. 2.   **ubi erat mansurus si ire perrexisset**: a contrafactual condition. The indicative imperfect periphrastic (*erat mansurus*) in the apodosis, substituted for *mansisset*, implies the certainty of Deiotarus's intention (*G&L* 254 r. 2–3; cf. 597 r. 2).

27 multorum dierum: genitive denoting extent of time. See *G&L* 365 n. 2.   **viam**: "along the road"; cognate accusative with *progressus esset*.   **cuius quidem hoc praeclarissimum est**: Supply *dictum*. *Cuius* = Deiotarus.   **quod**: introduces a clause in apposition to the preceding *hoc*.   **a Caesare tetrarchia et regno pecuniaque multatus est**: The verb governs an ablative of separation ("he was punished with the loss of . . ."). *Tetrarchia* refers not to Deiotarus's inherited position as leader of the Tolistobogii but, rather, to his position as tetrarch of the Trocmi, another Galatian tribe. Deiotarus took over as the leader of the Trocmi sometime after 52/51, upon the death (murder?) of Brogitarus, his son-in-law who had held the position. This move was confirmed by Pompey and the Senate but was later undone by Caesar as retribution for Deiotarus's support of Pompey in the Civil War. Caesar also levied a significant fine and took away control of the additional territories Pompey had bestowed on him (*Div.* 2.79; *B. Alex.* 67–68; Dio Cass. 41.63.1–4). After Caesar's death, Antonius claimed to have found a decree reassigning Deiotarus as tetrarch of the Trocmi (*Phil.* 2.93–96; *Att.* 14.12.1 = *SBA* 366.1; Strabo 12.5.1).   **auctoritatem et . . . libertatem atque . . . dignitatem**: *Auctoritas, libertas*, and *dignitas* are closely related concepts in C.'s political thought, and proper balance among them is critical for the maintenance of the ideal state (*Rep.* 2.56–59). The *auctoritas* of the Senate should be preeminent, and the people should possess *libertas* (freedom from tyranny), but not so much that mob rule could be instituted (see Wirszubski 1950, 3–9; Wood 1988, 149–50). Excessive *libertas* of the people diminishes the *auctoritas* of the Senate; this, in turn, results in the absence of *dignitas*, the respect that accrued to prominent individuals (esp. those who had held office; cf. *imperii* here). The homoeoteleuton with *variatio* of conjunctions adds emphasis. All three of these terms were deployed by both sides in the Civil War between Pompey and Caesar. Ancient writers are unanimous that the conflict between Caesar and Pompey was a war for personal *potentia* and *dignitas* (see Wirszubski 1950, 77–79 with references). In defending his allegiance to Pompey in this way, Deiotarus clearly aligns himself with the *optimates*, whom C. (*Sest.* 96–100) identified as the defenders of a balance between senatorial authority and freedom of the people.   **esse defensam**: technically dependent on *negat*, but the sense here indicates that *dicit* (*vel sim.*) should be supplied to govern this and the following two accusative + infinitive phrases. *Defensam* agrees with *dignitatem*, the last of the items in the series, but covers all three. See *G&L* 290.   **sibique eas aves . . . bene consuluisse**: "the birds had counseled him well."   **quibus auctoribus**: "on whose authority," sc. *aves*. Cf. *OLD*, s.v. *auctor* 3a.   **antiquiorem**: "preferable" (*OLD*, s.v. *antiquus* 10a).   **igitur**: rarely so far delayed in C. Its placement here emphasizes *vere augurari*.   **augurari**: As with *auspiciorum* a few lines above and *auspiciis* below, here is another instance of C. using a narrow technical term in a general way. Cf. 3n. *optumus augur*. Augury was a particularly Roman form of ornithomancy; Deiotarus was not a Roman augur.   **nam nostri quidem magistratus auspiciis utuntur coactis**: From Q.'s point of view, *auspicia coacta* are a sort of degenerate *auspicia impetrativa* (on which see 3n. *et inpetriendis . . . procurandis*).   **pulli**: The sacred chickens were kept by *pullarii*, mostly of freed status. When so ordered by a magistrate, the *pullarius* released the birds, who had been starved for some time, from their cage (*cavea*) and offered them a lump of food (*offa*) too big to swallow whole. This ensured that the chickens would give the best auspices possible, not only by eating greedily, but also by dropping some of their feed on the ground. It was a bad sign if the birds refused to come out of the cage or to eat (Liv. 6.41.8; Paul. ex Fest. 285L). The ritual is described in detail at *Div.* 2.71–73 (see Pease *ad loc.*). A grave relief depicting sacred chickens in the *cavea* can be seen in Turcan 1988, 2.19 and pl. 8 (*CIL* 14.2523; cf. Scullard 1981, pl. 6). See also Linderski 1986, 2155–56; Valeton 1890, 211–15.

28 quod autem scriptum habetis: It is not entirely clear whether Q. refers here to *libri augurales* available only to members of the college or, as is more likely, to one of the numerous works on augury written in the late republic that were circulated publicly. See Linderski 1985; Linderski 1986, 2241– 56; Rawson 1985a, 298–316.   † **aut tripudium fieri**: As the text of this passage stands, *aut* makes little sense. Correcting *aut* to *avi* (as proposed by Turnebus and followed by many others, including Valeton [1890, 212]) leaves the meaning incomplete: thus several commentators presume that an adjective agreeing with *avi* has fallen out. Wardle (*ad loc.*) proposes to add *omni* ("a tripudium results from ⟨any⟩ bird"), pointing to a parallel in an augural decree quoted by M. at *Div.* 2.73 and a passage in Festus (386L) ultimately deriving from the work of C.'s augural colleague Ap. Claudius Pulcher (on whom see 28n. *solidum* and 29n. *Appius collega tuus*). It is possible that the sentence originally aimed at an etymological connection between *solidum* and *solistimum* (matched by the etymology of *tripudium* offered by M. at *Div.* 2.72). But see 28n. *solidum*. A *tripudium* is a predictive sign that occurs when certain things, such as a rock, a living tree, or (as in this case) something carried by a bird drops to the ground without any human intervention (Fest. 284L with Paul. ex Fest. 285L; Fest. 386L; Serv., *A.* 3.90; Valeton 1890, 212). *Tripudium* is also used to describe the ritual dance of the Salian priests (e.g., Liv. 1.20.4) and the Arval Brethren (*CIL* 6.2104.32 = *ILS* 5039, from Rome) and may therefore refer to a halting, jerky movement like that of a chicken (*pullus*). This is difficult, however, to envision with respect to a rock or tree. M. offers a very different etymology at 2.72: *sed quia cum pascuntur necesse est aliquid ex ore cadere et terram pavire (terripavium primo post terripudium dictum est: hoc quidem iam tripudium dicitur).*   **ex ea**: sc. *offa*.   **solidum**: a difficult word. It can be equivalent to *terra* (e.g., Verg., *G.* 2.231 and *A.* 11.427), a meaning that is sensible here. Festus (386L), however, suggests a different, technical augural meaning when, drawing on the lost *De Augurali Disciplina* of C.'s augural colleague Ap. Claudius Pulcher (of which C. had a copy: see *Fam.* 3.4.1, 3.9.3, 3.11.4 = *SBF* 67.1, 72.3, 74.4), he reports that a *tripudium solistimum* can also occur when a *saxum solidum* (whole [?] rock) falls on its own.   **solistimum**: "most complete"; superlative of *sollus* (whole). This is a very rare word, used only to modify *tripudium*. A *tripudium solistimum* was a very positive sign.   **multa auguria multa auspicia**: Although there was a technical distinction between *auguria* and *auspicia*, many ancient writers treat the terms as synonyms, as early as Pl., *Sti.* 459–63. Modern scholars have offered various explanations of the difference between these two categories of signs; the most authoritative account is that of Linderski 1986, esp. 2294–96. Both *auspicia* and *auguria* were answers received from Jupiter. An *auspicium* was valid for only one day and applied only to the question of the timing for a course of action already settled on. In contrast, an *augurium* determined whether or not Jupiter approved of the course of action itself, a person inaugurated as a priest or magistrate, the selection of a place, or the performance of a ceremony. A further consequence of this distinction is that a positive or negative *auspicium* could always be undone if the god chose to send an oblative *auspicium* (see 3n. *et inpetriendis . . . procurandis*) after the initial sign had been given. The message conveyed through an *augurium*, however, was permanent. A negative *augurium* resulted in the abandonment of the project in question, while a positive one conferred Jupiter's approval in perpetuity and "the permanent status of *res* or *persona inaugurata*" (Linderski 1986, 2296).   As an augur, C. must have been aware of the difference between *auguria* and *auspicia*, but he is here quoting the elder Cato (d. 146 BCE). The origin of the quotation is unknown (Peter 1.95 frag. 132 = *FRH* 2.232 frag. 132). It is possible, though unlikely, that Cato, too, was a member of the college (see Astin 1978, 18 n. 13). Whether Cato was an augur or not, he is known to have dealt with augural issues in his oratory. Festus (277L = Jordan [1860] 1967, 67–68) preserves a fragment of a speech titled *De Auguribus*, and we have two fragments from *De Aedilibus Vitio Creatis* (Jordan [1860] 1967, 67) that deal with augural law as it pertained to the election of magistrates.   **quod**: Its antecedent is *multa auguria multa auspicia . . . neglegentia collegii amissa plane et deserta sunt.*   **Cato ille sapiens**: C. frequently describes the elder Cato as *sapiens* and associates him with *sapientia* (e.g., *Ver.* 2.2.5, 2.5.180; *Sen.* 4; *Off.* 3.16).   **Nihil . . . maioris rei**: "nothing of greater importance."   **ne privatim quidem**: "not even in private matters." Private auspices were a subject of antiquarian interest in the late republic. Aul. Gell. (7.6.10) quotes from a book on the topic, now lost, by C.'s friend P. Nigidius Figulus, an expert in arcane religious practice and the occult. See Rawson 1985a, 309–

12.   **quod etiam nunc nuptiarum auspices declarant**: "a fact that the takers of wedding auspices still prove." *Auspicia* were taken by *auspices* on the morning of the wedding, signifying the beginning of the wedding itself. By the late republic, the *auspex* could be a friend of the family and was not required to be a professional diviner. For further discussion and a collection of the relevant sources, see Treggiari 1991, 164; Boëls-Janssen 1993, 135–39; Hersch 2010, 115–19. Val. Max. 2.1.1 draws on this passage.   **qui re omissa nomen tantum tenent**: This same point is made at 3 and 95. The maintenance of practices no longer meaningful expresses the difference between then (*quondam*) and now (*nunc*), especially when the present situation is regarded as in some way specious or false (cf. Tac. *Ann.* 1.3). This is another instance of the theme of appearance versus reality.   **ut nunc extis . . . sic tum avibus magnae res inpetriri solebant**: Over time, extispicy did displace augury as the primary method of divination. The ease with which domesticated animals could be provided for sacrifice meant that politicians and generals in the field could obtain auspices when they desired them, rather than having to wait for Jupiter to send his birds.   **sinistra**: accusative plural. Positive signs were identified as *sinistra* because they appeared on the gods' left, that is, in the east. The gods were thought to live in the north, facing southward, with the east on their left. The augur, however, sat west of the *templum* (the field of vision in which he sought signs) and faced eastward to watch for signs, the north on his left and the south on his right. For this reason, signs appearing in the eastern portion of the *templum* were called *sinistra*—even if they appeared on the augur's right (cf. 2.82). The most favorable signs came from the northeast. For a detailed discussion, see Linderski 1986, 2256–96.   **in dira et in vitiosa**: technical terms for certain categories of unfavorable *signa*. *Dira*, popularly derived from *deorum ira*, were oblative signs that indicated terrible impending disaster. *Vitium* resulted from accepting auspices taken incorrectly (i.e., with some error in the ritual, as in the case of the elder Gracchus mentioned below: see 33n. *scriptum apud te* with M.'s response at 2.74; *N. D.* 2.10–11) or from disregarding auspices taken in the proper manner. See Linderski 1986, 2162–68. The following anecdote illustrates both *dira* and *vitiosa*.

29 **ut . . . perdiderunt**: *Ut* + indicative = "as." Q. refers to the consuls of 249 BCE, each of whom suffered a disastrous loss at sea during the First Punic War. This is a popular *exemplum* repeated by numerous sources (for which see Pease *ad loc.*; *MRR* 1.214, s.a. 249). The sacred chickens would not eat for Claudius when he brought them out on his ship before the battle of Drepanum in Sicily (no doubt the birds had motion sickness, a complaint not restricted to humans). In exasperation, he threw them overboard, saying

they should drink if they would not eat. Claudius's story combines the images of seamanship and political/military leadership with which Q. opened this portion of his argument (see 24n. *quid, gubernatores nonne falluntur*). It is reported that Junius, whose cognomen was (became?) Pullus, also failed to respect the auspices and lost his fleet near Camarina. M. returns to this anecdote twice (2.20, 71).   **inter se strepere . . .** : The source of the fragment (two trochaic septenarii) is uncertain, though it may come from the same source as the quotation at 24 (Ribbeck, p. 286; Pease *ad loc.*; Artigas 1990, 127–28), since the earlier quotation certainly and this one probably refers to the Greek departure from Troy. If they are taken from the same source, C. has quoted them out of order, since Agamemnon's command to set sail must have been issued before his men, in the fragment quoted at 24, can rejoice at starting for home (Timpanaro 1999, 254 n. 106). By returning to the Homeric *exemplum* that introduced this series of proofs, Q. brings this portion of the catalog to a neat close and clears the stage for a case in point that requires much more attention.   **strepere . . . obterere**: infinitives in their original context, as indicated by the meter, and here as well, dependent on *coepissent*.   **aperteque artem**: There is hiatus at the caesura, a coincidence not uncommon in archaic poetry.   **solvere**: "to weigh anchor" (*OLD*, s.v. 4).   **secundo rumore adversaque avi**: "to positive response yet with unfavorable auspices." The enclitic *-que* is adversative (*OLD*, s.v. 8). The positive response comes from the men.   **sed quid vetera?**: Supply *ego loquor* or something similar. Q. frequently uses phrases like this to mark the transition from one class of *exempla* to another (e.g., 46, 55, 97), implying greater authority and relevance for the new category. For a discussion of the weakening power of an *exemplum* as it recedes into the past, see Chaplin 2000, 164–67.   **M. Crasso quid acciderit**: refers to the annihilation in 53 of M. Licinius Crassus and seven legions under his command near the town of Carrhae in northern Mesopotamia. For sources, see Pease *ad loc.*; *MRR* 2.214–15, s.a. 55.   **dirarum obnuntiatione neglecta**: See 28n. *in dira et in vitiosa*. As consul along with Pompey in 55, Crassus received a five-year command in Syria, where he was expected to start a war with the Parthians. Pompey was assigned the two Spains. Despite vigorous public opposition to the Parthian campaign (some tribunes tried to prevent Crassus from levying troops), Crassus prepared to head east. In a last, desperate effort to hinder him, Dio Cassius says (39.39.6), the tribunes reported seeing dire portents while Crassus offered sacrifice before setting out, but Crassus ignored them; it is to this that Q. refers. Ateius, one of the tribunes, delivered the *obnuntiatio*, the official announcement of oblative signs (signs sent by the gods without a request from mortals).   **in quo**: "in which case."   **Appius collega tuus**: Ap. Claudius Pulcher, consul of 54 (*MRR* 1.221, s.a.) and son of the

Caecilia mentioned at 4, was already an augur when C. became consul in 63 (see 28n. *solidum* and below, 105). He was considered by his contemporaries to be unusually credulous and superstitious (see below, 105). When Claudius became censor in 50, he used his office to settle some old scores and to tighten lax standards of behavior.   **non satis scienter . . . C. Ateium notavit, quod ementitum auspicia subscriberet**: "he unwisely censured C. Ateius in that he [Claudius] wrote down that he had falsified the auspices." *Quod* introduces a clause of alleged reason, which takes its verb in the subjunctive: the assertion that Ateius falsified the auspices is Claudius's. Censors could remove an individual from the Senate or the equestrian order by leaving a mark of condemnation (*nota*) next to his name on the citizen list.   **fuerit hoc censoris . . . at illud minime auguris**: *Fuerit* is perfect subjunctive in a clause of concession, "granted that it was appropriate for a censor." *Censoris* and *auguris* are genitives of characteristic. Granting that Claudius may have acted appropriately as censor by expelling Ateius for falsifying the auspices, Q. maintains that Claudius made an augural mistake when he blamed Ateius for the disaster at Carrhae. The augural argument is complicated. All reported signs, whether legitimately observed or completely fabricated, are binding on both gods and men. In other words, any sign (real or not) is valid once it has been announced. See, e.g., Liv. 10.40.11; C., *Phil.* 2.83 and 2.88 with Linderski 1986, 2214. The *obnuntiatio* of a negative sign, however, does not cause the unfavorable event about which it warns. The recipient who disregards its message is responsible for the outcome. Thus, by falsifying the auspices (if that is what Ateius did; Q. steps back from endorsing this position), Ateius set up the possibility of Crassus's defeat, but it was Crassus's decision to ignore Ateius's warning that ensured the loss of the legions. M. takes up the example of Crassus at 2.22, 24, and 84. The issues raised by this episode are laid out clearly in Wardle *ad loc.* and Konrad 2004.   **ob eam causam populum Romanum calamitatem maximam cepisse**: Wardle (*ad loc.*, following Schäublin) is surely right that this phrase was taken from Claudius's notation (*nota*) next to Ateius's name in the citizenship rolls.   **veram . . . fuisse obnuntiationem**: dependent on *adprobavit.*   **provideris**: an indefinite second person.

30 quid eventurum esset nisi cavisset: an indirect question dependent on *monuit,* thus in secondary sequence. Because the whole sentence refers to the past, the protasis of the future condition within the indirect question is represented by the pluperfect subjunctive (*cavisset*), as it would be in *oratio obliqua* (*G&L* 656). The apodosis of the future condition is here represented by an imperfect active periphrastic (*eventurum esset*).   **aut illa obnuntiatio nihil valuit, aut si . . . valuit**: C. often uses the rhetorical device of dilemma (*complexio*), which presents an opponent with two unappealing alternatives. The first option here is that Ateius cannot be held responsible: the falsely manufactured pronouncement had no value at all precisely because it was false (and also because, as tribune, Ateius did not have the power to offer a binding *nuntiatio oblativorum* [see Linderski 1986, 2202 n. 199]). The second option is that Ateius's prediction was valid (as Claudius himself admitted was proved by events) and thus that responsibility for the ensuing disaster rested squarely on the shoulders of Crassus, who ignored the warning. Presenting his argument in this way makes clear the logical inconsistency of the counterargument (Craig 1993, 11) and emphatically caps the line of Q.'s argument that those who do not pay attention to the auspices are doomed.   **id valuit ut**: "it was valid in that."   **peccatum haereat non**: "no fault can stick"; a vivid image not duplicated elsewhere in Latin literature.   **lituus iste vester**: Q. again emphasizes M.'s membership in the augural college (cf. *auspicia vero vestra* at 25). The *lituus* was a curved staff of unknotted wood; it was Etruscan in origin and the most recognizable symbol of the Roman augurate. For images, see Torelli 2001, 274; Ryberg 1955, 60, pl. xvi, fig. 31. Through the augurs' role as guarantors of the validity of the auspices under which magistrates were elected, the *lituus* bore both religious and political significance. It appears on coinage of the republican period, both as an advertisement of the issuer's descent from an augur (e.g., *RRC* 1.273–76 [#242.1 and #243.1–5], 289 [#264.1], 300 [#285.2]) and, when paired with a pontifex's pitcher (*simpulum*), as an assertion of a general's claim to religiously sanctioned military and political power (Stewart 1997).   **nempe eo Romulus regiones direxit tum cum urbem condidit**: *Eo* is correlative with *unde* in the previous sentence. Here, *regiones* are the quadrants an augur marked out in the sky (*Leg.* 2.21; Var., *L.* 7.7–9; Liv. 1.18.6–10 with Ogilvie's commentary), not the *quattor regiones* into which the city was divided by Servius Tullius (Var., *L.* 5.45–54). The collocation of *tum cum*, "at the time when," is common in writings of C. and Ovid but far less so in those of other authors. The antiquity of augury and the authority of its earliest Roman practitioner lend it credibility. In his rebuttal, M. criticizes Romulus's primitive belief in augury as a tool for foreseeing events, though he defends the usefulness of augury to the state (2.70). M. also points out that the precise origins of augury were unclear (2.80; cf. his similar treatment of other forms of divination at 2.28, 50, 85).   **[id est incurvum . . . nomen invenit]**: A scribe's note has worked its way into the text. C.'s audience would have known what a lituus looked like (see 30n. *lituus iste vester*); Pease notes that *id est* often introduces a gloss.   **in curia Saliorum . . . inventus est integer**: The survival of the *lituus* is proof of the gods' power and of the validity of augury. This is the sole mention of a *curia Saliorum* on the Palatine (cf. Var., *L.*

5.155). The Salii at Rome were religious officials tied to the cult of Mars whose most prominent ritual duty was to dance through the streets carrying *ancila* (sacred shields) at the March festival of Quinquatrus and perhaps also again in October at the Armilustrum (D. H. 2.70–71). Valerius Maximus (1.8.11) mentions a *sacrarium Saliorum* in his version of the story, which appears as part of a catalog of sacred items that miraculously survived conflagrations (cf. D. H. 14.2; Plu., *Cam.* 32; D. Palombi, *LTUR* 1.335–36, s.v. "Curia Saliorum"; *NTDAR* 105, s.v. "Curia Saliorum Palatinorum"). The story also appears in the *Fasti Praenestini* of the Augustan era (= *Inscr. Ital.* XIII.2, 123).

31 Prisco regnante Tarquinio: the fifth king of Rome (and the first of Etruscan origin), thought to have ruled in 616–579. By tradition, he is more closely identified with divination than any other king except Romulus: there were divine signs of his own royal destiny and that of Servius Tullius, who grew up as a slave in his house (Liv. 1.34.8–9, 1.39.1–4); his wife, Tanaquil, is described as *perita ut volgo Etrusci caelestium prodigiorum mulier* (Liv. 1.34.9); he was responsible for the exauguration of older sacred precincts on the Capitol to make way for the temple of Jupiter Optimus Maximus (Liv. 1.55.1–6); and it was during his reign that the *Caput Oli* was discovered (see 23n. *in Chiorum lapicidinis saxo diffisso caput extitisse Panisci*).   **quis veterum scriptorum non loquitur**: Q. again appeals to antiquity to strengthen his argument. As it happens, C. is the oldest extant source (also at *N. D.* 2.9 and 3.14), but there is no reason to doubt that the story had been around long before.   **quae sit ab Atto Navio per lituum regionum facta discriptio**: "what regional division was made by Attus Navius with his staff." Navius is one of the more shadowy figures in the traditional accounts of Rome under the kings. His name is a mix of Italic and Etruscan elements: his praenomen may mark him as Sabine or Roman (see Wardle and Pease on 31; Ogilvie on Liv. 2.16.4; Scarsi 2005, 402 with bibliography), while his nomen is Etruscan. Q. omits an important part of the tradition: after coming to the king's attention, Navius came into conflict with Priscus over the king's plan to expand the cavalry that would have altered the *census* established and inaugurated by Romulus (Liv. 1.36.2–8; D. H. 3.70.1–71.5; Fest. 168–70L). Navius said that no changes should be made until the birds had been consulted. Tarquin then challenged Navius to demonstrate his powers by setting before him the task described in 32. C. knew this part of the story (*Rep.* 2.36); thus his silence here is probably intentional. By arranging the tale in this way, Q. turns Priscus's challenge into a clinical test of the validity of augury. In other versions that include the conflict over the census, itself presented as a conflict between Etruscan and Roman divination in Roman political life, the test is intended as an insult.   **una**: sc. *sus*.   **si recuperasset . . . esset in vinea**: a simple future condition in *oratio obliqua*,

dependent on *vovisse dicitur.*   **uvam**: an appropriate rustic offering (cf. Tib.
1.5.27).   **quae maxima esset**: Subordinate clauses in *oratio obliqua* have
their verbs in the subjunctive. The tense of the subjunctive is determined by
the tense sequence with the verb that introduces the *oratio obliqua*. See *NLS*
179.   **ad meridiem spectans**: "looking southward"; cf. Var., *L.* 7.7. Because
Navius divides the vineyard (not the sky, *contra* Pease) into quadrants,
he performs an *augurium stativum*, which sought divine guidance in the
selection of a thing or place (Serv., *A.* 3.84, 10.423). The birds were supposed
to appear over or settle on the object in question, and there was flexibility in
the direction the auspicant faced, hence Navius's unusual orientation here. For
a normal augury, the auspicant was required to face eastward. See Linderski
1986, 2280–86, esp. n. 536.   **vineam divisisset**: The interest of augurs in
vineyards is elsewhere attested by C. (*Leg.* 2.21 with Dyck 2004, 305–6). This
is almost certainly linked in some way to the role of Jupiter, whose signs the
augurs interpret, in the August festival of the *Vinalia rustica* (Var., *L.* 6.16; De
Cazanove 1995).   **abdixissent**: by refusing to alight. *Abdico* is a technical
term, appearing in its augural sense only here: *non addico* is more common
(cf. Liv. 1.36.3, 55.3).

32 ex quo: "wherefore, as a consequence."   **ille**: indicates, as often, a
change of subject.   **tum Attum iussisse experiri**: The *oratio obliqua*
(continued in the next sentence with *esse discissam*) depends on something
like *dicitur* above or *accepimus* below. It is not clear whether *Attum* is subject
or direct object, though the latter option is preferable. It is hard to imagine
the impoverished swineherd—still a *puer* in this version of the tale—giving
orders to the king of Rome. In other versions, however, it is Priscus who cuts
the stone (D. H. 3.71.4).   **et Tarquinius augure Atto Navio uteretur et
populus . . . ad eum referret**: Navius's skills are now sought out and revered
by the body politic, not just by the *vicini omnes* mentioned in 31, presumably
other impoverished residents of Navius's rural district. Navius's augury has
moved from the private realm to the public one.

33 supraque inpositum puteal accepimus: The *puteal*, an enclosure around
a sacred spot akin to the enclosure around the mouth of a well, was in the
Comitium, near the praetor's tribunal. In all likelihood, it was a *bidental*, a
place that had been ritually purified after being struck by lightning. Nearby
stood a statue, smaller than life size, thought to be of Navius himself (D.
H. 3.71.5), and a sacred fig tree (the *ficus Navia* [Fest. 168L]), which Plin.
(*Nat.* 15.77) identifies as marking a spot where *sacra* struck by lightning
had been buried. Bidentals are rare finds: one at Minturnae (identified
by an inscription: *[ful]gur / fulg[ur]*) contained damaged architectural
fragments in stone and terracotta, pottery, and animal bones (Livi 2006,

98–100).   **Negemus ... comburamus ... dicamus ... fateamur**: an
insincere statement. Hortatory subjunctives, like the first three in this passage,
often appear in a series. The exact significance of the last subjunctive is not
entirely clear (perhaps it was attracted into the subjunctive by what precedes,
or perhaps it expresses a potentiality), but the overall sense of this passage
is readily understandable.   **Negemus omnia, comburamus annales**:
To dismiss tales like that of Romulus's *lituus* and of Navius is to dismiss the
historical tradition of Rome. Originally, the *annales* were annual records kept
by the pontifex maximus (hence their designation as *annales maximi*) that
noted the names of magistrates and major public events. Over time, the term
came to be used for histories generally. The first literary work called *Annales*
was the epic poem of Ennius (on which see 23n. *Andromacham Enni*). Over
the course of the second century BCE, there was an effloresence of prose
histories of Rome that followed the year-by-year arrangement of the *annales
maximi*, tracing the development of the city from its origins. These works,
also called *annales*, formed the core of the Roman historical tradition of the
period of the kings and of the early republic.   **scriptum apud te**: Again,
Q. strengthens his argument by pointing out that his source is C. himself.
Q. probably refers here to *N. D.* 2.10–11, where the story is told in greater
detail and is cast somewhat differently. During the election of consuls for the
year 162, the *rogator*, the official charged with recording the oral vote of the
centuries (the constituent units of the centuriate assembly, the public body
that elected consuls, praetors, and censors) died suddenly. The presiding
magistrate at the elections, Ti. Sempronius Gracchus, consul in 163 and
father of the famous tribunes (*MRR* 1.397–98 and 440–42, s.aa. 177 and
163–62), ordered the voting to continue despite this, referring the matter to
the Senate only after he perceived public discomfort with his decision. The
Senate brought in the *haruspices* for consultation. They declared that the
rogator had not been *iustum* (legal or legitimate), indicating that Gracchus
had made some sort of error in holding the elections. Gracchus flew into
a rage, shouting, *itane vero, ego non iustus, qui et consul rogavi et augur et
auspicato? an vos Tusci ac barbari auspiciorum populi Romani ius tenetis et
interpretes esse comitiorum potestis?* Only later, after having left the city for
his province at the end of his consular year, did Gracchus recognize that he
had made an error, and he reported to the Senate that the new consuls had, in
fact, been *vitio creatos* (see 33n. *quod ... esset*). As in the last *exemplum* (see
31n. *quae sit ab Atto Navio per lituum regionum facta discriptio*), Q. passes
over a prominent aspect of the story that highlights the competition between
Etruscan and Roman divination in Roman political life. Any implication
of charlatanism in a form of divination endorsed by he Roman state would
complicate Q.'s position. At 2.75, M. echoes Gracchus's objections (as

presented in the passage from *N. D.*) about the competence of the *haruspices*
to comment on augural matters.   **cum tabernaculum vitio cepisset
inprudens**: concessive. The nominative adjective *inprudens* agrees with an
unexpressed subject (Gracchus) and is best rendered as an adverb in English.
A similar event is reported at Liv. 4.7.3. *Tabernaculum capere* is the technical
phrase for an augur setting up the tent from which he watched for signs; the
phrase is often shorthand for the whole ceremony of *auspicatio*, that is, the
taking of the auspices. *Tabernaculum vitio captum* could refer to an error at
any point during the *auspicatio* before the action in question was undertaken.
It need not be limited to an incorrect placement of the tent. On *vitium*, see
28n. *in dira et in vitiosa*.   **quod inauspicato pomerium transgressus
esset**: The verb is subjunctive in virtual *oratio obliqua*: the explanation is
Gracchus's. Consuls were elected by the *comitia centuriata*, which met in the
Campus Martius, outside the *pomerium*, the sacred boundary of the city that
separated a consul's civil powers and auspices from his military ones (see 33n.
scriptum apud te). As was proper, Gracchus took the auspices while in the city,
before crossing the *pomerium* on his way to the Campus Martius to hold the
elections. Before elections could be held, however, Gracchus had to return
to the city to take care of some other senatorial business. This meant that he
again crossed the *pomerium*, an act that canceled the *auspicia* he had taken
earlier. Since he did not take the *auspicia* a second time before returning to
the Campus Martius, every action Gracchus took upon his return, including
holding the elections, was *inauspicato* (*N. D.* 2.11). The *rogator's* death was an
indication that the elections were invalid.   **comitia consulibus rogandis**:
"the assembly for electing consuls." The dative of the gerundive is rare before
the age of Augustus, with the major exception of titles of *comitia* and *collegia*.
Cf. 3n. *et inpetriendis . . . procurandis*.   **confessione errati sui**: Gracchus
sent a letter to Rome admitting his error. The augurs ruled that the consuls
must resign office, which they did, and new elections were held (2.74–75; *N.
D.* 2.11). The great authority of the *auspicia* was confirmed in that the consuls
could not hold office if they had been elected under unfavorable *auspicia*;
authority accrued to the *haruspices* because their interpretation was proven
accurate.   **recentibus comitiis**: "not long after the election."

34–38 Oracles

Q. here expands on the two categories of divination that he introduced
briefly in 11–12 (see 11n. *duo . . . divinandi genera*), before he began the
long digression in 12–33. After reviewing the difference between natural
and artificial divination and touching briefly on haruspicy and astrology, Q.

turns to oracles, the first of three types of natural, or inspired, divination. The argument in this section is not linear but, rather, flows discursively over several points, with some repetition of earlier arguments. The unpolished, conversational quality of this passage is further underlined by several stylistic elements, including frequent structural repetition in consecutive sentences and several isocolic phrases (i.e., similarly structured phrases of equal length).

34 divinationum: The plural is rare in Latin, appearing only in *Div.* at 78, 90, and 93, each time referring to different forms of divination, rather than multiple instances of one type of prediction.   **artis**: "technical knowledge."   **qui novas res . . . persequuntur, veteres . . . didicerunt**: There is asyndeton between these two clauses, as well as hysteron proteron: they appear in an order that reverses their logical connection. One would need to have learned the ancient teachings before being able to make new pronouncements using conjecture. Their logical relationship is preserved in the different tenses of *persequuntur* and *didicerunt*. *Veteres* is contrasted with *novas res*.   **animi**: modifies both *concitatione* and *motu*.   **contingit**: I follow Pease in accepting the variant reading for the manuscript's *contigit*. Q. does not relegate the phenomenon to the past.   **non numquam**: "sometimes"; cf. 24n. *At non numquam*.   **ut Bacis Boeotius ut Epimenides Cres ut Sibylla Erythraea**: There is an anacoluthon (see 16n. *possit*) in the switch to a series of nominatives from the preceding *vaticinantibus*. This series constitutes an asyndetic tricolon, the first of several isocola in this passage that serve to underline the multiplicity of *exempla*. Written collections of prophecies, often attributed to divine or semidivine individuals, circulated in the ancient world from very early on. A collection attributed to Bacis was known as early as Herodotus (e.g., 8.20, 77). Epimenides of Crete, to whom numerous literary works were attributed, including oracles, appears to have been active in the seventh century (*Ath. Pol.* 1). Prophetic verses attributed to the many Sibyls known to the ancients were also available. Although it was often difficult to tell which Sibyl was supposed to have written a particular prophecy, the Erythraean Sibyl, who purportedly predicted the fall of Troy, worked her name into some of her verses (Var. ap. Lact., *Div. Inst.* I.6.7–12 = Cardauns 1976, 1.42–43, no. 56a). There were Sibyls in Italy at Cumae and Tibur, but inspired prophets, like the three named here, were largely a Greek phenomenon. Romans preferred to consult the words of the Sibyl collected in the Sibylline books, rather than the prophet herself.   **cuius generis oracla . . . non ea quae . . . ducuntur, sed illa . . . funduntur**: Q. distinguishes here between oracles whose pronouncements were given by a priest(ess) possessed by a divine force and oracles that communicated through divinatory lots. The two types of divination could coexist in a single sanctuary, as at Delphi (see Johnston 2008, 38–60, esp. 51–56).   **aequatis sortibus ducuntur**: "are drawn from uniform lots." Though not strictly a technical term, *ducere* is common in descriptions of cleromancy (lot divination). See Grottanelli 2005. The lots in a set were close in size and weight in order to make them as indistinguishable by touch as possible, thereby equalizing the chances that any one lot would be drawn from the urn. A number of the extant lots from the Roman world are small rectangular bronze strips with a perforation at one end (suggesting that a set would have been kept together, perhaps on a ring). On one side, they usually bear a terse expression that could provide a suitable answer to any number of questions or that would be capable of multiple interpretations. Photographs of *sortes* are found in *ILLRP Imagines*, p. 255 nn. 354–56.   **instinctu divino adflatuque**: Almost exactly the same phrase is used at 12.   **sortes quas e terra editas**: refers to the lot oracle at the sanctuary of Fortuna Primigenia at Praeneste, where the lots gained authority from the sanctity of the sanctuary itself, from their own divine origin and antiquity, and from the elevated social status of the man who discovered them. These factors distinguish the Praenestine lots from those used by the lower class *sortilegi* that Q. disparages at 132. The most extensive description of Fortuna's sanctuary and its ritual is found in M's response at 2.85–87, where he recounts that these lots, made of oak and inscribed in archaic letters, were discovered by the nobleman Numerius Suffustius, who, acting on instructions given to him in a dream, broke open a rock that contained them. Beyond saying that under Fortune's instruction (*Fortunae monitu*), a boy mixed the lots and then drew them, M. does not provide details for the method of consultation.   **quae tamen ductae . . . divinitus**: "even so, lots have been drawn so that they fall out in a way relevant to the question at hand—I believe that can happen by divine intervention." Q. does not connect the two phrases *quae . . . cadant* and *fieri . . . divinitus* grammatically, although the link between them is easy enough to understand. The anacoluthon enhances the lively feel of this passage, reflecting the loose style of conversation between intimates. **tamen**: The concession pertains to lots in general, not to the Praenestine lots specifically. **ductae**: that is, drawn at random. **divinitus**: M. offers a response to this specific point at 2.85, where he counters that lots speak to a specific question only as a result of *temeritas et casus* (randomness and chance).   **ut grammatici poetarum**: Similar comparisons are found at 39, 116. In addition to providing aristocratic boys with an early education in proper Latinity, *grammatici* introduced their students to great works of literature through detailed explication of texts, mostly poetry, line by line if not word by word. Poets and prophets were always closely related in the ancient mind (see *OLD*, s.v. *uates* 1–2). Their interpreters—for poets, *grammatici*; for prophets, priests or other diviners skilled in explaining their cryptic pronouncements—seem to have worked in analogous ways. There is a striking degree of similarity in the methods of diviners, especially those who interpreted written oracles, and allegorist literary critics (on which see Struck 2005). Both sought a hidden meaning beneath the surface of a text, most often written in hexameters. The comparison between grammarians and diviners was explicitly made by Panaetius (Athenaeus 634c–d = van Straaten 1962, 31, no. 93), the leading Stoic philosopher in the last half of the second century BCE.   **eorum**: sc. the gods.   **divinationem**: object of *ad* and defined by the intervening phrase. The use here is unusual: *divinationem* must mean something like "knowledge of the future" or "divine intention." Pease accepts the manuscripts' *divinationem* against the variant *divinitatem* proposed by Hottinger (and retained by Ax), arguing that Q.'s point is that interpreters of prophecy were able to reveal the underlying message from the gods, not that they are almost divine figures themselves. Thinking along these same lines, Schäublin, followed by Wardle, replaces *divinationem* with *divinam rationem*.

35 calliditas: "cleverness, craftiness"; also at 105. In the introduction (2), C. has already established an opposition between excessive learnedness, of which *calliditas* is a component, and belief in divination.   **pervertere**: takes as its object *res vetustate robustas*. *Pervertere* is an uncommon word in Latin generally but a favorite of C., in whose work most of its occurrences are found. It appears twice in this passage (see below, 38).   **Non reperio causam**: an interruption by Q.'s imaginary interlocutor. Their running conversation continues (cf. 23–24, 37, 60), serving as an organizing principle for Q.'s argument by introducing topics and also allowing him to cast his opponent's criticism in ways beneficial to his own position.   **obscuritate involuta naturae**: "enveloped in the obscurity of nature." The participle modifies an understood *causa*, the subject of *latet*.   **his**: points forward to forms of divination enumerated in the next sentence.   **adducar aut in extis . . . delirare aut . . . in fulgoribus errare aut . . . portenta interpretari**: *Adducar* + infinitive = *adducar ad credendum*. Though not truly isocolic, the structure of these three phrases is largely similar. Q. names the major methods of divination comprised by the *Etrusca disciplina*, on which see 3n. *haruspicum disciplina*. **delirare**: Used pejoratively throughout *Div.* (cf. 53, 2.90, 2.141) and elsewhere in C.'s *philosophica*, it is the opposite of true prophesying through divine inspiration.   **saepe fremitus saepe mugitus saepe motus**: another asyndetic tricolon. *Motus* is the culmination of *fremitus* (roaring) and *mugitus* (rumbling), which are almost certainly technical haruspicial terms for different types of noises coming from the earth (cf. C.,

Har. Resp. 20), although they are not used exclusively in this way. *Fremitus* is frequently used to describe the roar of a crowd, *mugitus* for the bellowing of cattle.

36 quid: "What?" Here and in the next question, this is an exclamation of surprise that anyone could deny the truth of the statement that follows.   **qui inridetur partus hic mulae**: "is the recent parturition of a mule being laughed at?" (*OLD*, s.v. *hic*[1] 3a). The postponement of the demonstrative *hic* emphasizes the word that follows. The Stoic doctrine of sympathy (συμπάθεια) posited a relationship among the constituent parts of the universe such that a change in one area necessarily affects a change in another, even if the two areas do not appear to be connected in any way. Sympathy was used to explain the efficacy of many divinatory practices where signs had no clear link to the events they foretold. In this case, there is no obvious connection between mules and the state of civil society, but the aberration of a mule giving birth can be a sympathetic indication of impending war (*partus malorum*). The sympathetic connection is underscored by the metaphorical link between the two "births" and by a similar sound in *mulae* and *malorum*. In Book 2, M. attacks the idea of cosmic sympathy, most significantly at 34–35 and 142–43.   **in sterilitate naturae**: A mule is a hybrid animal, a cross between a donkey stallion and horse mare. Though mules are almost always sterile, they can be fertile in rare instances. Plin., *Nat.* 8.173 suggests that prodigies of this type were regularly reported at Rome. Five are noted in the extant books and epitomes of Livy, including one in Obsequens's summary of 50/49 BCE (Obs. 65), the same notice that records the outbreak of civil war between Pompey and Caesar. It may be to this particular instance that Q. refers. M. mocks this *exemplum* at 2.49–50 and 2.61, saying that the event was not truly miraculous because it was not an impossible occurrence; people only treat it as a prodigy because it is rare. For more on mule prodigies, see MacBain 1982, 14–15.   **Tib. Gracchus P. filius**: This is the same Gracchus as in 33, on whom see 33n. *scriptum apud te*. This story also appears in Val. Max. 4.6.1; Plin., *Nat.* 7.122; Plu., *Ti. Gracch.* 1.4–5; and *Vir. Ill.* 57.4. For the history of this episode and its place within a family religious tradition, see Santangelo 2005.   **ut C. Gracchus filius eius scriptum reliquit**: Gaius is the famous tribune of 123 and 122 BCE, whose vigorous efforts at reforming Roman government, inspired by the efforts of his older brother Tiberius a decade before, were ultimately thwarted by more conservative elements. In his response at 2.62, M. says that the story was recounted by the younger Gracchus *ad M. Pomponium*, which presumably indicates a letter. It is possible, however, that M. means a book of Gaius's mentioned by Plutarch (*Ti. Gracch.* 8.9). C.'s opinion of Gracchus and his brother, the tribune of 133, is generally hostile with regard to their political position (e.g., *Dom.* 102; *Prov. Cons.* 18), although he is appreciative of their talent, their desire to serve the people, and their oratorical abilities. Gaius in particular had a reputation as a powerful orator (*Brut.* 125; *Har. Resp.* 41; Vell. 2.6.1; Tac., *Dial.* 18.2), and a collection of his speeches circulated until late antiquity. The extant fragments are collected in Malcovati 1976, 1.174–98.   **haruspices**: Private consultations of the prestigious *haruspices* used by the Senate are rarely recorded by our sources, but it is possible that a man of the elder Gracchus's elevated stature would have had access to them, rather than having to resort to the *haruspices* for hire disparaged by Q. at 132.   **si marem emisisset, uxori brevi tempore esse moriendum, si feminam, ipsi**: Brachylogy, where a missing word must be supplied from a corresponding word in the context, occurs twice in this sentence: *emisisset* governs both *marem* and *feminam*, and *esse moriendum* governs both *uxori* and *ipsi*.   **maturam**: "timely." Gracchus was much older than his wife (Plin., *Nat.* 7.122; Plu., *Ti. Gracch.* 1.5).   **P. Africani filiam**: Cornelia, daughter of Scipio Africanus and mother of twelve children, of whom only three survived to adulthood (the two tribunes and a daughter who married Cornelia's nephew, Scipio Aemilianus), was a force in her own right. She is credited with overseeing the education and inspiring the careers of her children (Plu., *Ti. Gracch.* 1.6–7; Tac., *Dial.* 28).   **inrideamus**: picks up the *inridetur* above.   **vanos futtiles:** asyndeton.   **eventus ac res**: "outcome of the affair"; hendiadys (cf. 20n. *artis scripta ac monumenta volutans*).   ⟨**condemnemus**⟩: probably dropped from the text because of its similarity to *contemnamus*. The following *condemnemus inquam* strongly suggests that Q. is repeating a word he has just said (cf. 105 for a similar construction). The preceding *contemnamus* marks the end of its period, whereas the restored *condemnemus* begins a new thought.   **Babylonem**: In addition to the Chaldeans (cf. 2n. *qua in natione Chaldaei non ex artis sed ex gentis vocabulo nominati*), Babylon gave rise to many other itinerant fortune-tellers, dream interpreters, and prophets. See Dickie 2001, 111–12.   **e Caucaso . . . servantes**: "observing from Mount Caucasus." *Servare* is a technical augural term for observing celestial phenomena and the flight of birds (Serv., *A.* 6.198). The phrase almost certainly refers not to the Caucasus proper (the area now covered largely by Georgia, Azerbaijan, and Armenia) but, rather, to the Paropamisus mountain range in the Hindu Kush in modern Afghanistan, which lies much closer to ancient Babylon. The Paropamisus was called the Caucasus by Greek writers and was the birthplace of Callanus, the Brahmin who was part of Alexander the Great's entourage (see 47n. *Callanus Indus*). **numeris**: "astrological calculations"; cf. Hor., *Carm.*

1.11.2–3. [et motibus]: In this context, one would expect that *motus* and *cursus* are synonyms, rather than that the former is a means of tracking the latter. Pease points out that the phrase looks like a corruption of *ex montibus*, which may have been a marginal gloss for *e Caucaso*, later inserted into the text in the wrong place.   **aut stultitiae aut vanitatis aut inpudentiae**: genitives of accusation in a tricolon.   **qui quadringenta septuaginta milia annorum ut ipsi dicunt monumentis conprehensa continent**: "who keep in record books the things they have observed over 470,000 years, so they say." Babylonian astrology was thought to be very old, with many ancient authors claiming that it was even older than Q. claims. See Wardle *ad loc.*   **mentiri iudicemus nec . . . pertimescere**: The jussive subjunctive launches *oratio obliqua*. The unarticulated subject of both *mentiri* and *pertimescere* is the preceding *hos* (sc. the Babylonians).   **saeculorum reliquorum iudicium quod de ipsis futurum sit**: "what will be the judgment of themselves made in future ages."

37 age barbari vani atque fallaces: Cf. 13n. *age*. Supply *sint*, a subjunctive to indicate a concession granted for the sake of argument. Though he adduces evidence from outside the Greek and Roman sphere when he finds it valuable, Q. can, for the sake of argument, set it aside.   **num etiam Graiorum historia mentita est?**: Use of the less common, poetic *Graiorum* lends greater solemnity to the *historia* and *exempla* that follow. Q. implies the superiority of Greek *exempla* over other foreign material, switching not only from barbarian to Greek evidence but from technical to natural divination.   **Croeso**: the last king of Lydia. Although not Greek himself, Croesus was important in the Greek historiographical tradition. He sent messengers to all the famous oracles in Greece and Libya to ask the same question so that he might determine which, if any, of the oracles were really able to prophesy (Herodot. 1.46–56). After comparing the various responses, he determined that the only true oracles were those of Apollo at Delphi and of Amphiaraus near Oropus in Boeotia. Croesus then sent messengers back to those two shrines, to ask if he should make war on the growing Persian power. Both oracles replied that he would destroy a mighty empire if he undertook such a campaign. Croesus took this to mean that he would be victorious. Unfortunately, his own empire was overthrown by the Persians in 546. He is another example of a supreme leader, like Pompey and Deiotarus (24–27), for whom foreknowledge did not translate into success.   **ut de naturali divinatione dicam**: "to talk about natural divination"; a parenthetical clause that expresses Q.'s reason for making the statement itself (*OLD*, s.v. *ut* 29a).   **quae Atheniensibus . . . Corinthiis**: another series of near isocola used to emphasize the number of cases adduced as evidence. Literary and epigraphic sources record consultations of the Delphic oracle by each of these peoples on numerous occasions over several centuries (see 3n. *Pythio . . . oraculo*). For a representative selection of references, see Pease and Wardle *ad loc*. Athenian consultation of the Delphic oracle in particular has been the subject of several studies, including Bowden 2005.   **Chrysippus**: the third leader of the Stoic school and the author of two volumes of divinatory *exempla* (one on dreams, the other on oracles), described by C. at 6 as *acerrumo vir ingenio*. His work is mentioned again at 39. M. attacks his authority at 2.115–16 and 2.134.   **sine locuplete auctore atque teste**: "without a trustworthy authority and source" (*OLD*, s.v. *locuples* 4). Cf. *Div.* 2.119; *Off.* 3.100; Apul. *Fl.* 16.38, 17.4.

38 "Idem iam diu non facit": another objection from the imaginary interlocutor. After centuries of being the most revered oracular shrine in the Greek world, the sanctuary at Delphi began to lose its authority in the fourth century BCE. Once it came under the control of the Aetolians in the early third century BCE, the oracle's pronouncements were increasingly thought to be subject to the political will of the power that possessed it. Although the oracle's advice was no longer sought regularly by states and cities after the death of Alexander, private individuals continued to consult it until the late third century CE.   **ut igitur nunc . . . sic tum**: "Well then, just as now . . . so at that time . . ." Q. again makes a pointed distinction between the present situation and older, better days.   **nisi summa veritate in tanta gloria non fuisset**: "if it had not exhibited the greatest truthfulness, it would not have enjoyed such renown." *Fuisset* governs both protasis and apodosis.   **vis illa terrae . . . evanuisse vetustate**: At 2.117–18, M. mocks this suggestion, arguing that the prophecies ceased not because the divine *vis* weakened but because men grew less credulous. Earthquakes and sedimentation appear to have, over time, blocked the release of the gases that caused the Pythia's frenzy. For an accessible account of recent geological findings, see Broad 2006, 107–200. For ancient explanations of the oracle's decline, see Pease *ad loc*.   **sed, ut vis, acciderit**: a compression of "but let it have happened however you desire" *vel sim. Sed* dismisses the explanations just offered (*OLD*, s.v. 2); *acciderit* is in the perfect subjunctive within an indirect question.   **uerax**: an uncommon word, often used in a prophetic context. Cf. Tib. 1.2.41, 3.7.119, 3.7.133; Hor., *Carm. Saec.* 25; Ov., *Her.* 16.280.

39–59 *Dreams*

The organization of this long section is not as tidy and linear as the earlier parts of Q.'s argument, but he never wanders very far from the topic at hand. This catalog of *exempla* is followed by a theoretical explanation of the ability of the soul to foresee events (60–64). Within the catalog, some attempt is made at grouping dreams by type of dreamer—political leaders and their mothers (39–51), philosophers (52–54), and figures from recent Roman history (55–59)—though the organization of the latter two sections is particularly loose. In many instances, consecutive *exempla* are linked by some shared detail, such as the repetition of the dream over several days or the appearance of unidentified divine messengers. Nearly all the dreams recorded here are also preserved in other sources, which indicates that they were established elements of the historical tradition. Where comparison can be made, Q.'s interpretations of individual dreams are in keeping with the general guidelines laid out in Artemidorus's *Oneirocritica*, the only extant ancient dream book (dated to the second century CE). While they are not immediately relevant to C.'s contemporary political situation, many of the *exempla* here have associations with Julius Caesar. In Book 2 (esp. 136), M. rebuts most of Q.'s historical dream *exempla* on the grounds that there is no way to verify that these dreams happened as tradition presents them or even at all. M. silently passes over the dreams Q. cites from poetic sources (Ilia, Hecuba, and Tarquin) and the philosophers' dreams.

39 omittamus . . . veniamus: Hortatory subjunctives introduce a shift to the second type of natural divination.   **quibus . . . ea . . . quae . . . illa**: The antecedent for all of these is *somnia*. The pleonasm (use of more words than necessary) of *illa*, a superfluous reinforcement of *quae*, contributes to the conversational tone.   **Chrysippus multis et minutis somniis colligendis facit idem quod Antipater . . . sed exemplis grandioribus decuit uti**: *Facit* is also understood in the relative clause *quod Antipater* (brachylogy). Q.'s criticism of Chrysippus and Antipater (on whom see 6) is echoed by M. at 2.144, where he cites examples that illustrate Antiphon's method of antilogical interpretation. Antiphon, whose identity is not certain (for the main schools of thought, see Gagarin 2002, 37–52; Pendrick 2002, 1–26), sought deeper, hidden meanings in dreams that were the opposite of what the dream appeared to indicate. **minutis . . . grandioribus**: "trifling . . . loftier"; terms often used to contrast different rhetorical styles (*Opt. Gen.* 9; *Orat.* 123; *De Orat.* 3.169; *Part.* 57). *Somniis minutis* are generic, not tied to any identifiable person, place, or event, whereas *somniis grandioribus* are associated with prominent historical individuals.   **explicata**: modifies *quae*.   **Dionysi mater**: The subject of the exemplum is dramatically positioned first, even though this sets it at an unusual distance from the *cum* clause of which it is the grammatical subject. Cf. 46, 48. Having criticized earlier writers for their attention to less worthy *exempla*, Q. begins with a dream associated with a prominent historical figure. Dionysius I, ruler of Syracuse from 405 to 367,

appears often in C.'s work (e.g., *Q. Fr.* 2.12[11].4 = *SBQ* 16.4), especially in
his later *philosophica*, as a tyrant who combined refined education with great
cruelty. He was known to have written tragedies and perhaps histories as
well (*Suda*, s.v. Διονύσιος, Σικελίας τύραννος). C.'s most extensive treatment
of Dionysius, *Tusc.* 5.57–63, was written shortly before *N. D.* and *Div.* and
has been read as a lightly veiled criticism of Caesar (Jaeger 2002; Verbaal
2006; see 46n. *matrem Phalaridis*). A tradition of hostile dreams concerning
Dionysius is preserved in Val. Max. 1.7 ext. 6 and Heraclides of Pontus (133
Wehrli).   **et doctum hominem et diligentem et aequalem temporum
illorum**: To distance this *exemplum* from *minutis somniis*, Q. emphasizes his
source's erudition and chronological proximity to the events. His appraisal
of the merits of Philistus, a fourth-century historian of Sicily and a close
associate of Dionysius, matches C.'s own opinion expressed elsewhere (e.g.,
Q. Fr. 2.12[11].4 = *SBQ* 16.4; *De Orat.* 2.57). Though C. uses *diligens* most
often to mean "careful or attentive to detail," it is possible that he is here also
playing on its other meaning, "devoted." Philistus's favorable attitude toward
tyrants earned him the label φιλοτυραννότατος (Plu., *Dio.* 36.3; cf. D. H.,
Pomp. 5). Philistus is the source of another anecdote about Dionysius at
73.   **satyriscum**: "a baby satyr." The story is also reported at Val. Max. 1.7
ext. 7, which is also the only other literary occurrence in Latin of *satyriscus*,
a term more common in Greek (for a similar Latin diminutive, see 23n. *in
Chiorum lapicidinis saxo diffisso caput extitisse Panisci*). The explanation
for the interpreters' response is not obvious. It is possible that there is some
play on the association of satyrs with the god Dionysus and, by an iota of
difference, with Dionysius. By making a satyr of Dionysius, the dream may
also be understood to foretell his unrestrained, tyrannical behavior.   **huic**:
that is, *matri*.   **galeotae**: Little is known about these diviners, who are most
frequently associated with Sicily (e.g., Hsych., s.v. Γαλεοί). Ancient attempts
to identify them as descendants of Galeos, a son of Apollo, are obviously
etymologizing (as in St. Byz., s.v. Γαλεῶται). Pease doubts that the word is of
Greek origin. It is similar to the Semitic root *g-l-y* (to open or reveal), which
sometimes appears in classical Hebrew (Amos 3:7), biblical Aramaic (several
occurrences in Daniel 2), and Phoenician in a mantic sense (Gaster 1973,
esp. 21–22). This may point to a Semitic origin, which is not an unreasonable
conclusion given the long-standing Carthaginian presence in Sicily.

40 Num te ad fabulas revoco vel nostrorum vel Graecorum poetarum?:
Q. is aware that mythological tales (*fabulae*) are, for M., the least credible
type of evidence (e.g., 2.80), but he forges ahead anyway (cf. 17–22 from
Consulatus Suus).   **apud Ennium**: Ennius's most important work, from
which the following fragment comes, is his epic poem *Annales*, an account

of Rome's history from Aeneas down to the author's own day. For this work, he eschewed the native Italic Saturnian meter used in earlier Latin epics by Livius Andronicus and Naevius, in favor of dactyllic hexameter, the meter of Greek epic and prophecy. To adapt the language and the meter to each other, Ennius developed rules on word placement and the handling of vowels and of the caesura and established the proper style and diction for subsequent Roman epic. He also wedded a native Italic aesthetic to this new Greek form, including the heavy use of alliteration, assonance, and consonance (all present in the fragment below) and other forms of sound patterning that are common in archaic Latin but rare in the refined Greek poetry of the Hellenistic period. The *Annales* presented a history of Rome that exemplified the *virtus* of the Roman elite: success in war, wisdom and restraint in peace, and excellence in speaking, all in pursuit of the greater glory of the Roman state. The poem presented the Romans to themselves at their best, linking Ennius's contemporaries to their noble ancestors. The *Annales* remained the quintessential school text until Vergil's *Aeneid* replaced it more than a century later.   **Vestalis illa**: This introduces the longest extant fragment of the *Annales* (corresponding to 34–50 in the edition by Skutsch, whose commentary on these lines informs that offered here): a speech by Ilia (so named at 56 and 60 Skutsch), the future mother of Romulus and Remus. In other versions of the tale, she is known as Rhea, Silvia, or Rhea Silvia (e.g., Liv. 1.3.11; D. H. 1.76.3; Ov., *F.* 3.11; Plu., *Rom.* 3.3). In the traditional story, the twins' great-uncle Amulius usurps the throne from his brother, their grandfather. To eliminate all threats to his rule, Amulius compels his niece to become a Vestal Virgin, thinking that she will never bear children as a chaste priestess. But Ilia catches the attention of the god Mars, who has already impregnated her by the time she delivers this speech. M. does not address this particular *exemplum* in Book 2.   **et cita cum tremulis anus attulit artubus**: *Et* connects the passage to whatever preceded it in Ennius. *Cita* is best translated adverbially (cf 33n. *cum tabernaculum vitio cepisset inprudens*). *Artubus* is ablative plural: *artus* is one of a handful of fourth declension nouns that retains the *u* of the stem in all cases and numbers. Assonance and alliteration appear in nearly every line of this passage, beginning here with the repetition of *c*, *t*, *a*, and *l*. Skutsch is right that *anus* mostly likely refers to a servant different from *Eurydica prognata* mentioned two lines below and that she is not, as Pease asserts, an older Vestal.   **memorat**: sc. Ilia.   **exterrita somno**: "frightened out of her sleep."   **Eurydica prognata, pater quam noster amavit**: *Eurydica* is an ablative of origin followed by the vocative *prognata*, and it is also the antecedent of *quam*. Ilia addresses her sister, whose presence was probably indicated by Ennius before our fragment begins. In Ennius and Naevius (D. H. 1.72–73; Serv., *A.*

1.273, 6.777), Ilia is the daughter of Aeneas, making Romulus his grandson; in the more canonical version, many generations of kings at Alba Longa separate Romulus from Aeneas (e.g., Cato frag. 9 Peter = *FRH* 2.158 frag. 6; probably also Fabius Pictor frag. 5 Peter = *FRH* 2.48-63 frag. 4.; Liv. 1.3.6–11; D. H. 1.71.1–5). Aeneas's Trojan wife is called Eurydice in earlier Greek sources; she is first attested as Creusa in the Augustan period (Verg., *A.* 2.562).   **corpus**: This would have been pronounced with a short *u* and no *s* sound. In archaic Latin, a final *s* after a short vowel and followed by a word beginning with a consonant was often omitted (e.g., *CIL* 1².8: *Cornelio L. f.*); hence it did not cause the lengthening of the preceding syllable. This is common in Ennius (see *ecfatus* and *somnus* in this same passage, *navibus* and *manus* in 67) and Lucilius, but it is almost unknown in poets of the late republic onward, with the exception of the archaizing Lucretius. From the end of the third century BCE onward, final *s* was written in inscriptions and (presumably) literary texts, but it was still omitted in pronunciation (see *Orat.* 161). See Halporn, Ostwald, and Rosenmeyer 1963, 64; Coleman 1999, 33–34.   **visus . . . videbar . . . videtur**: The repetition emphasizes that Ilia is reporting a dream. Forms of *videre* (equivalent to *somniare*; see Jacobs 2010, 323) are plentiful throughout Q.'s dream catalog and are common in dream reports generally. The dreamlike quality of Ilia's account is further enhanced by the rapid transition from one scene to the next. Ilia's dream has many elements in common with dreams reported in Greek epic and tragedy, as well as with other foundation legends. See Krevans 1993; Connors 1994.   **homo pulcher**: sc. Mars. The divine Mars was surely handsome, but *pulcher* has a further religious meaning of "blessed, ideal." See Skutsch *ad loc.* with Linderski 2006, 90–91.   **raptare**: "to drag off." Commenting on the delicacy of this passage, Skutsch (*ad loc.*) notes that there is "the merest hint" of rape in the verb. Accepting Skutsch's proposal that Mars visited Ilia while asleep in her bedchamber, Krevans points out that Ilia tells her dream while pregnant (1993, 265–66); supporting that argument is Q.'s placement of this *exemplum* between two dreams that are clearly pregnancy dreams.   **postilla**: appears again in 42. Comparable to *postea* and *posthac*, this form is found in early Latin but disappears from regular use in the classical period.   **germana soror**: *Germana* usually indicates identical parentage, which would make both women daughters of Aeneas and Eurydice. Skutsch, however, asserts that nothing prevents *germana* from being used for a half sister (the relationship he prefers to see here); citing *TLL*, s.v. IA1d, he takes *germana* as equivalent to *cara*.   **te . . . corde capessere**: This is a difficult phrase. Skutsch notes that the usual meaning of *capere* and its derivatives used with *corde* is "to understand you," which is not appropriate here. One expects something like "to see you" or "to embrace you," but such use is unparalleled. Skutsch's proposal to take it as "to reach you" is preferable to Wardle's literal "to grasp you in my heart." **semita nulla pedem stabilibat**: *Stabilibat* is an archaic form of the imperfect: the regular form *stabiliebat* is impossible in dactylic hexameter. The language emphasizes the wildness and desolation of the place (cf. 59n. *in locis solis*).

41 exim compellare pater me voce videtur / his verbis: The pleonasm of *voce* with *compellare* (and other verbs of speaking) is very old and often appears in extant Latin poetry—perhaps for metrical reasons. See *voce vocabam* six lines below. Aeneas does not actually appear to Ilia, as is made clear by *nec sese dedit in conspectum* four lines down. **post ex fluvio fortuna resistet**: The Tiber will save her twin sons, and Ilia herself will be thrown into the river after giving birth and being married to the river Anio, which intersects with the Tiber at Antemnae (I.xxxix Skutsch with commentary). Variants of this part of the story are told at Porph., *In Hor. Carm.* 1.2.17–18 and Serv., *A.* 1.273. **multa**: The singular *multum* is commonly used as an adverbial accusative, but the plural *multa* is used in some instances in poetry: there is one possible example in prose, Caecina in *Fam.* 6.7.2 = *SBF* 237.2. **caeli caerula templa**: This phrase appears several times in the extant fragments of Ennius. The image is adapted by many later poets, most notably Lucretius and Vergil. See Skutsch *ad loc.*

42 haec etiamsi ficta sunt a poeta . . . somniorum: Q. anticipates another objection. **sit sane etiam illud commenticium**: jussive subjunctive granting a concession for the sake of argument (*NLS* 112 n. i). **quia**: Though a causal clause is awkward here, the *quia* almost certainly belongs to Q.'s speech and not to the fragment. C. prefers quotations that are complete sense units; as Jocelyn (1967, 221) notes, his quotations "do not begin with adverbial clauses hanging in the air." Assigning *quia* to Q. leaves a partial first line of the quotation (cf. 24n. *profectione laeti . . . occaecat nigror*). **mater gravida . . .**: These iambic trimeters are thought to come from Ennius's tragedy *Alexander*, which seems to have dealt with a tradition that the infant Alexander (i.e., Paris) was abandoned at birth on the advice of seers. He was raised by herdsmen and was eventually welcomed back into the royal house by his brothers Hector and Deiphobus (see Jocelyn 1967, 202). Three other quotations also thought to be from this same play are found at 66–67, and there is another at 114. It is not clear who would have spoken the lines preserved here. Though not in the Homeric poems, Hecuba's dreams were part of the tradition about the fall of Troy (e.g., Eur., *Hek.* 88). **parere ⟨ex⟩ se**: The preposition was added by Bücheler and is accepted by Ax and Pease. Timpanaro and Schäublin, however, follow Jocelyn (1967, 77) in maintaining the more difficult manuscript reading. Cf. Ov., *Her.* 17.237–38. Jocelyn (1967, 223) explains that Ennius has here conflated two different constructions: *parere se . . . facem vidit* and *parere . . . facem visa est.*   **pater / rex ipse Priamus**: The asyndetic string of nominatives builds to a crescendo with the name of the ill-fated king. Priam appears several times in Q.'s argument (66, 85, 89).   **mentis metu / perculsus curis sumptus suspirantibus**: "struck with fear in his mind and sighing, consumed by worries." *Mentis* is genitive of the part affected, a less common variant of the accusative construction. The descriptive *suspirantibus* is transferred from its proper object, Priam, to another (hypallage). Note the consonance and alliteration of *m, p, c, s,* and *t.*   **exsacrificabat hostiis balantibus**: The verb appears only here in extant Latin; the force of the prefix and of the tense is not clear. Perhaps *exsacrificare* is a calque on Greek ἐκθύομαι = to expiate, but Jocelyn (1967, 197) notes a tendency in Roman tragedy to replace regular forms with an *ex-* compound. **hostiis balantibus**: "bleating victims"; = sheep (instrumental ablative; cf. *Div.* 1.101; Liv. 22.1.17). Note that the line ends with a rhyme: *suspirantibus / balantibus.*   **coniecturam**: See 12n. *animadversa et notata.*   **postulat pacem petens**: Alliteration of *p* also occurs with *puerum primus Priamo* and *pestem Pergamo* in this passage. *Pacem petere* is a common variation of the petitionary prayer formula *veniam petere*, "to seek indulgence" (Hickson 1993, 50–51). It is also used for seeking an end to hostilities. Cf. *pax deorum*, used to refer to the proper relationship between gods and men.   **quo sese vertant tantae sortes somnium**: indirect question dependent on *edoceret. Sortes* = "fate," not the physical lots used in divination (*contra* Jocelyn 1967, 225). *Somnium* is an archaic genitive plural.   **primus Priamo qui foret / postilla natus**: "who was to be born to Priam next." **primus . . . postilla**: literally "first afterward."   **temperaret tollere**: "should not bring up." *Temperaret* is subjunctive in an indirect command; the speaker changes to *oratio obliqua* in the next line. Some have taken this passage to refer to the Roman ritual of *tollere liberum*, in which a *paterfamilias* declared his paternity of a newborn child by lifting the baby off the ground and holding it aloft for all to see. But there is no evidence that the Romans ever actually practiced such a ritual: Shaw 2001 has demonstrated conclusively that it is a modern fiction arising from an over-reading of the sources.

43 sint . . . adiungatur: potential subjunctive followed by jussive subjunctive. Q. moves from a weaker (mythical) to a stronger (historical) category of evidence.   **Aeneae somnium**: The reference is not clear: nothing matching Q.'s description is preserved in the extant fragments of Fabius Pictor (on whom see next note), although Pictor does include a dream of more narrow scope (preserved in Diod. 7.5 = frag. 4 Peter = *FRH* 2.46 frag. 3). In the

Aeneid, Aeneas has several dreams: of Hector (2.268–301), of the Penates (3.147–78), of Mercury (4.553–72), and of the Tiber (8.26–67).   **in nostri Fabi Pictoris Graecis annalibus**: Q. Fabius Pictor, the first Roman to write history, was a senator during the Hannibalic War. His decision to write in Greek suggests that he intended to explain the Romans and justify their actions to the Greek world. References by ancient authors to annals written by Fabius in Latin are almost certainly to a later translation of the Greek original (*contra* Pease).   **eius modi**: introducing the result clause *ut . . . fuerint*.   **ei secundum quietem visa sunt**: "appeared to him (Aeneas) after he fell asleep." *Secundum* is the preposition governing the accusative. The phrase *secundum quietem* appears another five times in *Div.* (1.43, 48; 2.124, 126 [twice], 135) and only another three times in all of classical Latin. Each case concerns visions seen in dreams.   **Superbi Tarquini somnium**: The dream does not appear in the prose accounts (although Liv. 1.56.4–13 and D. H. 4.63.2–3 include other divine signs). Prophetic dreams are a common plot device in Greek tragedy, and Accius appears to have drawn specifically on dream imagery in Aeschylus, Sophocles, and Euripides, on which see Mastrocinque 1983; Manuwald 2001, 220–37; Erasmo 2004, 59–63. Parallels especially to the myth of Atreus have been noted (see below). It is possible that Accius draws on Etruscan motifs as well (Fauth 1976; Guittard 1986). As in Ilia's dream at 40–41, the narrative is compressed and shifts abruptly between scenes. M. does not address this dream in Book 2.   **in Bruto Acci**: The *Brutus* by Accius (170–c. 85), the most prolific Roman tragedian and an acquaintance of C. (*Brut.* 107), was originally composed for D. Iunius Brutus Callaicus, consul of 138 (*Arch.* 27; Val. Max. 8.14.2). The play was on C.'s mind at about the time *Div.* was written: a performance of it had been scheduled by M. Iunius Brutus, the assassin of Caesar who was a friend of C., for the *ludi Apollinares* that he, as praetor, was organizing for the summer of 44 BCE. Caesar's friends, M. and L. Antonius, saw the obvious propaganda value for Brutus of a production of a *fabula praetextata* (tragedy on a Roman topic) that treated the expulsion of the last king of Rome by the Roman people under the leadership of Brutus's most distinguished ancestor. Without consulting him, the Antonii substituted Accius's *Tereus* for the *Brutus* (*Att.* 16.5.1 = SBA 410.1). Their ploy failed to dampen popular enthusiasm for Brutus and Cassius, however: the crowd still cheered them at the performance of the *Tereus* (*Att.* 16.2.3 = SBA 412.3; *Phil.* 1.36; App., *BC* 3.24).   **ipse**: sc. Tarquinius.

44 quoniam quieti corpus: This passage of iambic senarii opens with alliteration. **quoniam**: "after."   **nocturno inpetu**: "at the onset of night"; cf. *N. D.* 2.97, *impetum caeli*. In prose, the phrase is used of nighttime military

attacks (*Cat.* 1.8; *Phil.* 11.7; Liv. 3.30.2, 39.36.10).   **visust in somnis**: On
the contracted form *visust* = *visus est*, see 40n. *corpus*. This use of the ablative
plural of *somnus* is frequent in *Div*.   **pecus lanigerum**: Accius was known
for a grandiose style that included elevated expressions like this one. For more
detailed discussion, see Boyle 2006, 113–19. *Lanigerum* appears first in Ennius
(perhaps in a satiric context; see Courtney 2003, 19) and then in many later
poets, including Lucretius, Vergil, and Ovid.   **duos consanguineos arietes
inde eligi . . .** : The whole rest of the quotation depends loosely on *visust* two
lines above (cf. the similar construction at 40n. *visus . . . videbar . . . videtur*).
There is anacoluthon in the frequent change of subject among the verbs in
the *oratio obliqua*, from the rams (here) to Tarquin, the surviving ram, and
the sun. The episode represents Tarquinius's treatment of his nephews. The
praeclariorem alterum is Brutus's more distinguished brother (cf. D. H. 4.68.2;
Liv. 1.56.7), who was murdered along with their father by Tarquinius. The ram
who butts Tarquin represents Brutus, who, in self-defense, decided to play the
fool in order to convince Tarquinius that he posed no threat. Brutus eventually
brought about Tarquin's overthrow. In both the Greek and Etruscan traditions
of oneirocriticism (dream interpretation), rams are symbols of good things to
come (Artemid. 2.12; Macr., *Sat.* 3.7.2; Fauth 1976, 484–85). In the myth of
Atreus, to which this passage bears strong similarities, Atreus's future kingship
is signaled by the gift of a golden lamb from Pan that was also associated with
a shift in the sun's course. See 45n. *ad dexteram . . . praepotens*.   **conitier**:
from *conitor*, "made for me." For the form and *linquier* below, see 20n. *volvier*.
The ram knocks Tarquinius over but does not kill him: an indication of the
king's imminent expulsion from Rome. After losing power, Tarquin attempted,
unsuccessfully, to retake Rome with the help of Etruscan allies. He is said to
have died at the court of Aristodemus of Cumae in 495 BCE (Liv. 2.21.5; D.
H. 6.21.3).   **in me arietare eoque ictu me ad casum dari**: an unusually
high number of elisions in a single line. **arietare**: "to behave like an *aries*"; = to
butt.   **dextrorsum . . . linquier cursu novo**: "shifted to a new path toward
the right." Cf. *OLD*, s.v. *linquo* 1d.

45 coniectoribus: interpreters of dreams and signs (Quint., *Inst.*
3.6.30).   **rex, quae in vita usurpant homines . . .** : The *coniectores* deliver,
in trochaic septenarii, a falsely reassuring response cast in appropriate
religious language (*verruncent, signum praepotens, auguratum*). The structure
of these lines, with asyndeton and the piling up of near synonyms, mimics
Latin prayer. This exchange between dreamer and interpreters is modeled
on the account of Atossa's dream in Aesch., *Pers.* 176–225 (Erasmo 2004,
59–63). It cannot be determined whether these lines immediately followed
Tarquinius's account of his dream in Accius.   **sed in re tanta haut**

temere inproviso offerunt: "but on such an important matter, things do not present themselves unexpectedly and without reason." Cf. *OLD*, s.v. *offero* 3a. The diviners draw a distinction between natural dreams that stem from daily experience and prophetic dreams. The circumstances and content of Tarquinius's dream mark it out as the latter.   **hebetem**: "dull"; a close synonym for the cognomen *Brutus*, which means "dull-witted." In analyzing the dream and its interpretation, other scholars have seen additional references to Brutus's praenomen and nomen, but these are not obvious (Wardle, pp. 221–22; Guittard 1986, 58–59).   **aeque ac**: "equally with."   **pectus egregium**: This etymological play on *ex grege* (cf. Paul. ex Fest. 21L, 70L) is asyndetic with *sapientia munitum*. Although the *coniectores* link the movement of the sun to the fate of the *populus Romanus*, it is possible that a link between the sun and Tarquinius would have been sensible to Accius's audience. Cf. Pompey's retort to Sulla that more people worship the rising sun than the setting sun (Plu., *Pomp.* 14.4).   **perpropinquam**: "very near"; a rare word, elsewhere used only at *Clu.* 23.   **verruncent**: "may they turn out"; a word appearing exclusively in prayer and divinatory contexts.   **ad dexteram . . . praepotens**: It is not clear what celestial phenomenon Accius had in mind, though it is clear that there was a reversal of the sun's course. This interpretation is supported by the parallel to a similar element in the myth of Atreus recounted by Euripides in several plays (*Or.* 1001–6; *El.* 726–42; *I. T.* 189–202, 816). The nature of the change in the sun's movement in Euripides is not clear either (see, e.g., Willink 1986, 253–57).   **auguratum est rem Romanam publicam summam fore**: Note the heavy use of assonance in the final syllables.

46 Age nunc ad externa redeamus: Cf. 13n. *age*. Q. signals a new topic. This new section of his argument continues patterns already established: the alternation between Greek and Roman (we go from Tarquin to Phalaris) and the sequence of pregnancy dream and kingship dream (the Phalaris *exemplum* is followed by the dream of Cyrus).   **matrem Phalaridis . . .** : This sentence has the same structure as the opening of the *exemplum* of the dream of the mother of Dionysius of Syracuse. See 39n. *Dionysi mater*. Phalaris, tyrant of Acragas (c. 570–c.549), was famous for his deviousness and his unique method for the disposal of his enemies: roasting them alive in a brass bull. A thorough treatment of the tradition about him is found in Hinz 2001, 19–126. For C., Phalaris is synonymous with tyrannical viciousness (e.g., *Ver.* 2.4.73, 2.5.145; *Tusc.* 2.18, 5.75, 5.87; *Fin.* 4.64, 5.85; *Off.* 2.26). As with the passages from Accius above, Julius Caesar may lurk behind the reference. In two letters to Atticus from the early days of the Civil War between Caesar and Pompey, C. likens Caesar to Phalaris (*Att.* 7.12.2, 7.20.2 = *SBA* 135.2, 144.2), and he

directly compares the two in *Off.* 2.26.   **Ponticus Heraclides**: Born in the
city of Heracleia on the Black Sea coast of Asia Minor, Heraclides moved to
Athens to study with Plato and possibly Aristotle. (On his relationship to the
Peripatetic school, see Gottschalk 1980, 2–6; Fortenbaugh in Schütrumpf
2008, vii–viii.) Heraclides had a penchant for the exotic and the fabulous,
and his fame seems to have been based more on his abilities as a writer than
on the strength of his philosophy. Q.'s favorable evaluation seems to be in
line with C.'s (*Tusc.* 5.8). Indeed, C. took Heraclides's dialogues as a model
(*Att.* 13.19.3–4 = *SBA* 326.3–4), and he cites him (albeit in neutral terms) as
an earlier authority on political philosophy (*Leg.* 3.14). Heraclides did not
enjoy universal approval, however (cf. the comments of Sallustius reported
in *Q. Fr.* 3.5[5–7].1 = *SBQ* 25.1 and of the Epicurean Velleius in *N. D.* 1.34
[with Gottschalk 1980, 96–97] and Plu., *Cam.* 22.3). It is not known from
which of Heraclides's numerous works this fragment comes, but it has been
assigned, with good reason, to his περὶ χρησμῶν (132 Wehrli).   **teneret . . .
videretur**: subjunctives in relative clauses in *oratio obliqua*.   **qui . . .
refervescere videretur**: *Qui = sanguis*. This is the only occurrence of
refervescere, "to bubble up," in classical Latin. This is a vivid image of roiling,
seething, and expanding liquid.   **quod matris somnium inmanis filii
crudelitas conprobavit**: *Inmanis* is nominative, giving the sentence a nicely
balanced arrangement (accusative-genitive-accusative, nominative-genitive-
nominative, verb). Q. frequently punctuates the ends of the *exempla* with the
assertion that the events happened as predicted (cf. 50, 52, 55–56, 58–59).
Phalaris was so strongly associated with cruelty and bloodthirstiness that
Q. need not elaborate further. The gist of the dream is clear even if some of
the details (e.g., why Mercury?) are not readily explicable.   **quid ego . . .
proferam?**: Q. shifts from pregnancy dreams of the mothers of political
leaders to a series of dreams of the leaders themselves. The loose but logical
connection of this passage to what precedes is discursive and contributes to
the sense of real conversation.   **magi**: This term, like *Chaldaei* (2n. *qua in
natione Chaldaei non ex artis sed ex gentis vocabulo Chaldaei*), was often used
by Greek and Roman authors as a generic (frequently derogatory) term for
practitioners of magic, but it is used here in the technical sense of Zoroastrian
priests. The *magi* originally served the Medean kings and continued as
members of the court, advisors, and interpreters of dreams and portents
for the Persian kings who succeeded them (see M. Schwartz, "The Religion
of Achaemenian Iran," in *CHI* 2.696–97; De Jong 1997, 396–402). They
were associated with several forms of technical divination, including dream
interpretation, pyromancy, and hydromancy.   **principi**: Cyrus II, the
Great, is identified as "first" since it was he who freed Persia from the control
of the Medes and first established the Persian Empire in the mid-sixth century

BCE. He is to be distinguished from Cyrus the Younger, on whom see 52n. *in ea militia*. In *Rep.* 1.43–44, Cyrus the Great is held up as the quintessential good king.   **ex Dinonis Persicis libris**: Dinon of Colophon (*FrGH* 690), father of Cleitarchus, the historian of Alexander, wrote a respected history of Persia in three books.   **cum se convolvens sol elaberetur et abiret**: Scholars have seen in Cyrus's dream a reference to *Khvarenah* (glory), a core concept of Zoroastrianism closely associated with rulers and etymologically linked to the sun and to fire. Those who possess *Khvarenah* enjoy success in life, but *Khvarenah* retreats from those who try to grasp it. De Jong 1997, 299–301.   **quod genus sapientium et doctorum habebatur in Persis**: The indicative marks this as Q.'s own parenthetical assertion.   **portendi**: It is common to use *portendere* in the passive with the thing foretold as its subject.   **septuagesimum**: sc. *annum*.   **quadraginta natus annos**: The standard idiom for expressing someone's age is *natus* + accusative of duration of time.

47 This *exemplum* is not a prophetic dream, but it is linked to what precedes by its focus on divination among barbarians and on a prediction for the length of a king's rule. The tale fits more neatly at 65, where Q. refers to it as part of his argument that the prophetic power of a soul increases as the soul nears death.   **barbaris gentibus**: Cf. 2n. *neque . . . neque*.   **siquidem**: "for"; introduces an *exemplum* that illustrates the general statement. See *OLD*, s.v. 4.   **Callanus Indus**: a Brahmin philosopher who joined Alexander the Great's entourage at Taxila (in modern Pakistan) in 326 and remained with him for almost two years. The story of his self-immolation was told by several of Alexander's close associates, on whose accounts (now lost) the versions of many later authors depend (e.g., Arr., *Anab.* 7.3.1–6; Plu., *Alex.* 69.6–8; Strabo 15.1.68; Ael., *V. H.* 5.6). Rather than live in ill health, Callanus chose to immolate himself, an act that Alexander only grudgingly permitted. Just before committing himself to the flames, Callanus predicted Alexander's death at Babylon. The sources for and variations in the tradition are collected and analyzed in Bosworth 1998. Though some judged Callanus's act insane (Diod. 17.107.5), others emphasized the equanimity with which Callanus faced death (e.g., C., *Tusc.* 2.52; Val. Max. 1.8 ext. 10).   **si quid vellet ut diceret**: "if he wished to say anything" (*G&L* 546 with 532 n. 3).   **optume**: an adverb; an enthusiastic affirmative response to Alexander.   **propediem . . . paucis post diebus**: Either Q. is hazy on the chronology, or, more likely, he has deliberately shortened the time between the deaths of Callanus and Alexander to make Callanus's prediction more dramatic (cf. 59n. *reditum . . . celerem*). Alexander did not die until a year and a half after his friend, in the spring of 323.   **discedo . . . revertar**: Q. acknowledges his digression but is not ready to leave it yet. He signals its end at 47 with *redeamus ad somnia* (cf. 46, 109).   **qua nocte . . . eadem . . . proxuma nocte**: The series of parallel constructions points up the simultaneousness of the events.   **constat**: "it is a fact that." Reports of portentous events coincident with Alexander's birth circulated early, probably within his own lifetime. C. gives a fuller version of the burning of the temple at Ephesus, attributed to Timaeus (350–260 BCE), at *N. D.* 2.69. See also Plu., *Alex.* 3.5–7.   **magos**: brings the digression full circle.   **pestem ac perniciem**: a frequent pairing in C. (e.g., *Cat.* 1.33; *Rab. Perd.* 2; *Leg.* 2.13; *Off.* 2.51).   **Haec de Indis et magis**: Supply *feruntur* (*vel sim.*).

48 Hannibalem: Cf. 39 *Dionysi mater*. Hannibal's visit to the sanctuary of Juno near Croton in southern Italy during the summer of 205 was documented by an altar and a Greek and Punic inscription mentioned by Livy (28.46.16) and seen by Polybius (3.33.17–18, 3.56.4). Neither historian relates the specific episode reported here, though Livy elsewhere notes the presence of a *columna aurea solida* in the temple (24.3.6). The omission in Livy is particularly striking since he makes it clear that he was using the same source as Q. cites here (28.46.14). For a more extensive discussion, see Jaeger 2006.   **Coelius**: In the last quarter of the second century BCE, L. Coelius Antipater produced a novel historical work, seven volumes dedicated to the Second Punic War, of which sixty-seven fragments survive (Peter 1.158–77 = *FRH* 2.384-423). This monograph was a departure from the popular annalistic histories (on which see 33n. *Negemus omnia, comburamus annales*) that began *ab urbe condita*. The value of Coelius's history was increased by his use of the Sicilian historian Silenus (*FrGH* 175; see 49n. *hoc item in*), who had traveled with Hannibal. C. rated Coelius highly, although more on stylistic grounds than for his reliability (*Brut.* 102; *De Orat.* 2.54). In contrast, Q. emphasizes Coelius's authority as a source at 55 (cf. 56, 78). This is the first of four dreams that Q. draws from Coelius's work; the others are recounted at 49, 55, and 56.   **quae esset in fano Iunonis Laciniae**: The verb in this relative clause is attracted into the subjunctive by *vellet*. The reader is probably meant to envision an entire sanctuary complex, even though *fanum* is technically just a sacred open area, often in front of the temple. Fridh (1990, 185) observes that C. prefers *fanum* to other terms for sacred locations when he is talking about the pillage of sacred sites. Juno Lacinia's temple was famously denuded of half its marble roof tiles by the censor of 174–173, Q. Fulvius Flaccus (*MRR* 1.404, s.a. 174), who transported them back to Rome to adorn his new temple of Fortuna Equestris (Liv. 42.3.1–11). Juno Lacinia is a Romanization of Hera Lacinia, whose sanctuary outside Croton served as a site of asylum and housed the treasury and main meeting place of the Italiote League, an organization of Greek cities in Italy headed by Croton. See Lomas 1993, 32, 128–29.   **extrinsecus inaurata**: The pleonasm underlines the distinction between *solida* and *inaurata*.   **tollere**: "to carry it off" (*OLD*, s.v. 10).   **secundum quietem**: See 43n. *secundum quietem*.   **eum quoque oculum . . . amitteret**: Hannibal had already been blinded in one eye by an infection in 217 (Liv. 22.2.10–11; Polyb. 3.79.12; Nep., *Hann.* 4.3). For Juno's threat to blind him completely, cf. the case of L. Caecilius Metellus, who, as *pontifex maximus* in the mid-third century BCE, was blinded after removing sacred items from the burning temple of Vesta (Plin., *Nat.* 7.141; Sen. Maior, *Con.* 4.2).   **buculam . . . faciendam**: This is the standard language of Latin dedicatory inscriptions: "he saw to it that a young cow was made . . ." The sanctuary was home to herds sacred to the goddess (Liv. 24.3.4).

49 hoc item in: points forward. *Item* indicates that Silenus (on whom see 48n. *Coelius*) is Coelius's source for both dreams of Hannibal. This dream is also reported at Liv. 21.22.5–9, Val. Max. 1.7 ext. 1, and Sil. Ital. 3.163–221.   **is**: Silenus.   **Hannibalem, cum cepisset Saguntum**: The Carthaginian sack of Rome's ally Saguntum in Spain in 219 was the catalyst for the Second Carthaginian War. Q.'s version of the dream emphasizes the divine sanction of Hannibal's mission in Italy. On the literary tradition of the dream, see Devillers and Krings 2006.   **quo illum utentem**: *Illum* denotes a change of subject (= Hannibal). The antecedent of *quo* is *ducemque unum*.   **ne respiceret**: Looking backward in dreams was an indication of difficulties ahead and of an unexpected return home (Artemid. 1.36). Hannibal's failure to heed the warning foretells his ultimate failure to accomplish his task.   **arbusta virgulta tecta**: The asyndeton hastens the speed of the prose, illustrating the speed of the monster.   **retro atque a tergo**: "behind him and at the rear of his army." These terms can be synonyms, but repetition here would not add anything to the dramatic impact of the image. *A tergo* is common in a military context.   **ne laboraret**: "he should not worry about" (*OLD*, s.v. 7).

50 Agathoclem: He may be the Stoic philosopher of Cyzicus of the late third and early second centuries (so Jacoby, *FrGH* 472 F 7), but this episode is not easily placed in his known works. Following *RE* 1.759 (Agathokles 25), Pease posits a Sicilian historian of the same name. Less attractive than either of these options is Wardle's proposal (following Heeringa) that C. has misread his source and inadvertently created a history by Agathocles, the tyrant of Syracuse, whose garrison troops Hamilcar was besieging in 309 BCE (Diod. 20.29.2–30.3) when this event is supposed to have taken place.   **visum esse audire vocem**: This introduces the indirect statement *se postridie* *cenaturum Syracusis. Visum esse* makes clear that the prediction (*vocem*) came to him in a dream (cf. 40n. *visus . . . videbar . . . videtur* and 2.137). Our other source for the story, Diodorus, attributes it to a μάντις (20.30.2). Cf. Liv. 1.56.12.   **Siculos**: There was a phalanx of Greek allies in Hamilcar's army (Diod. 20.29.6).   **Plena exemplorum est historia, tum referta vita communis**: Cf. 86. As Wardle (p. 234) notes, "the words reinforce, somewhat indirectly, the idea that prophetic dreams are not fictional or literary, or the preserve of the famous, but are a common, universally attested, and credible phenomenon." Cf. M.'s rebuttal at 2.136. Q. advances his argument: he is able to draw a handful of authoritative *exempla* from history, but the relative plentifulness of prophetic dreams in everyday life makes them even more powerful evidence for the validity of dream interpretation.

51 At vero: a strong adversative, distancing Decius's dream from the *vita communis*.   **P. Decius ille Quinti f.**: consul in 340 (*MRR* 1.135–36, s.a.); *f.* = *filius*, a standard abbreviation.   **tribunus militum**: As the most senior officer in a Roman legion, a military tribune reported directly to the consul who was the commander in the field. The office was prestigious, held by men of equestrian and sometimes senatorial rank. Military tribunes could command troops, exact levies, and administer the military oath to new recruits. See Lintott 1999, 139–40. A more detailed version of Decius's exploits is provided at Liv. 7.34.1–37.3 (see Oakley's commentary).   **M. Valerio A. Cornelio cos.**: "when M. Valerius and A. Cornelius were consuls," that is, 343 BCE. This is the standard way of dating by eponymous magistrates. The abbreviation *cos.* preserves the archaic form of the noun *cosol* (cf. *CIL* 1².8 and 581.18 [*cosoleretur*]).   **quod extat in annalibus**: On the importance of *annales*, see 33n. *Negemus omnia, comburamus annales.* This is the earliest extant account of this episode.   **devovit se**: Liv. 8.9.4–11.1 (see Oakley's commentary) is the *locus classicus* for Decius's devotion of himself and the army of the Latins, against whom the Romans fought in 340 at the battle of Veseris. *Devotio* entails the recitation of a prayer formula whereby one consecrates one's enemy—and sometimes oneself—to the gods of the underworld (Macr., *Sat.* 3.9.9–16). Decius's son and perhaps also his grandson were said to have performed this same ritual (or to have attempted to do so) at the battles of Sentinum in 295 (Liv. 10.28.1–18) and Asculum Satrianum in 279 (Zon. 8.5), respectively. The episode of 295 is possibly a doubling of the original tale, and that of 279 probably is.

52 Sed veniamus nunc . . . : Q. again introduces a new category of evidence with a jussive subjunctive.   **Est apud Platonem Socrates . . .** : Cf. Pl., *Crit.* 44a–b; D. L. 2.35. Q. begins with the most authoritative philosophical source.

For C.'s high opinion of Plato, see 5n. *cum Socrates . . . cumque.* Socrates spoke to Crito while awaiting execution in 399 for having corrupted the youth of Athens.   **post tertium diem**: "in two days." Contrary to modern practice, Greeks and Romans counted inclusively: today is the first day, tomorrow the second, and the day after tomorrow is the third. This pertains only to ordinal expressions (i.e., expressions that designate a position within a series—e.g., "first," "second," and "third") and can be seen in the use of *nundinae* for Roman market days, which occurred at intervals of eight days (nine days by inclusive reckoning). For cardinal numbers (e.g., 1, 3, 5), used in simple counting and enumerating the number of items in a set, the Romans counted exclusively just as we do. Hence *triennium* in 51 means a period of three years (343–340 BCE).   **pulchritudine eximia feminam**: Divine messengers are often distinguished by size or beauty (cf. 53).   **Tertia te Phthiae tempestas laeta locabit**: *Tempestas* is equivalent to *dies*. This is probably C.'s own rendering of Achilles's prediction of his own return home at Hom., *Il.* 9.362–63 (εἰ δέ κεν εὐπλοίην δώῃ κλυτὸς ἐννοσίγαιος / ἤματί κε τριτάτῳ Φθίην ἐρίβωλον ἱκοίμην [If the revered Earth-Shaker grants clear passage, I would come to fertile Phthia on the third day]), rather than a translation of Socrates's quotation of the line at Pl., *Crit.* 44b2, which excludes some of the elements of the original included here. C. has omitted the reference to Poseidon and transferred the descriptive ἐρίβωλον from Phthia to the *tempestas*. *Laeta* is a good choice for ἐρίβωλον since its primary meaning is "fertile," though it is used here in the sense of "favorable" or "propitious." Cf. 18n. *laeto mactasti lacte Latinas* and and 85n. *pulmo incisus etiam in bonis extis*. Note the alliteration and sound patterning of *t* and *l*. In the *Crito*, Socrates takes the line to mean that his soul will return home two days hence. A ship from Delos was expected to return to Athens the day after Socrates tells Crito of his dream. Socrates expected to die the next day after that. For the positive import of the dream (Socrates's death will be an occasion for joy), see Harte 2005, 249–51.   **quod ut est dictum sic scribitur contigisse**: "it is written that it happened just the way it was said."   **qui vir et quantus**: "What a man! How great he was!" Q.'s enthusiasm for Xenophon, a contemporary of Plato who also studied with Socrates, is more effusive than C.'s generally positive opinion of him (e.g., *De Orat.* 2.58; *Orat.* 32; *Sen.* 58). C. was clearly familiar with several of Xenophon's philosophical works, especially his *Cyropaedia*, a fictionalized biography of Cyrus the Great (on whom see 46n. *principi*) that expatiates on the ideal form of leadership and governance.   **in ea militia**: "during the military service." Xenophon's *Anabasis* is an account of his time in Persia as one of ten thousand Greek mercenaries serving with Cyrus the Younger in his attempt to take the Persian throne from his brother, Artaxerxes III. After Cyrus's death in battle at Cunaxa in 401, the generals in charge of the Greek forces were executed. Xenophon took command of the remnants of the mercenary force and led the survivors homeward as far as Byzantium. He records two of his own dreams (3.1.11, 4.3.8).

53 delirare: See 35n. *delirare*.   **singulari vir ingenio Aristoteles et paene divino**: Q.'s high opinion of Aristotle matches C.'s (e.g., *Orat.* 172; *De Orat.* 2.152; *Tusc.* 1.7; cf. 8n. *cum ambulandi causa in Lyceum venissemus*). The Aristotelian fragment that follows (ignored by M. in his rebuttal) presents a positive view of prophetic dreams that cannot be reconciled with the far more reserved and critical position of Aristotle's *De Div. per Somnum* and *De Insomniis* (van der Eijk 1994, 91–92; 2005, 179–92). The passage may come from Aristotle's lost work entitled *Eudemus* (37 Rose), a dialogue that would have presented varying opinions. It may also derive from a Stoic source that has recast Aristotle to look as if he accepted the Stoic position (Harris 2009, 163–64). In addition to its obvious relevance to Q.'s argument, the anecdote contributes indirectly to the theme of tyrants that runs through this section. It also evokes the larger program of C.'s philosophical works, namely, the use of philosophy to improve the governance of the state. As a young man, Eudemus of Cyprus studied with Plato, but he seems to have spent the latter part of his life fighting tyranny. Eudemus eventually died while fighting alongside other Academics on behalf of Dion, a friend of Plato who led the effort to liberate Syracuse from Dionysius II, son of the tyrant named at 39 (Nep., *Dion* 9.6; Plu., *Dio* 22.5; H. D. Westlake in *CAH²* 6.693–706). Emphasis on escape from tyranny is underscored in this passage by the frequent appearance of the word *tyrannus*.   **cum scribit**: introduces a long, complicated passage of *oratio obliqua* that extends all the way to *esse rediturum*, broken down here by phrases and outlined to clarify the multiple layers of subordination.

> *cum scribit*
> > *Eudemum . . . Pheras venisse*
> > > *quae erat urbs . . . autem . . . tenebatur*
> > *in eo igitur oppido . . . aegrum Eudemum fuisse*
> > > *ut omnes medici diffiderent*
> > *ei visum . . . iuvenem dicere*
> > > *fore*
> > > > *ut perbrevi convalesceret*
> > > *paucisque diebus interiturum Alexandrum tyrannum*
> > > *ipsum autem Eudemum . . . esse rediturum*

Pheras . . . quae erat urbs . . . tum admodum nobilis: Pherae enjoyed a brief period of prominence and power under a series of tyrants from Lycophron (ruled c. 406–c. 395) until Philip of Macedon took control of the city in 352 BCE (Diod. 15.60.1–61.5). The city's strength declined under Alexander (d. 358), the tyrant who figures here. On Alexander's death, see *Inv.* 2.144; *Off.* 2.25–6; Plu., *Pel.* 35.5–12.   **egregia facie iuvenem**: Cf. 52n. *pulchritudine eximia feminam.*   **illa**: = *et convaluisse Eudemum et ab uxoris fratribus interfectum tyrannum.*   **scribit Aristoteles**: governs an *oratio obliqua* in three parts: (1) *illa quidem prima . . . consecuta et convaluisse Eudemum et . . . interfectum tyrannum,* (2) *quinto autem anno exeunte . . . ad Syracusas occidisse,* (3) *ex quo ita illud somnium esse interpretatum.* Q. reminds us that Aristotle is the authority for the details of the dream, the accuracy of its predictions, and its proper interpretation. More than previous *exempla*, this anecdote reveals the looseness of possible interpretation.   **cum esset spes**: concessive.   **illum**: sc. Eudemus.   **ex quo**: "wherefore."

54 Adiungamus . . . divinum Sophoclem: Q. again announces a change in topic with a jussive subjunctive. C. was a great admirer of Sophocles's work (cf. *Orat.* 4). This tale, with some variation, is also found in a fragment of Hieronymous of Rhodes preserved in the *Vita Sophoclis* (31 Wehrli). Hieronymous was a follower of Aristotle who wrote in the third century BCE. For a general treatment of the development of such anecdotes about major poets as context and explanation for their works, see Lefkowitz 1981, esp. 75–87, 160–63. Hieronymous is frequently cited as a source in C.'s philosophical works; thus he may be the source here. It cannot be determined whether the tale originated with Hieronymous or whether he merely recorded a story already in circulation.   **ubi idem saepius, ascendit in Arium pagum detulit rem**: a very compressed sentence that suggests the speed with which Sophocles finally acted. Supply *somniavit* (*vel sim.*) after *saepius*. *Detulit rem* = "reported the matter." Note the asyndeton of *ascendit . . . detulit*. The repetition of dreams was a phenomenon recognized in ancient oneirocriticism: if the same dream appeared to a person in a short period of time, he was to understand that each occurrence conveyed the same meaning (Artemid. 4.27). The motif of the repeating dream as a sign of escalating urgency and impending danger offered authors an opportunity to inject tension into their narratives. Cf. 55n. *iterum esse idem iussum et monitum*; Herodot. 7.12–15. The council of the Areopagus met on the "Hill of Ares" (hence its name), to the west of the Athenian acropolis. Its members (*Areopagitae*) were former magistrates (ex-archons) who served as an advisory council to the current archons of the city. The Areopagus also served as a court for certain types of serious offense, including religious transgressions (MacDowell 1978, 27–29). Temple theft (ἱεροσυλία) was punishable by death, interdiction from burial within Attica, and confiscation of property

(MacDowell 1978, 149). It is not clear what punishment was meted out in this case. For a discussion of Roman attitudes toward the Areopagos in the late republic, see Rawson 1985b, 44–67.   **quaestione adhibita**: "after an investigation was conducted."   **Indicis Herculis**: "Hercules the Discloser." Aside from this notice and the fragment from the *Vita* (see above), we have no other reference to this deity.

55 Sed quid ego Graecorum: Cf. 29n. *sed quid vetera?*   **nescio quo modo**: *Nescio* + interrogative pronoun can be used in place of an indefinite pronoun ("I don't know how," i.e., "somehow"), and in such cases, it does not affect the construction that follows. Hence *delectant* remains indicative. M. mirrors Q.'s sentiment at 2.8.   **Omnes hoc historici, Fabii Gellii sed proxume Coelius**: Supply *scribunt*. **proxume**: "with the greatest accuracy" (*OLD*, s.v. *proxime* A5b). Wardle (*ad loc.*) cites Liv. 25.23.12 as a comparandum. The plurals *Fabii Gellii* are probably generalizing ("people like Fabius and Gellius"), as there was only one prominent annalist by each name: Q. Fabius Pictor, who wrote *annales* (see 33n. *Negemus omnia, comburamus annales*) in Greek in the early part of the second century BCE, and Cnaeus Gellius, who wrote *annales* in at least thirty-three books. By indicating a whole class of writers like Fabius and Gellius, Q. points toward the popularity of the story in the annalistic tradition. The versions of authors earlier than C. are now lost, but the later accounts of at least eight other authors (most famously Liv. 2.36.1–37.1) survive, albeit with some important variation in the details. C. presents a patrician version of the tale by setting it in the Circus Maximus at a performance of the *ludi maximi* (both strongly associated with Rome's aristocratic class in the early republic), whereas Val. Max. 1.7.4 preserves an alternate tradition that sets the story firmly in a plebeian context, identifying the location as the Circus Flaminius and the games as the *ludi plebei*. Wardle (*ad loc.*) offers a catalog of extant versions, as well as a detailed reconstruction of the development of the story.   **cum bello Latino ludi votivi maxumi primum fierent**: Rome fought several wars with the Latins, the last ending in 338 BCE. The war referred to here ended in 493. Liv. 2.36.1–37.1 and D. H. 7.71.2 date the first performance of the *ludi maximi* to two years or so after the war ended. Thereafter, the *ludi* were held annually over several days in September, during which period also fell the *dies natalis* of the temple of Jupiter Optimus Maximus on the Capitoline. The coincidence underlines the close relationship between the games and the chief god of the Roman state, who is not identified here but is named in other versions. The games are *votivi* because they were vowed by the consul Aulus Postumius before his victory at the major battle of Lake Regillus in 496 (D. H. 6.10.1, 7.71.2). In addition to athletic competitions, the games eventually included theatrical performances and other stage entertainments. See Liv. 7.2.4–13 with Oakley's extensive commentary.   **civitas ad arma repente est excitata**: There was a surprise attack by the Volscians (Liv. 2.37.1–39.1).   **instaurativi constituti sunt**: "renewed games were arranged." The adjective *instaurativi* appears only here; the verbal and substantive forms are far more common. *Ludi* were religious rituals and, like all Roman rituals, had to be performed with great precision. When a ritual was not performed properly—because of either some error or, as here, external circumstances—the entire rite had to be performed again from the beginning, regardless of cost. Failure to follow the ritual prescription in all details would anger the gods. Livy records numerous multiple *instaurationes ludorum*, as many as seven times in one case (33.25.2).   **servus per circum . . . furcam ferens ductus est**: A common punishment for a slave guilty of a mundane offense was to humiliate him by making him process through a public place with his arms fastened to the projecting ends of a *furca* (a Y-shaped pole) placed on his back (cf. Pl., *Cas.* 389; *Cist.* 247; *Men.* 941–43). **circum**: sc. *circum maximum*, the only major circus in Rome in the early fifth century and the site of the *ludi maximi*. The crowd had gathered for a chariot race.   **cuidam rustico Romano**: Later authors identify him as the plebeian T. Latinius (Liv. 2.36.2; D. H. 7.68.3), Atinius (Lact., *Div. Inst.* 2.7.20), or Annius (Macr., *Sat.* 1.11.3). The latter version is preferred by Ogilvie (on Liv. 2.36) since the Annii were a prominent plebeian family in the mid-fourth century, that is, close to the date of 279 that Macrobius gives for the story.   **visus est**: The subject is *qui diceret*. Unidentified divine figures also appear in 49 and 52–53. Nearly all other accounts identify the apparition as Jupiter.   **praesulem**: "lead dancer," that is, the unfortunate slave. *Praesul* is a very rare word (including the variants *praesultator* and *praesultor*), appearing in extant Latin almost exclusively in the context of this particular episode. The sole exception is a reference to the ritual dance of the Salii (in a fragment of Lucilius preserved in Fest. 334L). In Liv. 7.10.3 (see Oakley's commentary), the taunting behavior of a Gallic warrior is described as *praesultat* (a form attested only there).   **ludis**: dative of purpose.   **eum**: sc. *rusticum Romanum*; subject of *iussum esse*.   **idque ab eodem iussum esse eum senatui nuntiare**: This is the second part of the message conveyed by the divine apparition.   **illum non esse ausum**: Until this point, Q. has relayed the story in direct speech, quoting indirectly only the message relayed in the dream. Now Q. switches to *oratio obliqua*, loosely dependent on *omnes hoc historici [scribunt]*, for the rest of the tale.   **iterum esse idem iussum et monitum . . .** : The second time around, Jupiter raises the stakes.   **ad amicos**: that is, his *consilium* (cf. Liv. 2.36.6, *consilio*, with Ogilvie's commentary). Though the public *consilia* (advisory councils) of generals and magistrates are common in Roman historical narratives, the private *consilia* of ordinary citizens are not. A *paterfamilias* had absolute control over his household, but his power was tempered by the entrenched expectation that he would consult with family and close friends in making any important decision. For more detailed discussion, see Lacey 1986, 137–40.   **somnio comprobato**: The Senate is persuaded by the farmer's ability to walk after relaying the message from his dream, not by the message itself.   **memoriae proditum est**: See 2n. *memoriae prodiderunt.*

56 Gaius vero Gracchus . . . : The adversative *vero* (always postpositive) distances this exceptionally well documented *exemplum* from the previous one. The jump from the early fifth century to the late second century is rather abrupt, but the *exempla* are linked in that they come from the same source, Coelius. On the Gracchi, see 36n. *ut C. Gracchus filius eius scriptum reliquit.*   **quaesturam petenti**: Six years after his brother's death, Gaius was a successful candidate in 127 for a quaestorship in 126. See *MRR* 1.508, s.a. 126.   **quam vellet cunctaretur**: "however much he should delay." *Quam vellet* is equivalent to *quamvis* in *oratio obliqua*. Wardle (*ad loc.*) explains this as a reference to the fact that Gaius did not pursue political office until several years after he met the minimum age requirement.   **eodem sibi leto**: Both brothers met their ends in violent conflicts with their political opponents, and their bodies were dumped into the Tiber. The tragic quality this lent to their stories was not lost on ancient authors (e.g., Vell. 2.6.7; Plu., *Ti. Gracch.* 20.4; Plu., *C. Gracch.* 17.6).   **ante quam tribunus plebi C. Gracchus factus esset**: The prediction is more impressive because it occurred early in Gaius's career, before it was clear that he was destined to follow the same path as his brother.   **se audisse scribit Coelius et dixisse multis**: echoes *multis dixit* above. A pronoun (*eum, illum*), subject of *dixisse* and referring to Gracchus, has been lost. Coelius's report is strengthened by the fact that Gracchus himself was the source. It gains even more authority from the fact that a number of other people who heard about the dream from Gaius himself could confirm Coelius's report.   **quae creberrume commemorantur a Stoicis**: In the earlier catalog (at 6) of Stoics who wrote on divination, C. mentions only one work dedicated to prophetic dreams, that of Chrysippus, in which the next two *exempla* were probably included.   **unum de Simonide**: Cf. Val. Max. 1.7 ext. 3. The *oratio obliqua* introduced here depends loosely on *commemorantur*. Simonides of Ceos was a Greek poet of the late sixth and early fifth centuries whose work is known only from fragments (for the major collections, see West 1992, 2.114–37; Poltera 2008). On his biography in antiquity, see Lefkowitz 1981, 49–56. C. cites Simonides most frequently as a model of productive old age and exceptional memory (*Sen.* 23; *Tusc.* 1.59) and credits him with inventing the *ars memoriae*, a system for improving one's ability to retain information (*Fin.* 2.104; *De Orat.* 2.351–54). The tale told here may have been invented as an explanation for epigrams attributed to Simonides, namely, *Anth. Pal.* 7.77 and 7.516. But Page (1981, 299–300) suggests that our anecdote came first and that the epigrams were written in the Hellenistic period to flesh out the growing biographical tradition.   **cum ignotum quendam . . .** : The *cum* clause extends to *navem conscendere* and separates *unum de Simonide* from the core of *oratio obliqua* of which it is the subject. This is a standard pattern in Q.'s recounting of dreams. Cf. the dreams of the mother of Dionysius (39), the mother of Phalaris (46), and Hannibal (48).   **quem sepultura adfecerat**: "whom he had provided with burial." See Bodel 1994, 32.   **Simonidem redisse, perisse ceteros**: Chiasmus and asyndeton stress the distinction.

57 Alterum ita traditum clarum admodum somnium: "The other dream is very clear and is handed down thus." All modern translators render *clarum admodum* as "very well known" *vel sim.*, but the other meaning of *clarus* ("clear" or "manifestly comprehensible"; cf. 19, 106; *Cat.* 1.6; *De Orat.* 3.157) is surely also at play here, since there is physical evidence to confirm the dream's meaning and accuracy. Cf. 10n. *clara et perspicua*. This is the least prestigious evidence Q. has put forward (the identity of its source is vague, and it is not tied to known individuals or to a particular time), but its vividness and clarity compensate for its other shortcomings (cf. Val. Max. 1.7 ext. 10). The rest of the anecdote is in *oratio obliqua* dependent on this phrase.   **una**: "together."   **alterum ad coponem devertisse, ad hospitem alterum**: Cf. 56n. *Simonidem redisse, perisse ceteros*. The travelers' choice of accommodation reflects a difference in economic status, a distinction highlighted by the chiasmus. Wealthier individuals could afford to stay at a respectable inn (*hospitium*) run by a *hospes*, whereas those of lesser means had to stay at a lower-class establishment called a *copona* (the colloquial spelling of *caupona*). The owners of such inexpensive hotels are often presented as dishonest and dangerous (e.g., Var. in Non. 16L; Apul., *Met.* 1.7–13). That the Arcadian travelers had a choice of accommodation is an indication of the size and importance of Megara, a settlement along two main roads running between central Greece and the Peloponnese. Smaller, less traveled cities could not support more than a single inn. For more, see Casson 1974, 87–90, 197–218.   **qui ut cenati quiescerent**: "As soon as they had eaten and fallen asleep." The verb is in the subjunctive because this is a relative clause in *oratio obliqua*; *ut* has a temporal meaning. The perfect passive participle of *cenare* has a deponent sense.   **concubia nocte**: "right after he fell asleep"; cf. Sisenna ap. Non. 130L.   **qui erat in hospitio**: Although we are still in *oratio obliqua, erat* is indicative because the relative

clause is explanatory.   **rogare ut . . . mortem suam ne inultam esse
pateretur**: *Ut* and *ne* are often used in combination for *ne*. In C., they are
usually found closer together than they are here.   **se interfectum . . . esse
coniectum . . . iniectum**: a parenthetical explanation for the *oratio obliqua*
launched by *rogare*. The proper disposal of garbage (including human waste)
and the bodies of those too poor to be given proper burial was to haul them
out of urban areas in wagons and to dump them outside town walls. For
further discussion, see Bodel 1994, 30–59.   **petere ut**: parallel to *rogare*
and dependent on *visum esse*.   **hoc vero eum somnio commotum mane
bubulco praesto ad portam fuisse**: "moved by this (second) dream, he was
at the gate, ready for the wagoneer." The pace of the narrative—hastened by
asyndeton and the series of short periods—heightens the drama of the final
scene. Seeming to realize that he has lingered over setting up the story, Q.
now races toward the critical revelation. The interlocking word order of *hoc
vero eum somnio commotum* (*abab*) illustrates the confusion of the man's
emotional state.   **divinius**: Cf. 59, 63, 106. With Timpanaro (*ad loc.*), I
take this to mean "more prophetic," rather than "more divinely inspired." See
OLD, s.v. 6.

58 sed quid . . . quaerimus: Q. signals that he is moving to another category
of material. Here he lays out the most powerful examples he can muster,
recent instances from the most authoritative sources, M. and himself. The
historicity of these dreams cannot be denied.   **me, cum Asiae pro cos.
praeessem, vidisse in quiete**: goes back to *narravi*. *Me* is the subject of *vidisse*.
On Q.'s governorship, see 8n. *Q. fratre*. Having reached the rank of praetor in
Rome, Q. was eligible, at the end of his term of office, to be sent to one of the
provinces. With the exception of the years immediately after its annexation
in 133, the province of Asia (on what is now the west central coast of Turkey)
always had governors who were ex-praetors endowed with consular *imperium*,
that is, supreme power over the military and the right to interpret and execute
law within the province. The title *pro consule* indicates that the holder was
given a more important task and a more independent position than another
magistrate designated *pro praetore*. See Brennan 2000, 2.609–10, 619–21.
Q.'s dream is similar to a portent about the future of the Syracusan tyrant
Dionysius I at 73.   **eos eventus rerum**: This may be a pointed reference
to C.'s exile and eventual return home (see Intro. p. 4), but it may also refer
more generally to his political fortunes. While Q. was in Asia, C.'s position in
Rome had become increasingly precarious. As Q. was preparing to leave for
home early in 58, Clodius introduced a bill to exile all those who had executed
Roman citizens without trial; the bill was aimed at C. personally, for his role in

suppressing the Catilinarian conspiracy (*Att.* 3.1–4 = *SBA* 46–49; *Q. Fr.* 1.2.16 = *SBQ* 2.16).

59 Venio nunc ad tuum: sc. *somnium*. Q. plays his strongest card last: the source is M. himself, and as Q. emphasizes at the end of the anecdote, M. seemed to have taken comfort from his dream. If we can trust the report of Sallustius's account, it might be an indication that the historical C. was, at least on one occasion, willing to put stock in divination. In Book 2, M. counters this anecdote (2.136–40) at the theoretical level, arguing that dreams are made up of vestiges of our waking thoughts and that they are not in any way predictive of the future. The story is also told by Val. Max. 1.7.5.   **Sallustius**: Even if M. were to deny it, Q. has another authority to say the event actually happened. Cn. Sallustius, of equestrian rank, is frequently mentioned in C's letters (see Shackleton Bailey's commentary on *Att.* 1.11.1 = *SBA* 7.1). He was one of several friends who accompanied C. into exile, traveling at least as far as Brundisium (*Fam.* 14.4.6 = *SBF* 6.6).   **in illa fuga nobis gloriosa patriae calamitosa**: Note the antithesis of *gloriosa . . . calamitosa*, emphasized by asyndeton. C's reaction to exile— anguish, depression, and anger come through clearly in his letters from 58 and 57—indicates that he thought it anything but *gloriosa*. Cf. *Sest.* 53. Q. is patently flattering his brother. For a more detailed discussion, see Kelly 2006, 110–25.   **campi Atinatis**: "in the area around Atina." Timpanaro (*ad loc.*) points out that this is probably Atina in Lucania (modern Atena Lucana), which C. would have passed on the Via Popilia on his way to Brundisium before departing for the East. There was another town of same name in the area of modern Frosinone, but this is not far from C's hometown of Arpinum (where he more likely would have stayed).   **arte et graviter**: "deeply and heavily"; cf. *OLD*, s.v. *arte* 4a.   **iter instaret**: "the journey was at hand"; that is, "it was time to go."   ⟨se⟩: that is, Sallustius.   **hora secunda fere**: that is, about two hours after dawn.   **in locis solis**: "in remote places"; cf. 40n. *semita . . . stabilibat*.   **C. Marium cum fascibus laureatis**: Marius held the consulship an unprecedented seven times, including five consecutive terms from 104 to 100, and was awarded triumphs over Jugurtha and the Cimbri and Teutones. Despite these successes, he remained a controversial figure. Marius allied himself with unscrupulous politicians, was a protagonist in Rome's first civil conflict (with Sulla in 88), and dealt very harshly with his enemies after he and his allies took control of the city in 87. C. often uses Marius as an *exemplum* of the fickleness of Fortune, often in the context of Marius's exile from Rome, with notable disregard for the consul's more reprehensible actions (e.g, *Red. Pop.* 19–20; Carney 1967). C. also wrote

an epic poem about him (on which see 106n. *in Mario*). Marius appears
here with all the symbols of a victorious general. All Roman magistrates
endowed with *imperium* (dictators, consuls, praetors) were accompanied by
attendants called *lictores* as a symbol of their power. The *lictores* carried the
fasces, bundles of rods that were symbols of the magistrates' ability to compel
obedience. When a consul was outside the city with his troops, an ax (*securis*)
was added to the *fasces* as a symbol of his ability to execute a soldier without
trial. A victorious commander was entitled to wrap his *fasces* with laurel (*Pis.*
97; Plu., *Luc.* 36.3). C. himself earned this privilege in 51 while governor of
Cilicia (*Att.* 5.20.3 = *SBA* 113.3; *Fam.* 2.10.2–3 = *SBF* 86.2–3; *Lig.* 7; see also
the exchange between C. and the younger Cato at *Fam.* 15.4–6 = *SBF* 110–12).
For more on the symbolic power of the *fasces*, see Marshall 1984.   **bono
animo te iussisse esse**: The unexpected order of *iussisse esse* (cf. *esse dixisses*
just above) results in the awkward consonance of *ss* but highlights the forceful
nature of Marius's command: he does not comfort or request.   **lictorique
proxumo tradidisse**: Supply *te*. Of the twelve lictors who attended a consul,
the *proximus lictor* (sometimes called the *primus lictor*) had the honor of
standing closest to the magistrate, and it was to him that the consul gave his
orders. Cf. Liv. 24.44.7–10; Val. Max. 2.2.4a–b.   **monumentum suum**:
When C. awoke from his dream, he probably assumed that Marius referred
to his tomb. It was only later, when news of C.'s recall came from Rome,
that the *monumentum* was revealed to be the temple to *Honos et Virtus* that
Marius had built with spoils from his victories over the Cimbri and Teutones
(D. Palombi, *LTUR* 3.33–35, s.v. "Honos et Virtus, Aedes Mariana"; *NTDAR*
190, s.v. "Honos et Virtus (Mariana), Aedes (2)"). Val. Max. 1.7.5 incorrectly
identifies the *monumentum* as an otherwise unknown temple to Jupiter
built by Marius. The choice of location for the vote to recall C. underlined
the parallel between Marius's saving of the republic through his generalship
and C.'s saving Rome from Catiline through his statesmanship. The events
around C.'s exile and return to Rome, as well as C.'s presentation of them, are
discussed in Kaster 2006, 1–14, with a detailed treatment of their complex
chronology at 393–408.   **in eo**: sc. *monumento*.   **tum et se exclamasse
Sallustius narrat**: We are no longer in M.'s dream.   **reditum . . . celerem**:
Sallustius was overly optimistic: C.'s exile lasted eighteen months. Cf. Q.'s
misleading *celeriter* below.   **te ipsum visum somnio delectari**: Not only
did Sallustius hear M. recount his dream immediately after the fact, but
he also saw M.'s reaction to it. M. cannot deny that he took his dream as a
positive sign, nor can he fault others for doing the same. But in his rebuttal,
M. dismisses his reaction as a sign of his desire to bear his own exile with
the same fortitude with which Marius bore his (2.140).   **ut**: "how";
introduces an indirect question. See *OLD*, s.v. A1b.   **optumo et clarissimo**

viro consule: P. Cornelius Lentulus Spinther (*MRR* 2.199, s.a. 57), some of whose correspondence with C. is preserved in the collection *Ad Familiares*. This effusive praise and the hyperbolic tone of this entire passage match C.'s portrayal of these events elsewhere (e.g., *Pis.* 34; *Sest.* 144; *Red. in Sen.* 8; *Dom.* 7).   **frequentissimo . . . plausu comprobatum**: Cf. 23n. *Andromacham Enni* and *Sest.* 117. The outburst happened during a theatrical production at the *ludi Apollinares*. The city was crowded as people responded to the Senate's decree that all those from the towns of Italy who wanted C. to return should come to Rome for the vote.   **dixisse te nihil . . . divinius**: See 57n. *divinius*. Q. cites C.'s own words to round off this final, most authoritative *exemplum*. This quotation may be a further indication that C. was not as hostile to divination as M. appears in Book 2.

60–71 *The Ratio of Natural Divination*

The long discussion of dreams begun in 39 is capped by a brief attempt to explain the prophetic ability of the soul. This is the closest Q. ever comes to offering an explanation of the mechanics of any type of divination. Earlier (12), he had disavowed the need for a comprehensible *ratio*; accordingly, Q.'s main interest here is the authority of the philosophers he cites rather than the details of the mechanisms of prophecy. Starting from prophetic dreams, Q. broadens his focus to include the prophetic powers of those on the verge of death (at 63) and inspired prophecy (at 66). His main contention is that people have an inherent prophetic power that is enabled in certain circumstances: when one who has lived temperately dreams, is close to death, or is in a state of frenzy. Each of these circumstances is vividly illustrated.

60 At multa falsa: another anticipated objection. Cf. 24n. *At non numquam*. Q.'s defense against this charge does not satisfy M., who brings up the point again at 2.127–28.   **immo obscura fortasse nobis**: Cf. 35. The gods do not send false dreams; if some dreams erroneously predict future events, the fault is man's: either he does not understand the message sent, or, as Q. argues below, he hinders his own ability to receive truly prophetic dreams by tainting his body. Q. is able to cite to his advantage both the clarity of signs (10n. *clara et perspicua*) and their ambiguity.   **sed sint falsa quaedam**: See 29n. *fuerit hoc censoris . . . at illud minime auguris*.   **contra vera quid dicimus**: "Why do we protest against those that are true?"   **integri**: "in a clean state," that is, not full of food and drink.   **vide quid Socrates in Platonis politia loquatur**: The quotation that follows is a paraphrase of *Rep.* 571c–572b, despite Q.'s claim at the end of 61 to have repeated Plato's very words. The Platonic passage draws on an earlier tradition that emphasized the link between a person's physical state and his dreams, exemplified by a portion of the Hippocratic treatise *De Victu* that discusses dreams as symptoms of certain types of malady (on which see van der Eijk 2004). Plato's innovation is that he gives greater prominence to the relationship between a person's psychological and moral state and the nature of his dreams. In its original, Platonic context, this passage is part of a discussion of the tyrannical man, who can be identified by his immoderate behavior and desires, which, among other consequences, lead him to have violent, depraved dreams. Q. turns the passage into a defense of the prophetic potential of dreams. For a connection between tyranny and dreams of incest, see Grottanelli 1999.   **cum dormientibus ea pars animi . . . illa autem . . . cum sit**: The *oratio obliqua* dependent on *dicit enim* begins with two long, parallel circumstantial *cum* clauses that each contain a relative clause modifying its subject. The Platonic soul is made of parts that are not always in perfect harmony (their exact number is a vexed question: see Vander Waerdt 1985, 284–86). In *Rep.* 439d–e, Socrates lays out a tripartite soul consisting of reason (νοῦς, *ratio*), which is drawn toward knowledge and truth and guides a person's life; spirit (θυμός, *ira*), concerned with honor and ambition; and appetite (ἐπιθυμία, *cupiditas*), which desires food, drink, sex, and money. Elsewhere, however (e.g., *Leg.* 653b–c, 904b–c), Plato discusses the soul as comprising two parts (as Q. does here), variously described as divine and human, rational and irrational, or immortal and mortal. The different ways of dividing the soul can be reconciled: the human, irrational, mortal part of the soul in the bipartite division comprises the spirited and appetitive parts of the tripartite division. The variation of Plato's presentation is matched by C., who shifts between discussing the Platonic soul as bi- or tripartite, even within a single work (e.g., *Tusc.* 1.20, 4.10).   **mentis et rationis**: "intellect and reason." The phrase is repeated twice more in 60–61. Cf. *ratione et scientia* (4), *mentis et consilii* (61), and *rationis atque intelligentiae* (70).   **feritas . . . atque agrestis inmanitas**: These qualities are incompatible with the practice of divination (1–2).   **potu atque pastu**: These technical, agricultural terms (a variation of *cibo et vino* above) contribute to the characterization of this part of the soul as an untamed animal (*feritas, agrestis inmanitas, exsultare*).   **exsultare eam in somno inmoderateque iactari**: *Eam = illa . . . in qua feritas quaedam sit atque agrestis inmanitas*. Q. finally arrives at the main part of the indirect statement that was introduced by *dicit enim*. After this point, he forgets that he is in *oratio obliqua*, and for the rest of his paraphrase of Socrates, which does not conclude until the end of 61 (signaled by *haec verba ipsa Platonis expressi*), he slips back into *oratio recta*.   **cum matre corpus miscere**: "to have sex with his mother"; a Graecism from Plato's ἐπιχειρεῖν μείγνυσθαι (*Rep.*

571d).   **miscere . . . trucidare . . . cruentari . . . facere**: All depend on
videatur. Q. embellishes Plato, making the dreams more gory and vile.

61 at qui salubri et moderato cultu atque victu quieti se tradiderit: "But
the man of healthful and modest lifestyle and habit who gives himself over
to rest." The ablatives are descriptive. This relative clause begins a sentence
so long and complicated that Q. loses direction part of the way through
it. This first portion does not connect grammatically to the second (*tum
eveniet . . . ut illa tertia pars . . . praebeat*), from which it is separated a long
way. The meandering structure and grammatical disjointedness (anacoluthon)
contribute to the conversational quality of Q.'s speech. Real conversation rarely
follows a linear path, often jumping from one topic or construction to another
before the speaker has finished with the first. Similar breaks are also found
at 9, 18, and 34. Note, however, that *qui* is picked up in the next sentence
by *ei*.   **ea parte animi quae . . . eaque parte animi quae . . . illa etiam
tertia parte animi, in qua**: These three long ablative absolutes, each of which
contains at least one relative clause, describe the circumstances under which
the moderate man goes to sleep.   **saturataque bonarum cogitationum
epulis**: a translation of Plato's ἑστιάσας λόγων καλῶν καὶ σκέψεων. This
image, not found elsewhere in classical Latin, became popular among
Christian writers.   **quorum utrumque**: sc. *inopia* and *satietas*.   **sive
deest naturae quippiam**: "whether nature lacks something."   **vegetam . . .
acremque**: Cf. *Fin.* 2.45.   **tum ei**: picks up *qui* at the beginning of 61.

62 Epicurum igitur . . . namque Carneades: The two most important
opponents of divination are also mentioned together at 109 and 2.51.
Epicurus, who treated dreams solely as a physical phenomenon and
argued that divination did not exist, is the philosopher most ridiculed
by C. (see 5n. *Xenophanes . . . Epicurum*), and Q. gives him only passing
mention.   **concertationis studio**: "because of his penchant for argument";
ablative of cause. *Concertationis* is rare in classical Latin, used only by C.
and the elder Pliny.   **modo ait hoc modo illud**: "sometimes says this,
sometimes that." Q. refers to the Academic practice of holding no fixed
position on most major issues (cf. 7n. *etenim . . . comparemus*). Because C.
elides the verb in this phrase at *N. D.* 1.47, some editors have preferred to
remove it here. But cf. *Att.* 2.15.1 = *SBA* 35.1; *Luc.* 121.   **at ille, quod
sentit**: Supply a verb of speaking. Q. articulates an anticipated defense of
Epicurus (cf. the anticipated objections at 24 and 60).   **qui ut rationem
non redderent**: concessive; cf. 10n. *ut sint di.* Q. admits the main weakness of
his position: even Plato and Socrates cannot meet M.'s (anticipated) demand
for a real explanation for how divination works.   **auctoritate tamen hos**

minutos philosophos vincerent: The verb is a potential subjunctive. Q.'s position stands in sharp contrast to C.'s expectations of his own readers: in *N. D.* 1.10, C. explicitly criticizes those who fail to evaluate the *ratio* of an argument and accept it simply on the *auctoritas* of the one who endorses it.   **iubet**: Supply *nos*. This is Q.'s interpretation: the passage in Plato does not give instructions for the proper conduct of one's life.   **ex quo etiam Pythagoricis interdictum putatur ne faba vescerentur**: The followers of Pythagoras were famous for avoiding certain types of food—mostly meat and fish, but also some produce (Riedweg 2005, 67–71; Garnsey 1999, 85–89)—for ideological reasons. The exact rationale behind—indeed, even the existence of—the Pythagorean restriction on beans (κύαμοι) was debated in antiquity. Aristotle proposed several explanations (ap. D. L. 8.34–35 = 195 Rose): beans' destructive power and their similarity to genitalia, the gates of Hades, the nature of the universe, or the nature of oligarchy. Pliny (*Nat.* 18.118) thought the reason was that beans dulled the senses and caused sleeplessness. Cf. Gel. 4.11.1–14.   **tranquillitati mentis quaerenti**: The hypallage (see 42n. *mentis metu / perculsus curis sumptus suspirantibus*) gives this passage an elevated, poetic tone, to humorous effect.

63 a societate et a contagione corporis: "from its connection to, and the influence of, the body." *Contagio* does not imply here disease and contamination. Cf. 110, 129, 2.33.   **meminit praeteritorum praesentia cernit, futura providet**: Note the chiasmus in *meminit praeteritorum praesentia cernit*, which forms a unit of past and present and highlights *futura providet*. The unity of all three possibilities is emphasized by asyndeton. Dreams, like all forms of divination, can clarify past and present events, as well as predict the future.   **dormientis ut mortui**: The association of sleep and death goes back to Homer, who identifies Sleep as the brother of Death (*Il.* 14.231), a genealogy followed in Verg., *A.* 6.278. Descriptions of death as unending sleep are as common as those of sleep as a temporary death (e.g., Pl., *Apol.* 40c–d; Catul. 5.5–6; Lucr. 3.909–11; *Tusc.* 1.92, 97; *Sen.* 80 [a paraphrase of Xen. *Cyr.* 8.7.21]).   **quod multo magis**: introduces prophecy by the ghosts of the departed and waking prophecy by those on the verge of death. The logical connection of these to prophectic dreams is that an individual's capacity for prophecy strengthens as his soul is loosened from the body: the soul is freed from the body temporarily in sleep, and the permanent separation of the soul from the body occurs gradually as death approaches. Thus the ability of the *animus* to foresee the future increases as one approaches death, reaching its full potential *post mortem*.   **faciet . . . excesserit . . . est**: *Animus* is the implied subject of each verb.   **divinior**: "more able to divine"; cf. 57n. *divinius*.   **id ipsum . . . instare mortem**:

"this very thing . . . that death presses upon them." **itaque is . . .
tumque . . . eosque**: *Is* is dative plural. The sentence is neatly shaped into three
independent but closely connected clauses. Cf. Lucr. 1.132–35 with Bailey's
commentary; Pl., *Rep.* 330d–e.   **vel**: intensifies *maxume*.

64 illo etiam exemplo confirmat Posidonius: See 6n. *noster
Posidonius*. Most editors agree that *etiam* indicates that Posidonius is
the source for both this section and the discussion in 63. This cannot
be proved, however, and it should be noted that 63 is not included in
Edelstein and Kidd's edition of the fragments of Posidonius (1988–89;
frag.108).   **aequales**: "coevals."   **deinde deinceps**: "and then in turn"; a
rare collocation.   **deorum adpulsu**: This is the critical element of natural,
as opposed to technical, divination.   **provideat . . . sit . . . conloquantur**:
subjunctives in informal *oratio obliqua*. Q. makes it clear that these three
reasons are Posidonius's.   **ipse per sese**: "all on its own."   **quippe
qui deorum cognatione teneatur**: "inasmuch as it is possessed of a kinship
with the gods." *Quippe qui* introduces an explanatory relative clause. Cf.
G&L 626 n. 1; *OLD*, s.v. *quippe* 2c. The idea of a close relationship between
the human soul and divinity is widespread in ancient philosophy, including
Stoicism, which sees the human soul as part of the divine spirit or energy
(πνεῦμα) that pervades the universe. Q. touches on this point also at 70 and
110. Cf. *N. D.* 1.27.   **inmortalium animorum**: refers to δαίμονες (divine
beings that delivered messages from the gods), ἥρωες (surviving souls of the
human dead), or some combination thereof).   **insignitae notae veritatis**:
The essential meaning of the phrase is the same whether *insignitae* is taken
with *notae* or with *veritatis*. On the importance of the clarity of divine signs
for Q.'s argument, see 10n. *clara et perspicua*.   **idque, ut modo dixi . . .
augurentur**: Q. reiterates his point before introducing a series of new *exempla*.
augurentur: Cf. 27n. *augurari*.   **ut modo dixi**: at 63.

65 ex quo: Supply *modo*.   **de quo ante dixi**: at 47.   **qui . . . Achilli
mortem denuntiat**: *Il.* 22.355–60, which mirrors the prophecy of the dying
Patroclus to Hector at *Il.* 16.851–54.   **neque enim illud verbum temere
consuetudo adprobavisset, si ea res nulla esset omnino**: "Indeed, common
usage would not have endorsed that word without good cause, if there were
no substance to it at all." *Neque* and *temere* reinforce one another. *Illud verbum*
points forward to *praesagibat* but may also mean "a saying," anticipating an
entire verse. On etymologies, see 1n. *a divis . . . a furore*.   **praesagibat**:
For the shortened imperfect, cf. 40n. *semita nulla pedem stabilibat*. Q. slightly
alters the line from Pl., *Aul.* 178 (*praesagibat mi animus frustra me ire quom
exibam domo*), suggesting that C. has given the line from memory.   **sagire**

enim sentire acute est . . . : A nearly identical definition, including the illustrative examples of *sagae* and *sagaces canes*, is preserved in Paul. ex Fest. 303L with 250L. *Sagire* appears only here in extant Latin.   **sagae anus**: *Saga* is an imperfect synonym for *anus*. The latter is a general, often neutral term for an old woman, whereas Paulus ex Fest. 232L and 427L link the *saga* to the performance of rituals. In the literature of the late Roman Republic and early Roman Empire, the *saga* is usually a combination of witch and procuress (*lena*), often a figure with excessive libido (e.g., the old women in Tib. 1.2, Prop. 4.5, and Ov., *Am.* 1.8); she becomes an object of abuse and derision. Cf. Non. 33–34L.   **sagaces dicti canes**: because of their superlative senses of smell and hearing; a stock phrase.

66 Inest igitur: resumes the argument interrupted by the discussion of *praesagire*.   **furor**: Cf. 1n. *a divis . . . a furore*.   **"Sed quid oculis . . .** : *Quid* is an adverbial accusative. This first of three quotations, all presumed to be from the same scene of Ennius's *Alexander* (on which see 42n. *mater gravida . . .*), consists of trochaic tetrameters delivered by two speakers. The first two lines most likely belong to the leader of the chorus (Jocelyn 1967, 207; Wardle *ad loc.*), but many editors (Pease, Freyburger and Scheid, Timpanaro, and Schäublin) assign them to Hecuba. The rest of this quotation belongs to Hecuba's daughter, Cassandra, the quintessential inspired prophet (cf. 85, 89, 2.112).   **oculis rapere . . . ardentibus**: "to seize with burning eyes." The intransitive use of *rapere* is highly unusual, but the image is not uncommon in tragic or mock-tragic contexts (e.g., *Har. Resp.* 39; *De Orat.* 3.162; Pl., *Pseud.* 596; Verg., *G.* 1.183; Juv. 10.331–33). Timpanaro prefers Lambinus's emendation to *rabere* (to rave), but *oculis rabere* is unparalleled in extant Latin.   **ubi illa paulo ante sapiens virginali modestia?**: "Where is that modesty, rational and proper to a young woman, that was here a short while ago?" The manuscripts' reading of this line presents metrical difficulties, particularly the hiatus at *paulo ante* and the question of whether *virginali* is ablative or, as is more likely, nominative singular (with the archaic omission of the terminal *s*). See 40n. *corpus*. Editors do not agree how to emend it, but the essential meaning is clear. For a detailed discussion, see Jocelyn 1967, 210–11; Jocelyn stands alone in obelizing *virginali*. The theme of modesty and shame runs throughout this passage (*pudet, miseret, piget*). According to tradition, Cassandra was granted her prophetic powers by Apollo, who sought to win her for himself. When she refused his advances, Apollo cursed her with forever having her true prophecies disregarded (Aesch., *Ag.* 1203–13). Her fits of ecstasy are often presented as the result of unwanted divine influence (e.g., Aesch., *Ag.* 1173–77).   **Mater, optumatum multo mulier melior mulierum**: *Optumatum* is genitive plural and is picked up

by *optumi* and *optumam* further on in the quotation. Although the form
optimus, -a, -um was more common in early Latin, the third declension
form is also found (e.g., *Fam.* 7.6.1 = *SBF* 27.6.1 [see commentary], either
quoting from Ennius's *Medea* or merely using Ennian vocabulary; cf. Jocelyn
1967, 118). Note the alliteration in this line, not just of initial *m*, but also of
l and *r*.   **missa sum superstitiosis hariolationibus**: "I have been turned
loose by inspired prophecies." The precise meaning of *missa sum* is not clear.
Jocelyn points to the replacement of compound verbs with simple forms in
tragedy and proposes to understand *emissa sum* or *immissa sum*. In early
Latin, *superstitiosus* is a neutral word for those in an ecstatic state (e.g., 2.115;
Pl., *Am.* 323; Pl., *Cur.* 397; Pl., *Rud.* 1139; see also 132n. *superstitiosi . . .
vates*). By the late republic, however, it came to be used pejoratively of those
deemed excessively credulous (e.g., 126; *Dom.* 105; *N. D.* 2.72, 3.92 ; Liv.
6.5.6 with Oakley's commentary). *Hariolatio* appears securely elsewhere
only in Gel. 15.18.3.   **neque me Apollo**: With Ax, I have retained the
manuscripts' reading, even though the negative *neque* makes little sense
given that the passage emphasizes Cassandra's discomfort and shame. No
alternative has won consensus. Pease accepts Ribbeck's emendation of *namque
Apollo*, while Timpanaro and Schäublin prefer *meque Apollo*, proposed by
Grotius.   **fatis fandis**: dative of purpose.   **ciet . . . pudet . . . piget . . .
dolet**: So many consecutive rhyming line endings are unparalleled in ancient
drama (Jocelyn 1967, 214). Cf. 20n. *monebant . . . ferebant . . . iubebant . . .
vereri . . . teneri*.   **virgines . . . aequalis**: See 64n. *aequales*.   **patris
mei meum factum pudet**: "My father is ashamed of my deeds." That *meum
factum* is genitive plural is guaranteed by *Orat.* 155. This appears to be the
only occurrence of *pudet* with two genitives. Note that the polyptoton of *mei
meum* continues into the next line with *mea . . . me . . . mei*. There is synizesis
(a combination of two separate vowel sounds into a single sound) in *mei* and
meum (also *tui* and *mei* in the next line).   **extra**: "apart from."   **men
obesse, illos prodesse, me obstare, illos obsequi**: "To think that I am a
hindrance, that they prosper you! That I oppose you, that they obey!" *Men*
= *me* + enclitic *-ne*. Here is a line of four exclamatory accusative + infinitive
constructions. Note the rhyme of *obesse prodesse* and the heavy repetition
of *ob-*.   **o poema tenerum et moratum atque molle**: *Moratum* is used
here in the sense of "well suited to her character (*mos*)" (cf. Quint., *Inst.*
4.2.64). More commonly, however, C. uses *moratus* in a political context, to
describe the civilized state (*Mil.* 93; *Brut.* 7; *De Orat.* 1.85; *Rep.* 5.1) and the
men who should lead it (*Leg. Agr.* 2.84; *De Orat.* 2.184). Q. is thinking of the
play as a written text (*poema*), rather than as a live performance (*fabula*). See
Goldberg 2000, 51–53. C.'s enthusiasm for this passage, indicated by the string
of positive adjectives he has given Q. to describe it, probably accounts for its

inclusion: Q. has to admit that it is not immediately relevant (see next note). *Tener* and *mollis* come to be identified most strongly with the aesthetic ideal of the neoteric and elegiac poets who, in the two or three generations after C., reacted against the weighty epic tradition represented by Ennius. For C., *teneritas* (suppleness) and *mollitia* (softness) are characteristic of youth (*Fin.* 5.58; *Leg.* 2.38) and are generally positive qualities in some of the arts (e.g., *Orat.* 64 [philosophy], *Fin.* 5.3 [poetry], *Brut.* 70 [sculpture]), yet they are antithetical to forceful, effective oratory (*Brut.* 38, 274–6; *De Orat.* 3.176) and to the proper behavior of a citizen of the *res publica* (*Mil.* 42).   **Sed hoc minus ad rem**: "but this is less to the point." *Hoc* = Q.'s praise for the passage just cited.

67 illud . . . expressum est: points back to the passage just quoted.   **ut vaticinari furor vera soleat**: stands in apposition to *illud quod volumus* (sc. *dicere*). Cf. 47n. *si quid vellet ut diceret.*   **adest, adest . . .** : The second syllable of *adest* is short. This fragment (in trochaic septenarii) is also from Ennius's *Alexander*, presumably from the same scene as the previous quotation. The imagery of this waking vision recalls that of Hecuba's dream at 42.   **deus inclusus**: recalls *praesagitio . . . inclusa* above (66).   **iamque mari magno classis cita / texitur; exitium examen rapit**: "and now a swift fleet is constructed on the open sea; it speeds along a swarm of troubles." *Exitium* is genitive plural (cf. *meum factum* in 66). These lines are in dactylic quatrains. The phrase *mare magnum* also appears in Enn., *Ann.* 434 Skutsch and is picked up by later poets from Lucilius onward. *Classis cita* appears only here and in Vergil (*A.* 5.33, 66). Note the alliteration and consonance of *mari magno, classis cita*, and *texitur* with *exitium examen*. C. quotes this line also in *Att.* 8.11.3 = *SBA* 161.3, in a passage on those who had set out with Pompey at the beginning of the Civil War.   **fera**: modifies *manus*, "multitude," "horde," "host."   **velivolantibus**: "sailing." The verb is preserved only here; the adjective *velivolus* is more common.   **navibus . . . manus**: The final syllable of each word is short. See 40n. *corpus.*

68 tragoedias loqui videor et fabulas: Again, Q. signals his transition from weaker, more literary evidence to something more authoritative. He distinguishes between *fabulas* and *tragoedias*. Though *fabula* is sometimes used for theatrical productions (e.g., Var., *L.* 6.55; Quint., *Inst.* 2.4.2), it is most often a general term for fictional narratives. In this instance, *fabulas* refers to the *exempla* Q. took from genres other than drama.   **ex te ipso . . . audivi**: This phrase launches a complicated series of nested indirect statements.

ex te ipso . . . audivi

   C. Coponium ad te venisse Dyrrhachium . . . cum primo hominem prudentem
      atque doctum
      cum praetorio . . . praeesset
   eumque dixisse
      remigem quendam . . . vaticinatum (esse)
         madefactum iri . . . Graeciam sanguine
         rapinas . . . et conscensionem . . . fugientibusque . . . respectum . . . fore
         sed . . . reditum ac domum itionem dari
   tum neque te ipsum non esse commotum
   Marcumque Varronem et M. Catonem . . . vehementer esse perterritos
      qui tum ibi erant doctos homines
   paucis sane post diebus . . . venisse Labienum
      qui cum interitum exercitus nuntiavisset
   reliqua vaticinationis brevi esse confecta

This is the best evidence Q. can adduce: M. is the original source, and Q. heard it directly from him. In early August of 48, C. was at Dyrrachium, Pompey's main base on the Adriatic, while Pompey moved off to engage Caesar in the final battle of the Civil War at Pharsalus (C., *Fam.* 9.18.2 = *SBF* 191.2; Liv., *Per.* 111; Plu., *Cic.* 39.1). C. was there to meet the remnants of Pompey's force, including Coponius (see below), as they fled in the aftermath of his defeat. M. addresses this *exemplum* at 2.114, arguing that what Q. takes as a message sent by the gods was really just the articulation of what was anticipated by those who best knew the relative strengths of Pompey's and Caesar's forces.   **C. Coponium**: Having been elected to the praetorship for 49 (*Att.* 8.12a.4 = *SBA* 162a.4; *MRR* 2.257, s.a. 49), Coponius was prorogated *cum praetorio imperio* for 48 (cf. 58n. *me, cum Asiae pro cos. praeessem, vidisse in quiete*), during which time he shared command of Pompey's Rhodian fleet with C. Marcellus (Caes., *Civ.* 3.5.3). Coponius's family came from Tibur and had enjoyed Roman citizenship for two generations (*Balb.* 53). He was long known to C. and Pompey; indeed, he may have been responsible for helping Pompey gather artwork for his theater in Rome in the early fifties (Plin., *Nat.* 36.41). He survived Pompey's defeat, fell afoul of Antonius in the aftermath of Caesar's death, but survived the proscriptions through his wife's efforts (App., *BC* 4.40).   **cum primo hominem prudentem atque doctum**: "a man especially sensible and learned." This use of *cum primo* is unique in extant Latin (see *TLL*, s.v. *cumprimis*; Pease *ad loc.*). Q.'s description is in keeping with C.'s mention in 56 BCE of Coponius and his brother as *adulescentes humanissimi et doctissimi, rectissimis studiis atque optimis artibus praediti* and with his assertion of their great affection for the Academic philosopher Dio (*Cael.* 24). Q. adds this description here to underline that Coponius was not someone of excessive credulity (cf. the description of Varro and Cato below). **quinqueremi**: the standard Roman warship during the republic, rowed by oarsmen in groups of five. **madefactum iri . . . Graeciam**: "Greece was going to be drenched." Latin uses the supine in *-um* + *iri* for a future passive infinitive. **conscensionem . . . respectum incendiorum**: picked up by *conscendistis . . . respicientes . . . incenderant* in 69. The Rhodians got the *propinquum reditum ac domum itionem* that was foretold: they abandoned their Roman allies shortly after Pharsalus. *Conscensio* (embarkation) appears only here in classical Latin. More common is a verbal phrase like *in naves imposito* (Caes., *Civ.* 3.103.1; Liv. 30.45.1, 45.34.8). **neque te ipsum non esse commotum**: "you yourself were somewhat upset." Cf. 24n. *At non numquam.* M.'s reaction was milder than that of his companions. **Marcumque Varronem et M. Catonem**: Roman praenomina are written out before an enclitic. M. Terentius Varro (116–27 BCE) had long been a supporter of Pompey and had served with him during his campaign against the pirates (66–62 BCE). In fact, Pompey awarded Varro the naval crown for his distinguished service (Plin., *Nat.* 7.115). C. was a great admirer of Varro (e.g., *Phil.* 2.103; *Brut.* 60, 205), who composed numerous works on a wide range of topics; only his *De Re Rustica* and *De Lingua Latina* now survive in substantial amount. Varro is mentioned often in C.'s letters, and eight addressed to him survive. He is also the dedicatee of C.'s *Academica* (*Fam.* 9.8 = *SBF* 254) and appears as an interlocutor in it. On Cato, see 24n. *summus imperator nuper fugit.* **Labienum**: T. Labienus held the high-ranking post of *legatus pro praetore* during Caesar's campaign in Gaul in the fifties (*MRR* 2.198, s.a. 58), but sided with Pompey in the Civil War that erupted in 49. After the defeat of the republican forces at Pharsalus in August 48, Labienus escaped to Dyrrachium with the remnants of his cavalry, made up of Gallic and German allies (Frontin., *Str.* 2.7.13; Dio Cass. 42.10.3; *B. Afr.* 19.3). Appian erroneously asserts that Labienus went to Spain (*BC* 2.87). Labienus then put his forces at Cato's disposal and continued to fight for the republican cause until his death in the final battle with Caesar at Munda in 45 (*B. Hisp.* 31.9; Vell. 2.55.4; App., *BC* 2.105). Labienus's head was brought to Caesar (App., *BC* 2.105). **brevi**: "in short order." An important theme of Q.'s argument is the swift fulfillment of a prophecy as proof of its accuracy and potency. Note the repetition of phrases like *paulo ante* and *subito* in the anecdotes that follow.

69 Nam: introduces Q.'s own interpretation of events. Pompey fled immediately to Egypt, where he was murdered by agents of Ptolemy XIII

(Plu., *Pomp.* 77.1–79.5), and other leaders of the republican forces scattered across the Mediterranean. The bulk of their forces moved to their naval base at Corcyra (Dio Cass. 42.10.1–3). When it was learned that Pompey had fled, Cato asked C. (who, as proconsul, outranked him) to take command of the republican forces. After C. refused (for which he was nearly killed by Pompey's son), Cato took charge himself (Plu., *Cic.* 39.1–2). Cato fought on for several more years, before committing suicide rather than submit to Caesar at Utica in north Africa in 46. For his part, C. refused to join in any more fighting after Pharsalus and soon returned to Italy after having been pardoned by Caesar, an act of which he was not very proud (e.g., *Att.* 11.5.1–4 = *SBA* 216.1–4; Plu., *Cic.* 39.3–5).   **ex horreis . . . constraverat**: Dyrrachium had been Pompey's supply base.   **quia sequi noluerant**: Supply *vos* as the object of *sequi*.

70 oracla: here in the sense "predictions." Similar definitions are found at 11 and 34.   **quae carere arte dixeram**: **Cratippus noster**: See 5n. *Cratippusque familiaris noster*. M. responds at 2.107–9.   **una ratio est, qua Cratippus noster uti solet**: This launches a series of three parallel clauses in *oratio obliqua*: (1) *animos hominum . . . esse tractos et haustos*, (2) *humani autem animi eam partem . . . non esse . . . seiugatam*, (3) *eam . . . vigere*. The subjects of clauses 2 and 3 are further described by relative clauses beginning with *quae*. The Peripatetics conceived of a bipartite (rational and irrational) soul. See Vander Waerdt 1985 and 6on. *cum dormientibus ea pars animi . . . illa autem . . . cum sit*.   **quadam ex parte extrinsecus**: "to a certain extent, from outside themselves." The notion that human souls are derived and drawn off (*tractos et haustos*) from the divine is common to many philosophers, including Plato (e.g., *Phlb.* 30a), the Stoics (Epict. 1.14.5–6), and Pythagoras (C., *Sen.* 78).   **quae sensum quae motum quae adpetitum habeat**: The repetition of *quae* highlights the three distinct properties of the first of Cratippus's two parts of the soul.

71 expositis exemplis: Cratippus proved his argument just as Q. does.   **si sine oculis non potest extare officium et munus oculorum, possunt autem aliquando oculi non fungi suo munere**: "if the function and duty of sight cannot exist without eyes, and moreover sometimes the eyes cannot perform their function . . ." This is the first of two parallel conditional statements, each of which comprises a long protasis in two parts connected by *autem* and a single apodosis.   **qui vel semel ita est usus oculis . . . is habet sensum . . .**: "the man who even once so used his eyes . . . retains a sense . . ." Cratippus argues that a single, verified performance of a cognitive function (sight in Cratippus's first instance, divination in the second) is sufficient to establish the possibility of future performances of that function. If a man sees

something once, it is possible he will do so again. Although the proof is not
identical, the ultimate source for this appears to be Pl., *Men.* 81d. See Tarrant
2000 for further discussion. Cf. 2.107; *Tusc.* 3.15.   **cum divinationem
habeat**: concessive.   **semel aliquid esse . . .** : introduces the *oratio obliqua*
dependent on *satis est*.   **nihil fortuito cecidisse videatur**: "it appears
to have happened in no way by chance." At 9, Q. defined divination as the
prediction of events that would otherwise be thought to have happened at
random.

72–78 Technical Divination

Q. finally turns his attention to artificial divination. He begins with an
assertion that there are specialists who possess knowledge that allows them to
interpret signs sent by the gods, but the argument then moves away from this
to a catalog of portents, many of which do not, in the telling at least, require
experts for interpretation. The catalog includes mostly Greek *exempla*, but
the Roman stories of Sulla and Flaminius are strategically placed for dramatic
effect (see below). The catalog will be reconfigured and expanded in M.'s
rebuttal at 2.54–68.

72 vero: a strong adversative, marking the shift to technical divination, the
second major category of divination that Q. identified at 11.   **animadversa
ac notata**: Cf. 12n. *animadversa et notata*. Cf. also 25, 131.   **ut supra dixi**:
at 12 and 34.   **in quo haruspices augures coniectoresque**: Although he
has switched to the singular, the antecedent of *quo* is *genera divinandi*. Cf.
the groups of diviners listed at 12.   **haec inprobantur a Peripateticis, a
Stoicis defenduntur**: The antecedent of *haec* is *genera divinandi*. Chiasmus
emphasizes the distinction between the positions of the two schools
(discussed at 5–6).   **quorum alia sunt posita in monumentis et
disciplina . . . alia autem subito ex tempore**: Q. further subdivides artificial
divination into those forms based on principles of interpretation preserved in
written records and those performed extemporaneously.   **et haruspicini
et fulgurales et rituales libri**: Of these three collections, we are best informed
about the *libri rituales*, which dealt with the rituals for founding cities,
consecrating religious places, organizing the body politic and the army, and
ceteraque eiusmodi ad bellum ac pacem pertinentia (Fest. 358L). The *libri
haruspicini* are mentioned only here. It is possible that they were a subset of
the *libri Tagetici* that preserved the teachings of the boy prophet Tages (de
Grummond 2006b, 28). The *libri fulgurales* included instructions for dealing
with signs sent through thunder and lightning (e.g., Amm. Marc. 23.5.13)

and, presumably, guidelines for interpretation like those in the brontoscopic
calendar preserved in Ioannes Lydus's *De Ostentis* 27-38 (now available in an
English translation by J. M. Turfa in de Grummond and Simon 2006, 173-90).
It is likely that Q. refers both to the original texts (which were not available
to the public) and to the exegetical and other scholarly works that sprang up
around them. E.g., a contemporary of C., L. Tarquitius Priscus, translated
Etruscan works on portents, and Lydus's Greek version of the Etruscan
calendar purports to be a translation of a Latin work by another of C.'s
contemporaries, Nigidius Figulus, the author of numerous works on aspects
of divination. For a thorough discussion of the lively production of works
on divination in the late republic, see Rawson 1985a, 298-316.   **vestri
etiam augurales**: Q. again stresses M.'s membership in the augural college
(cf. 25). There were *libri augurales* that were *reconditi*, that is, available
only to members of the college (*Dom.* 39; Serv., *A.* 1.398, 2.649). But as in
the case of the *Etrusca disciplina*, there was also a flourishing tradition of
scholarly exegesis that circulated more widely. We know of at least six works
on augural law, including one by C. himself, written in the last century of
the republic. None has survived.   **subito**: Cf. 68n. *brevi*.   **ut apud
Homerum Calchas**: Supply *fecit* or a similar verb. Calchas is one of the most
powerful prophets of Greek literature and was especially skilled in reading
bird signs.   **auguratus est**: used in a general sense. Q. refers to an episode
recounted by Odysseus at *Il.* 2.299-330, but his presentation passes over the
horror of the original: a snake streaked with blood emerged from under an
altar as the Greeks offered sacrifice at Aulis; it then consumed, with great
drama, a sparrow and her eight chicks, before it miraculously turned into
stone. M. mockingly responds to this *exemplum* at 2.63 by quoting the *Iliad*
passage in a translation that emphasizes the fear the *signum* struck into the
Greeks.   **et ut in Sullae scriptum historia . . .**: The hyperbaton, where the
participle interrupts the prepositional phrase, highlights the main source of
the anecdote: Sulla wrote a memoir in at least twenty-two books at the end
of his life. Many of the twenty-one remaining fragments (collected in Peter
1.195-204 = *FRH* 2.472-91) attest to Sulla's belief in prophetic signs and
dreams and in divine sanction for his actions. The placement of this anecdote
immediately after a tale from Homer imbues it with a heroic and tragic
character. The two *exempla* are clearly linked by the appearance of a snake
from underneath an altar and by the unexpressed horror lurking behind each
tale. While it is possible that the event in question occurred in 89 (Wardle
ad loc. follows App., *BC* 1.121, the only ancient source to date the event to
that year), it is more likely that it dates to the following year, when Sulla was
consul (Val. Max. 1.6.4; variant accounts are also found in Plu., *Sulla* 9.6 and
Liv. frag. 16 = Aug., *Civ. D.* 2.24). Ultimately, however, chronological precision

is not necessary for this *exemplum* to be effective. In the early 80s, the Social War, a conflict between Rome and its former Italian allies, was nearing its end. As the Romans gained the upper hand in that war, the threat of a civil war between the two most powerful Roman generals, Sulla and Marius, grew. Threat turned to reality when Marius and his allies in Rome maneuvered to have the command of the imminent war against Mithridates transferred from Sulla to Marius. In 88, Sulla lifted his seige of Nola, a Samnite stronghold in Campania, and led his six legions against Rome to regain the Mithridatic command—the first time in Roman history that the city was taken in hostile fashion by its own troops. Although the sign is cast here as presaging Sulla's successful sacking of the Samnite camp, C.'s readers would have had in mind this other, far more important and far more disastrous connection of Sulla, Nola, and victory.   **te inspectante**: The story actually carries the authority of two eyewitnesses, Sulla and M., which contrasts sharply with the mythical status of the former anecdote. C.'s service under Sulla in the Social War is also recorded in Plu., *Cic.* 3.2. C. himself mentions additional service under Pompeius Strabo (*Phil.* 12.27). In 88, C. would have been an eighteen-year-old serving in some junior capacity in Sulla's army, but we cannot recover the precise nature of his position. It would be of great interest to know if he was one of the ἄρχοντες (generally translated as "junior officers") who defected from Sulla before his march on Rome (App., *BC* 1.57 with Levick 1982). Only a single quaestor joined Sulla and the rank-and-file soldiers in their attack on the city.   **anguis emergeret**: Symbolic of Sulla's impending sally. Sulla is also identified with a snake at 106. For other serpentine *signa*, see 36, 79, 2.62.   **C. Postumius haruspex**: Sulla's personal *haruspex* who served him for several years, rather than one of the *haruspices* consulted by the Roman Senate in a public capacity. He is reported to have given Sulla another positive prediction at Tarentum in 83 (Aug., *Civ. D.* 2.24), and he may be the unnamed *haruspex* who interpreted a sign for Sulla at the Piraeus in 86 (Obs. 56b).   **florentissuma Samnitium castra**: "the most powerful Samnite camp"; cf. *OLD*, s.v. *florens* 3b. Pease (*ad loc.*) rightly adduces *De Orat.* 1.38 (*civitatem . . . florentissimam*) and *Phil.* 12.16 (*exercitu florentissimo*) in support of the manuscript reading over Val. Max. 1.6.4, which clearly relies on this passage but reads *fortissima* (which Wardle appears to follow).

73 in Dionysio: "in the case of Dionysius." See 39n. *Dionysi mater.* The connection of this anecdote to what precedes and what follows is not obvious, but its placement here reinforces the reading of the previous *exemplum* as pointing to Sulla's despotic behavior. M. takes up this and the next few anecdotes at 2.67–69.   **equus voraginibus non extitit**: "the horse did not stand out from the watery depths"; cf. Q.'s dream at 58 and the fall of

Flaminius's horse at 77. Possession of a horse was a sign of rank and status; accordingly, equine portents are most often associated with leaders (see Hyland 1990, 239–40). As at 58, the horse's disappearance and consequent re-emergence indicate the vicissitudes of its rider's career.   **examen apium**: In both Greek and Roman contexts, swarms of bees are usually harbingers of disaster (e.g., Herodot. 5.114; Plu., *Dio* 24.2–4; C., *Har. Resp.* 25; Liv. 21.46.1–w), though not always of utter destruction (e.g., Plin., *Nat.* 11.55; Verg., *A.* 7.64–70). See MacInnes 2000. Dreaming of bees could be positive for farmers, beekeepers, and, in some circumstances, generals and craftsmen; for everyone else, dreams of bees foretell death by a mob or by soldiers (Artemid. 2.22). This prodigy was taken to be very positive by Dionysius's supporter Philistus, but it may well have been taken by others as a sign of the cruelty with which Dionysius would rule Syracuse. Wardle (*ad loc.*) sees it as a sign of the bodyguard of six hundred men given to Dionysius shortly after he met his troops at Leontini.   **ostentum**: "sign"; another word with a technical divinatory meaning (on the difficulties of recovering which see Moussy 1990) that C. often uses as a general term. Cf. 76n. *portentum.*   **vim**: "meaning."   **paucis post diebus regnare coeperit**: mirrors *paulo ante quam regnare coepit* at the beginning of 73. Q. continues to emphasize the speed with which signs are proven to be true. Cf. 68n. *brevi.*

74 paulo ante Leuctricam calamitatem: Q. refers here to the defeat in 371 of the Spartans by the Thebans under the leadership of Epaminondas and their allies at Leuctra in Boeotia, the first major blow to Spartan military supremacy. In his rebuttal of this point at 2.54–57, M. is somewhat sympathetic to the Spartans, but in other works, C. casts the battle as the overthrow of tyranny (*Off.* 2.26; see also *Att.* 6.1.26 = *SBA* 115.26 with commentary).   **in Herculis fano arma sonuerunt Herculisque simulacrum . . . manavit**: Wardle identifies this *fanum* with a shrine at Sparta mentioned by Paus. 3.15.3, which housed a statue of Herakles in arms. The clanging weapons may have been those of the statue itself or, more likely, armaments that adorned the temple; cf. *armaque quae fixa in parietibus* in the next sentence. Shields, weaponry, and other types of military equipment were common offerings at Greek and Roman temples (see, e.g., Paus. 1.27.1, 2.14.4; Iriarte et al. 1997). Sweating statues and clanging weapons are frequent harbingers of armed conflict (cf. 98, 2.58; Liv. 22.1.8–14, 23.31.15, 27.4.14, 28.11.4; Obs. 54; Apollon., *Arg.* 4.1280–87).   **at eodem tempore . . . cumque eodem tempore . . . eademque tempestate**: *At* contrasts the *signa* at the Spartan shrine of Hercules with those at his Theban temple. The simultaneity of the Herculean *signa*, along with the roosters at Lebadia and other occurrences, makes them all the more impressive and, for a believer in

divination, less likely to be the result of chance.   **Callisthenes**: nephew
of Aristotle, companion of Alexander the Great, and the author of several
historical works, including the *Deeds of Alexander* and a *Hellenica*, from
which this fragment comes (*FrGH* 124 F 22a), in ten books covering the
period 386–356. He was executed on Alexander's orders for allegedly taking
part in the Conspiracy of the Pages in 327. In a catalog of philosophers
who ran afoul of tyrants (*Rab. Post.* 23), C. refers to Callisthenes as *doctus*.
Elsewhere, however, C. is very critical of his value as a historian, contrasting
him negatively with Philistus (*Q. Fr.* 2.12[11].4 = *SBQ* 16.4).   **clausae**
repagulis: "bolted shut."   **quae fixa in parietibus fuerant ea sunt humi**
inventa: Note the chiasmus. *Ea* is not necessary, but its presence points up
the drama of the discovery.   **Trophonio res divina fieret**: "a rite was
being performed in honor of Trophonius." The hero Trophonius was a master
builder thought to be responsible for numerous important sites, including
the threshold of Apollo's oracle of Delphi and his own oracle at Lebadia in
Boeotia. The elaborate ritual observed at Lebadia is described in detail by
Pausanias (9.39.5–14), who had himself consulted the oracle. After several
days of preparation, the consultant made a sacrifice to Trophonius, his
children, and other gods. The entrails of the animal were inspected by an
ἀνὴρ μάντις to discover the god's will. If the god consented, the consultant
descended into a cave where he consulted Trophonius directly (i.e., without
a priest or other intermediary). The oracle was active in the period of the late
republic and for several centuries afterward.   **gallos gallinaceos**: domestic
chickens. Cf. Plin., *Nat.* 10.49. Paus. 4.32.5–6 records a variant account of the
Theban consultation that does not include chickens. M. counters this example
by belittling the notion that so humble a bird would convey so important a
message and by arguing that there is nothing unusual about cocks crowing
at any time of day or night (2.56–7).   **nihil**: adverbial.   **avis illa victa**
silere soleret, canere si vicisset: Q. switches from the the plural *gallos* to the
singular *avis* because he is now talking about the species in general, rather
than a particular group of chickens. *Soleret* governs the infinitives in both
clauses. Note the chiastic arrangement and asyndeton of *victa silere soleret,*
canere si vicisset. This has the feel of an oracular pronouncement, concise and
balanced.

75 multis signis Lacedaemoniis . . . denuntiabatur: Although Q. has been
careful to include *signa* given to both sides at the battle at Leuctra, the
emphasis is on the portents of impending doom for the Spartans, in terms
of number (five signs sent to the Spartans, including three from Delphi and
Dodona, compared to two for the Thebans) and of placement: the catalog
begins and ends with dire predictions of Spartan defeat.   **namque et . . .**

corona ... stellaeque: *Namque,* a strengthened *nam,* introduces the next set of *exempla* as proof of the preceding statement. The following *et . . .-que* are coordinate.   **in Lysandri, qui Lacedaemoniorum clarissimus fuerat, statua:** Cf. Plu., *Lys.* 1.1–2, 18.1. Lysander led the Spartans to ultimate victory over the Athenians in the Peloponnesian War. In addition to being a symbol of Spartan supremacy, Lysander's statue is connected, through Lysander's claim of descent from Hercules (Plu., *Lys.* 2.1), to several other signs sent before Leuctra and listed in the passage. Q.'s positive assessment of Lysander matches that of C. in other works (e.g., *Sen.* 59) but contrasts sharply with the depiction in *Off.* 1.109, where Lysander is grouped with Sulla and Crassus as powerful men who stopped at nothing to achieve their goals. Similarities between the careers of Sulla and Lysander also struck Plutarch, who paired them in his *Lives* of famous Greeks and Romans. Lysander comes off the better of the two in Plutarch's *Comparison.*   **in capite corona subito extitit ex asperis herbis et agrestibus:** Cf. Plu., *Mor.* 397F. Grass growing in an unusual spot is taken by the superstitious to be a bad sign in Plu., *Mor.* 168F. For Q., the sudden appearance of the grass contributes to the impact of the sign. For trees growing *in capitibus statuarum vel aris,* see Plin., *Nat.* 17.244. At *Div.* 2.68, M. rationalizes this sign as the result of seeds dropped by birds.   **stellaeque aureae, quae Delphis erant a Lacedaemoniis positae post navalem illam victoriam . . . :** Cf. Plu., *Lys.* 18.1; *Mor.* 397F. Twin stars were used to represent the twin deities, Castor and Pollux, protectors of sailors and cavalrymen, by at least the fifth century (A. Hermary, *LIMC* 3.577 and 587, s.v. "Dioskouroi" nn. 114 and 233). Castor and Pollux were twin sons of Leda, queen of Sparta. Pollux's father was supposed to have been Zeus, while Castor was the son of the king of Sparta, Tyndareus. After Castor's death, Pollux pleaded with Zeus to let him share in Pollux's immortality. The battle mentioned here (*post navalem illam victoriam*) was fought between Sparta and Athens off the coast at Aegospotami in 405, and it brought an end to Athenian naval power. The divine twins made several battlefield appearances on behalf of both Greek and Roman forces (see *N. D.* 2.6 and 3.11 with Pease's commentary), the most famous of which is their simultaneous epiphanies at the battle between the Romans and the Latins at Lake Regillus in 496 and at the *lacus Iuturnae* in Rome, where they announced Rome's victory (D. H. 6.13.1–3; Liv. 2.19.3–2.20.13).

76 portentum: best rendered as "sign." As with *ostentum* in 73 above, to which *portentum* is often opposed (e.g., Fest. 284L), its original, technical meaning is lost. There were, in fact, four major categories of divine signs: *ostenta, portenta, prodigia,* and *monstra* (cf. 93). Scholarly efforts, both ancient and modern, to recover the fine distinctions among them have not resulted in any clarity. While the differences may have been of great importance to the *haruspices* as they decided how to respond to a sign, the Romans generally treated the terms as synonyms. Cf. Moussy 1977 and 1990; Engels 2007, 259–82.   **Spartiatis**: members of the class at Sparta that enjoyed full rights.   **oraclum ab Iove Dodonaeo**: Cf. 3n. *Pythio . . . oraculo*. Ancient sources mention six or seven different methods of consultation at Zeus's oracle at Dodona in Epirus; this passage is the only description of this particular ritual. See Johnston 2008, 60–72. The only practice attested archaeologically is the writing of questions addressed to Zeus or to Zeus and Dione (his female counterpart at Dodona). About fourteen hundred lead tablets survive preserving questions to the gods that could be answered with a simple yes or no. Johnston sugggests that sanctuary officials (a priestess in this case) put the questions into one jar and put pebbles or other markers indicating affirmative or negative responses into another. First a question and then the answer would be drawn. This is a more elaborate version of regular lot divination where it appears that only a single urn containing the answers was used (see Klingshirn 2006, 140–47).   ⟨vas⟩ **illud**: The word for the container that held the *sortes* has fallen out. At 2.69, M. refers to an *urnam*.   **simia, quam rex Molossorum in deliciis habebat**: *In deliciis habebat* = kept as a pet. The Molossi were a group of tribes in central Epirus, a region in northwestern Greece (see N. G. L. Hammond, "Illyrians and North-West Greeks," in *CAH*[2] 6, esp. 430–36). At some point after the mid-fifth century, they took control of the oracle at Dodona (Strabo 7.7.11). It is not clear why their king or, at least, his ape would have been present at the sanctuary, though it is possible that the high-ranking, public nature of the Spartan delegation played a role. Ape portents are not numerous in the ancient sources (see McDermott 1938, 149–53), and those recorded tend toward the negative. The conflict between Antonius and Octavian was, according to Dio Cass. 50.8.1, foretold by a disturbance caused by an ape in the temple of Ceres at Rome.   **ad sortem**: "for the drawing of lots."   **dissupavit**: "scattered."   **dixisse dicitur**: polyptoton.   **de salute . . . esse non de victoria cogitandum**: The Spartans are admonished for asking the wrong question.

77 C. Flaminius cons. iterum: Among Roman authors, the story of Flaminius's rash behavior and his flagrant disregard for the warnings sent to him before the battle of Lake Trasimene against Hannibal in 217 BCE became a favorite *exemplum* of the ill fortune awaiting those who do not properly reverence the gods. The Romans lost two-thirds of Flaminius's army and Flaminius himself. Most of the survivors were captured. The tale is recounted by at least fifteen different authors (references are collected in *MRR* 1.242, s.a. 217; see also Konrad 2004), most of whom include the portents mentioned

here. The most famous account is found in Liv. 21.63.1–22.7.14. C.'s source
is Coelius (on whom see 48n. *Coelius*; frag. 20 Peter = *FRH* 2.394 frag. 14b),
who is mentioned in 78 specifically as the source for the earthquake in the
north of Italy. Cf. *N. D.* 2.8. M. takes up this *exemplum* several times (2.21,
67, 71).   **rei publicae**: probably objective genitive, but the dative is also
possible (cf. *N. D.* 2.8).   **exercitu lustrato**: "after he had reviewed the
troops and purified them" (cf. 102; *Att.* 5.20.2 = *SBA* 113.2; *Fam.* 15.4.3 = *SBF*
110.3; *Phil.* 12.8; *B. Afr.* 75.1; Liv. 23.35.5). In addition to inspecting his troops
before beginning a campaign or a battle, a Roman general also performed a
ritual cleansing of his army. This ritual, the *lustratio exercitus*, comprised two
elements. First, there was a procession of a ram, a pig, and a bull around the
army or its camp (the area that defined the army as a unified community).
This was followed by the sacrifice, called a *suovetaurilia*, of the three animals.
The ritual is commonly depicted in Roman reliefs (see Moede 2007, 170–
72; Ryberg 1955, 104–19, pls. XXXIV–XLI, figs. 52a–61b). It most often
took place in the Campus Martius at Rome at the beginning of a campaign,
though it could also be performed in camp when the whole army was present.
At the conclusion of a census, the censors at Rome performed a lustration
of the Roman people nearly identical to the *lustratio exercitus*, also in the
Campus Martius; but instead of leading the people off to war, the censors
led them back into the city in a procession. The founders of Roman colonies
performed the same ceremony for colonial settlers, probably in the Campus
Martius, before leading them off to their new home. See Eckstein 1979, 91–
93; Gargola 1995, 72–82.   **castra movisset**: "he struck camp."   **Iovis
Statoris**: The message is that Flaminius should stay where he is (so Wardle *ad
loc.*). Jupiter Stator (the Stayer) is best known as the deity to whom Romulus
built a temple after the god stopped a rout of Roman forces by the Sabines
(Liv. 1.12.1–10 with Ogilvie's commentary; D. H. 2.50.3; Plu., *Rom.* 18.8–
9). Jupiter Stator had two temples in Rome in the historical period, both of
which were vowed by generals in battle. See F. Coarelli, *LTUR* 3.155–57, s.v.
"Iuppiter Stator, Aedes, Fanum, Templum"; A. Viscogliosi, *LTUR* 3.157–59,
s.v. "Iuppiter Stator, Aedes ad Circum;" *NTDAR* 225, s.v. "Iuppiter Stator,
Aedes (1)" and 225–26, s.v. "Iuppiter Stator, Aedes (2)."   **ipse et equus . . .
sine causa repente concidit**: The verb agrees with its nearest subject. The
stumble itself is unremarkable (as M. notes at 2.67), but Q. is careful to
point out that there was no explanation for it.   **nec eam rem habuit
religioni obiecto signo, ut peritis videbatur, ne committeret proelium**:
"and although that sign had been given, he did not, in contradiction of the
opinion of the experts, consider it an impediment to joining battle." **religioni**:
"impediment"; dative of purpose (*G&L* 356). See *OLD*, s.v. 2. **peritis**: It is
likely that the religious specialists, such as the *pullarius* mentioned in the

next sentence and possibly *augures* and/or *haruspices*, were already in the camp when Flaminius took over the army at Arretium from the previous year's consul.   **cum tripudio auspicaretur**: "when the auspices had been taken through observing the chickens"; cf. 27–28.   **pullarius**: a keeper of the sacred chickens. See 27n. *pulli*.   **pascerentur**: has a middle sense (*OLD*, s.v. *pasco* 6a).   **Flaminius**: Ellipsis of the verb hastens the pace of the sentence, illustrating the general's exasperation and impatience.   **vero**: ironic.   **signa**: He means the military standards. Each century (in this period, a group of sixty soldiers) in the army had as its symbol a *signum*, a long staff decorated with discs, wreaths, and other items and topped most often by an ornamental spearhead or a sculpted hand. In the next sentence, the military *signum* becomes a divine *signum*.   **signifer primi hastati**: the standard-bearer of the front line of the legion.   **nec quicquam proficeretur**: "it was no help."   **neglexit**: echoes *neglexit* at the beginning of 77. The object is easily supplied from the ablative absolute.

78 Coelius: Cf. 48n. *Coelius*.   **in Liguribus Gallia**: The asyndeton implies a unity of these two places and separates them from the other two items in the series (*compluribusque insulis totaque in Italia*).   **ut multa oppida conruerint . . . influxerit**: Result clauses in secondary sequence often take the perfect subjunctive to emphasize the completed nature of the action. The widespread, seemingly unnatural destruction is in keeping with Hannibal's dream at 49.   **Fiunt certae divinationum coniecturae a peritis**: picks up the *peritis* in 77. See 34n. *divinationum*. Q. had wandered away from the argument that he began at 72 (there are specialists who can interpret signs with reasonable, regular accuracy), but he returns to it here.   **Midae**: Ael., *V. H.* 12.45. Midas ruled Phrygia in the late eighth century.   **divitissumum fore praedictum est; quod evenit**: Within one hundred years of his death, he had become a legendary figure synonymous with vast wealth (Roller 1983).   **at Platoni . . . apes in labellis consedissent**: *At* introduces a new subject and contrasts two similar signs that carried different meanings. Although the story of Plato and the bees probably predates the late republic, this is the earliest extant version of it, also reported at Val. Max. 1.6 ext. 3; Plin., *Nat.* 11.55; and Ael., *V. H.* 10.21 and 12.45. Several later biographies of Plato contain fuller accounts (a full list of citations can be found in Riginos 1976, 17). The motif of bees settling on (or perhaps making honey on) the lips of infants as a sign of future literary greatness is widespread: similar tales are also told about Homer, Hesiod, Pindar, Sophocles, Menander, Vergil, and Lucan (see citations in Pease *ad loc.* and Riginos 1976, 19–20).

79 quid, amores ac deliciae tuae Roscius num aut ipse aut pro eo Lanuvium totum mentiebatur?: There is hendiadys in the phrase *amores ac deliciae* ("your darling love"; cf. 20n. *artis scripta ac monumenta volutans*), which is in apposition to *Roscius . . . ipse*. The combination of the two substantives is rare, appearing in classical Latin only in C. (*Phil.* 6.12, 13.26; *Cael.* 44; *Att.* 16.6.4 = *SBA* 414.4) and Gel. 7.8.6, and it often carries a mocking tone. At *Div.* 2.66, M. claims that the story about Roscius is fictitious. The comic actor Q. Roscius Gallus was one of two prominent men in this period from the town of Lanuvium in the Alban hills south of Rome (the other being T. Annius Milo, tribune of the plebs in 57). Roscius rose above the low status accorded his profession at Rome (see 80n. *ad leviora veniamus in Aesopo familiari*) and traveled in the most elite social circles, being on intimate terms with both Q. Lutatius Catulus, the consul of 102 BCE, who wrote flattering verses about him (preserved in *N. D.* 1.79), and Sulla (Plu., *Sulla* 36.2), who bestowed on him the golden ring that signified equestrian status (Macr., *Sat.* 3.14.11–13). Roscius appears frequently in C.'s works, often as the embodiment of physical grace and charm necessary for truly effective public speaking. It is possible that C. had studied elocution with him at some point (see Fantham 2002, 364–67; 2004, 83–84). Their friendship was close (Macr., *Sat.* 3.14.11); C. defended Roscius in 66 in a lawsuit brought by his former partner (*QRosc.*; see also Lebek 1996, 36–41).   **cunabulis**: *variatio* for *cunis* above.   **in Solonio [qui est campus agri Lanuvini]**: The relative clause is perhaps incorrect and certainly unnecessary (see Wardle *ad loc.*). Fest. 296L puts Solonium along the via Ostiensis that ran west from Rome to Ostia. It is possible that there was a second Solonium *aliunde ignotum* near Lanuvium, which lies about fifteen kilometers southeast of Rome. Either way, C.'s contemporary readers would not have needed the gloss: Lanuvium was a popular place for prominent Romans to maintain country homes (see Schultz 2006, 220 n. 48).   **puerum dormientem circumplicatum serpentis amplexu**: Snakes have thus far been signs of foreboding (36 and 72), but the snake here foretells future greatness. As with the story of the infant Plato and the bees, this is a common motif. In promoting this story, Roscius elevated his own status by putting himself in the company of Greek heroes, such as Herakles, who were also visited by snakes in their infancy; later on, the story was told about certain Roman emperors as well (see Pease *ad loc.* for sources).   **ad haruspices rettulit**: private *haruspices* for hire, rather than the prestigious diviners who were consulted by the *res publica*. Cf. 36n. *haruspices*.   **nobilius**: an ambiguous word that could mean not only "better known" but also "more noble (aristocratic)."   **hanc speciem Pasiteles caelavit**: Winckelmann rightly emended the manuscripts' *Praxiteles*, the name of a famous fourth-century Athenian sculptor, to *Pasiteles*, the name of a versatile Greek artist from southern Italy contemporary with C. and admired by Varro (Plin., *Nat.* 35.156). We cannot recover the scene Pasiteles depicted or the type of item he employed.   **noster expressit Archias**

versibus: The verses are lost. Nearly everything we know about Archias comes from the speech C. delivered on his behalf in 62 (*Arch.*) to defend him against accusations of unlawfully claiming Roman citizenship. Originally from Antioch, Archias became a Roman citizen through the efforts of the Licinii Luculli, the most prominent member of whom was L. Licinius Lucullus, consul of 74. C. had hoped that Archias would write an epic about his own consulship (*Att.* 1.16.15 = *SBA* 16.15), a project that the poet seems to have begun (*Arch.* 28) but that apparently never materialized.

79–81 Concitatio Animi

Without signaling a shift, Q. moves from technical back to natural divination as he turns to a discussion of inspired prophecy. The abrupt transition may be explained by the association of both artistic inspiration (Q. has just been talking about an actor, a sculptor, and a poet) and prophetic inspiration with *concitatio animi*. The relationship between artistry and prophecy is articulated below.

Quid igitur expectamus? an dum in foro nobiscum di inmortales, dum in viis versentur dum domi?: How obvious do the messages from the gods have to be before M. will accept them? Apart from a few earlier *exempla* (e.g., the Dioscuri at 75), Q. mentions waking visions only here and at 81. The small part they play in Q.'s argument reflects their relative unimportance in Roman religious life: there is only a little epigraphic evidence for the phenomenon (Renberg 2003, 27–67), whereas dream encounters with the divine are amply attested. Q. disavows waking visions in the next sentence.   **autem**: "but."   **tum . . . tum**: "first . . . then."   **nam terrae vis Pythiam Delphia incitabat, naturae Sibyllam**: Note the imperfect. On the cessation of Pythian prophecy at Delphi, see 38. The prophecies of the Sibyl were thought to date to the period of the monarchy at Rome (see Intro. pp. 7–8).   **quam sint varia terrarum genera?**: This builds on *vim autem suam longe lateque diffundunt* above. The implicit logical connection is that by permeating the earth with their power, the gods have created the geographical and climatic variety that was commonly believed to have influenced the development of national characters and cultural practices, including divinatory practice. See Thomas 2000, 75–114; Isaac 2004, 55–109. We have already seen how the terrain in Assyria affected the development of astrology (2), and Q. has just stressed (as he did earlier at 38) that the Pythia's prophetic power was derived from the peculiar quality of Delphi. Now Q. uses geographical variety to explain why some locations are more conducive to prophecy than others. At

Div. 2.96, M. turns the argument that geography shapes ethnic tendencies to a different purpose: he uses it to argue against the absolute determinism of astrology. **mortifera quaedam pars est, ut et Ampsancti in Hirpinis et in Asia Plutonia quae vidimus**: Plin., *Nat.* 2.207–8 lists several such sites, including the famous sanctuary of Mefitis, an Italic goddess strongly associated with sulfurous water, in the Ampsanctus river valley near the sulfurous lake at what is now Rocca S. Felice, in the territory of the ancient Hirpini in the central Apennines (see Edlund-Berry 2006, 175–79). Verg. (*A.* 7.563–71) describes the Ampsanctus valley as a place where the underworld and the surface of the earth converged. Commenting on Vergil's passage, Servius (*A.* 7.563 with 565) says that the stench of the sulfur was so strong that sacrificial victims did not have to be killed at the site: they died from the stench alone. *Plutonia* are caves thought by the Greeks to lead directly to the underworld because of the sulfur fumes they emitted. The plutonium near Hierapolis (modern Pamukkale in southwest Turkey) was a popular tourist attraction in the ancient world (Strabo 13.4.14; Dio Cass. 68.27.3; see also Ustinova 2009, 84–87) and would have been a small detour from C.'s route to the province of Cilicia in 51 BCE (e.g., *Att.* 5.13.1, 5.14.1 = *SBA* 106.1, 107.1; *Fam.* 3.5.1 = *SBF* 68.1). Although Q. did not accompany C. on that journey, he was with him for part of his time in Cilicia (*Att.* 5.11.7, 5.21.9 = *SBA* 104.7, 114.9) and may have visited the site at some point then. Or he may have gone there earlier, during his own governorship of Asia (see 8n. *Q. fratre*). **aliae pestilentes aliae salubres aliae quae acuta ingenia gignant aliae quae retusa**: The variety of environments is emphasized by the anaphora of *aliae*. **disparili**: an uncommon synonym for *dispar*.

80 The connection of this portion of the argument to what precedes is not obvious. The passage appears to develop the specific argument that environment can cause prophetic *furor* into a wider discussion of other factors that can produce the same effect. **Fit etiam saepe . . . saepe . . . saepe etiam**: Repetition stresses the prevalence of the phenomenon. **flexanima tamquam . . . in tumulis Teucrum commemorans suum**: Var., *L.*7.87 identifies Pacuvius as the author of these two iambic senarii, and it is generally agreed that they come from his *Teucer* (D'Anna 1967, 158; Artigas 1990, 129–31; Schierl 2006, 509–11), a possible source also for passages cited at 24 and 29. The identity of the speaker here is unknown, but the reference to *Teucrum . . . suum* indicates that the subject is Hesione, Teucer's mother, or perhaps his wife (see Pease *ad loc.*). *Flexanima* is a poetic word appearing only in one other fragment of Pacuvius (*De Orat.* 2.187), in Catul. 64.330, and in Apul., *Flor.* 3.1. Like many adjectives in Latin, it can be both passive (i.e., translated "turned in her mind"), as here, and active (i.e., translated "mind-turning"). *Tumulis* could refer to tombs, but given the strong association of Dionysus and his festivals with highland regions, it probably means "hills." The frenzy of the worship of Dionysus could bestow prophetic powers (Eur., *Bacch.* 298–301).   **illa concitatio declarat vim in animis esse divinam**: This argument is made elsewhere in the dialogue. See 34, 118; 2.27, 35, 117, 134.   **negat enim . . . Democritus . . . quod idem dicit Plato**: Cf. *De Orat.* 2.194; Hor., *Ars* 295–97; D. Chr. 53.1. See 5n. *Democritus.* The sentiment is amply attested in the Platonic corpus (e.g., *Apol.* 22b–c; *Phdr.* 245a; *Leg.* 682a, 719c).   **quem si placet appellet furorem**: *Si placet* is parenthetical. The antecedent of *quem* is *concitatio* two sentences above. It has been attracted to the gender of *furor*.   **ut in Phaedro Platonis**: *Phdr.* 244a–c.   **oratio . . . actio**: "style . . . delivery." *Actio* includes both physical movement and spoken delivery. On the distinction between these two terms, see *Brut.* 239; *Orat.* 54. Q. has already made a comparison between the work of the diviner and that of the statesman (24).   **vehemens et gravis et copiosa**: picks up *saepe vocum gravitate et cantibus ut pellantur animi vehementius* at the beginning of 80.   **ad leviora veniamus, in Aesopo familiari**: Aesopus was the greatest tragic actor of his day; see 23n. *Andromacham Enni.* The move from oratory to stage acting is logical: both professions required impeccable delivery, grace, theatricality, and persuasiveness. The close relationship between them is illustrated by Plutarch's claim (*Cic.* 5.4) that, in his youth, C. took Aesopus and Roscius as models for delivery. See Fantham 2002, 367–68. The two fields, however, were not treated equally. Oratory was the province of aristocratic young men aspiring to political careers; actors were often slaves, freedmen, or free non-citizens. Even citizen actors were liable to corporal punishment by Roman magistrates, a reflection of the fact that they did not enjoy full civic rights (Tac., *Ann.* 1.77; Suet., *Aug.* 45.3; Edwards 1993, 123–26). This discrepancy in status stems from a key difference in the relationship the professions were to maintain between words and thought. An orator's speech should reflect his own thoughts and feelings, whereas actors were expected to convey emotions and thoughts that were not their own. Therefore, the actor's techniques of persuasion and entertainment were useful tools for the orator, but only up to a certain point. In *De Orat.*(1.18, 129–30), C. makes it clear that an orator should project *gravitas*, the opposite of the *levitas* of a stage actor (Gunderson 2000, 111–48).   **vultuum atque motuum**: "of his expressions and movements." *Vultuum* appears to indicate that Aesopus sometimes performed without a mask, contrary to common practice.   **sensu mentis**: a difficult phrase that must mean something like "his mental senses" or "his mind's understanding" (so Wardle *ad loc.*). It also appears in *Att.* 4.3.1 = *SBA* 75.1; there is no need to follow Pease in emending the text here. Aesopus is reported to have so strongly felt the emotions of the characters he played that, on an occasion when he was acting the role of Atreus, he accidentally killed another actor on stage (Plu., *Cic.* 5.5).

81 Q. returns to the topic of divine epiphanies that he raised briefly at 79.   **quod contigisse Brenno dicitur**: *Dicitur* distances Q. from this story (as does *ferunt* in the next sentence), also reported in Paus. 1.4.4 and 10.22.12–23.10; Val. Max. 1.1 ext. 9; and Just., *Epit.* 24.6–8. When the Gauls invaded Greece in 279 BCE, Brennus approached the shrine at Delphi with an enormous force. The small number of Greek defenders, however, were encouraged by the vision of a young man and two maidens, taken to be Apollo, Athena, and Artemis (Diod. 22.9). The gods' visible presence is also recorded in two inscriptions from Cos and Delphi, discussed in Renberg 2003, 29–30.   **melancholici dicerentur**: Ancient medical specialists identified as *melancholia* a condition commonly identified in modern interpretations as depression. Its most prominent features were unfounded fear and anxiety, and it was strongly associated with exceptional intellectual or artistic abilities (Radden 2000, 3–51). C. equates *melancholia* with *furor* at *Tusc.* 3.11. In *EE* 1248a39–b3, Aristotle mentions the predisposition of melancholics toward prophetic dreams; but in *Div. per Som.* 463b12–18, he says that melancholics are prone to vague dreams. See van der Eijk 2005, 143–47. The most extensive treatment of melancholy in the Aristotelian corpus is in the pseudo-Aristotelian *Problemata* (30.1, 954a34–955a40), which Pease (*ad loc.*) identifies as a possible source for C. here. But the other works mentioned are more likely candidates (van der Eijk 1993, 225–28).   **ego autem haut scio an nec cardiacis hoc tribuendum sit nec phreneticis**: a cautious assertion, that is, "I do not know for certain that it ought not be ascribed to a digestive or mental condition" or "I am inclined to think that it ought to be ascribed . . ." The *cardiaca passio* is a stomach disorder for which madness was a symptom, whereas *phrenitis* is characterized by fever and mental derangement (Cael. Aur., *CP* 1.53–56, 2.161–64, 2.171). Aristotle discusses physiological causes of melancholy, but he does not refer directly to either of these specific conditions, nor does he cite them as causes of an enhanced ability to foresee the future (*Mem.* 453a14–31). Here, Q. does not directly contradict Aristotle's position on melancholic divination, but he questions a possible physiological explanation. This comment goes back to his remark at 60 that an individual's impaired physical state can bring about dreams that are *perturbata et confusa* rather than *vera*.   **animi enim integri, non vitiosi . . . corporis**: chiastic antithesis.

82–83 Reassertion of the Existence of Divinatio

This condensed, complicated passage can be broken down into five discrete
sections: (I) Q. establishes an initial proposition (*si sunt di neque ante
declarant hominibus quae futura sint*) and enumerates five (i–v) alternative
explanations for it, each introduced by *aut*; (II) Q. emphatically declares each
of the five explanations false, expanding his counterstatements to i, iii, and iv
with supporting arguments; (III) having eliminated all possible explanations
for the initial proposition, Q. declares that proposition false, at 83 (*non igitur
sunt di nec significant futura*); (IV) Q. then reasserts the first half of his initial
proposition (*sunt autem di*) as unarguable truth and concludes *significant ergo*
(this is a restatement of one of the basic tenets of Stoicism, that the existence
of the gods necessitates the existence of *divinatio* and vice versa; see 10n. *ut et
si divinatio sit, di sint, et si di sint, sit divinatio*); (V) Q. moves on to a second
argument (*et non, si significant, nullas vias dant . . .*) to prove the existence of
divinatio. M. refutes this passage point by point at 2.101–6.

82 Quam quidem esse re vera hac Stoicorum ratione concluditur: The
antecedent of *quam* is *divinatio*. *Quam . . . esse* is the subject of *concluditur*.
re vera: "in actuality"; modifies *esse*. **Stoicorum**: identified as Chrysippus,
Diogenes, and Antipater at 84.　　　　**at neque non**: introduces a series of
five counterarguments to the five alternative explanations just offered. Each
counterargument begins with a double negative that functions as an emphatic
positive.

83 non igitur: Q. declares the initial proposition false.　　　　**frustra enim
significarent**: a contrafactual apodosis for the unexpressed protasis *si nullas
vias darent nobis*.

84–87 Summary

Much of this section repeats in detail portions of both C.'s introduction to
Div. as a whole and Q.'s argument, especially at 12. This blending of voices
complicates efforts to distinguish C.'s personal opinion from Q.'s argument. The
main points reiterated here are (1) that the inexplicability of the link between
signs and the events they foretell does not mean that the link does not exist and
(2) that divination draws its authority from its extreme antiquity and from its
universal practice by the peoples of the world.

84 et Chrysippus et Diogenes et Antipater utitur: See 5n. *Zenoque et ii qui
ab eo essent profecti* and 6n. *Cleanthes . . . Chrysippus*.　　　　**si ratio mecum**

facit . . . : "if reason is on my side . . ." Q. thus begins to enumerate the major
types of evidence and authorities he has adduced, in a long series of isocola
that reaches a crescendo with a nod toward the political world (*si sapientissimi
viri qui res publicas constituerunt qui urbes condiderunt*). He stresses the
arguments both *consensu omnium* and *e vetustate*. At 2.81, M. mocks the
consensus omnium: it might be evidence of nothing more than universal
foolishness.   **an dum bestiae loquantur expectamus**: *Dum* + subjunctive
= "until." Q. expresses his growing exasperation, demanding to know what
kind of evidence his opponent needs to hear (cf. 79). For the Romans, a
talking animal was not an adynaton (an impossibility) but a rare occurrence
taken as a sign of divine displeasure (e.g., Plin., *Nat.* 8.183, 10.50; Liv. 3.10.6,
24.10.10, 35.21.4, 41.13.2).

85 quae . . . ratio quae causa: "what explanation . . . what cause." Q. has
repeated frequently that the validity of divination is established by the
accuracy of predictions even if the causal link between a sign and the event
it foretells is obscure. Cf. 12, 16, 25, 35, 109, 127.   **quid enim habet
haruspex cur . . . quid augur . . . quid astrologus**: Supply *causae* with *quid*
in each instance, reading "What rationale does the haruspex have to explain
why . . . ; what does the augur have . . . ; what does the astrologer . . ." This
passage, all the way down to *cur fiat quidque quaeris* at 86, is a long series of
anticipated objections from an imaginary interlocutor (as at 24, 37, 60, and
62), all cast as indirect questions, sometimes without an introductory clause
like *quid habet*.   **pulmo incisus etiam in bonis extis**: "a lung presenting
a fissure even among propitious entrails." Q. refers to a naturally occurring
abnormality and not to a cut made by the knife used to open the animal's
thorax (Pease *ad loc.*). In extant Latin, the phrase *bonis extis* appears elsewhere
only at 2.38. Positive *exta* are more often described as *laeta*.   **dirimat
tempus et proferat diem**: "interrupts the opportunity for action and defers
it to another day."   **cur a dextra corvus a sinstra cornix faciat ratum**:
The object of *faciat ratum* (validates) is an unexpressed *auspicium*. Cf. 12n.
Iuppiterne cornicem a laeva corvum ab dextera canere iussisset.   **stella
Iovis aut Veneris coniuncta cum luna . . . salutaris sit, Saturni Martisve
contraria**: This is one of the basic principles of astrology: Jupiter, Venus,
and the moon are essentially positive in their influence on future events,
while Saturn and Mars are negative (Barton 1994, 92–109).   **quid deinde
causae sit cur Cassandra furens futura prospiciat, Priamus sapiens hoc
idem facere non queat**: *Sit* is attracted into the subjunctive by the preceding
series of indirect questions. The asyndeton and the parallel structure of these
two clauses highlight the distinction between *furens* and *sapiens*. Q. uses
Cassandra as an *exemplum* of inspired prophecy at 66–67.

86 sed non nunc id agitur: "but this is not at issue at the moment."   **ut, si**: "For example, it is as if" (*OLD*, s.v. *ut* 6a).   **magnetem lapidem**: another undeniable yet inexplicable phenomenon in the natural world (cf. 13n. *Mirari licet quae sint animadversa a medicis herbarum genera*). The magnet was discussed by ancient writers, mostly as a novelty item used at dinner parties (an excellent discussion is found in Wallace 1996, 178–87). Philosophers often used the mystery of the magnet to make plausible other anomalies, such as irregular nouns (S. E., *M.* 1.226) and substances that can pull thorns and poisons out of the human body (Galen, *Nat. Fac.* 1.14.44–56 = Kühn 2.44–56, also available in the Loeb Classical Library volume by A. J. Brock). Plato (*Ion* 533d–e) uses magnetism as a metaphor for the power of divine inspiration that flows from the Muse to Homer and eventually to the audience.   **adliciat et trahat**: "attracts and draws along."   **quae nuper inventa est**: Philosophy, which has a history extending back six centuries before M. and Q.'s debate, is a relatively new discipline compared to the long-lived practice of divination at Rome.   **communis vita**: Cf. the appeal to everyday experience at 50.   **in quo modo esset auctoritas**: "provided that he had authority."

87 dixi de Pythagora de Democrito de Socrate . . . : In fact, the catalog of philosophers at 5–6 was presented by C. himself, not Q. The lapse may result from the speed with which C. composed this work: there are comparable errors in other works from the same period (e.g., *N. D.* 2.73; *Ac.* 1.46; *Fin.* 5.21). Even so, the nature of the mistake indicates that C. easily confused the opinions of the character Q. with his own, which suggests that they were not as far apart as has been argued. Where Q. has mentioned some of the philosophers listed here, his statements either have been neutral or have echoed the opinion expressed by C. in the introduction.   **unus dissentit Epicurus**: singled out by both Q. and C. for special derision. See 5n. *Xenophanes unus . . . reliqui vero omnes praeter Epicurum.*   **quid vero hoc turpius, quam quod idem nullam censet gratuitam esse virtutem?**: "Really, what is more shameful than this, the fact that the same man thinks no virtue is exercised without self-interest?" The colloquial double comparison using both ablative *hoc* and adverbial *quam* is found in other dialogues (*De Orat.* 1.169, 2.302; *N. D.* 1.38; *Fin.* 1.19). This is an *a fortiori* attack on Epicurus: if he was wrong about a matter so important as the nature of virtue, then surely he was wrong about divination. Q. refers to Epicurus's view of moral virtue as a means to an end, namely, pleasure (*Letter to Menoeceus* 132).

87–89 Hereditary Divination and Aristocratic Birth

Q. introduces two closely related themes. The first is the greater authority attributed to diviners of elevated social status and to those who could claim descent from well-established families of seers. The second is hostility toward low-class diviners who expect payment in return for their services.

87 eumque ducem classium fuisse ad Ilium, auspiciorum credo scientia non locorum: *Scientia* is ablative of means; *credo* is parenthetical. Q. paraphrases Hom., *Il.* 1.68–72.

88 Amphilochus et Mopsus Argivorum reges fuerunt sed iidem augures . . . : The combination of kingly and divinatory power is not uncommon (e.g., Romulus at 3). Amphilochus was a mythical member of the historical family of Melampodids, who claimed descent from another mythical seer, Melampus. Amphilochus served with the Greeks at Troy and afterward traveled with Calchas to Claros (Quint. Smyrn. 14.365–69). Calchas died after losing to another seer, Mopsus, in a mantic competition (Strabo 14.1.27). Mopsus founded an oracle of Apollo at Claros before he and Amphilochus immigrated to Cilicia, where they founded cities and another oracle at Mallus (Strabo 14.5.16; Herodot. 3.91.1). The nature of the relationship, if one exists, between the Mopsus of Greek myth and the kingly "house of Mopsus" that is attested for Cilicia by epigraphic evidence from the eighth century BCE is not clear. See Flower 2008a, 42–45.   **Amphiaraus et Tiresias**: Both figure prominently in Greek tragedies of the Theban cycle, where their advice to the rulers of the city (Tiresias in Sophocles's *Oedipus Tyrannus* and *Antigone* and in Euripides's *Bacchae*) and those who besieged it (Amphiaraus in Aeschylus's *Seven Against Thebes*. and Euripides's *Supplices*) is disregarded to disastrous effect. Amphiaraus is the father of Amphilochus.   **qui sui quaestus causa fictas suscitant sententias**: The source for this is unknown (Jocelyn 1967, 145). The bias against seers for hire, who might alter their predictions to ingratiate themselves with their patrons, is repeated at 92 and 132 and echoed by M. at 2.85.   **quorum de altero**: sc. Tiresias.   **solum sapere, ceteros umbrarum vagari modo**: a paraphrase of Circe's instructions to Odysseus at *Od.* 10.492–95.   **Amphiaraum autem sic honoravit fama Graeciae**: "Moreover, Amphiaraus enjoyed such fame in Greece."   **deus**: placed in an emphatic position before *ut*.   **atque ut ab eius solo in quo est humatus oracla peterentur**: The Amphiareion, the oracular shrine that stood on the site where Amphiaraus had been swallowed by the earth (Soph., *El.* 837–39), was at Oropus, a city north of Athens. It flourished in the fourth century BCE and continued to be a popular pilgrimage site through the Hellenistic period. C. was familiar with the shrine: he had been part of a senatorial committee that ruled, in 73, that the sanctuary was exempt from taxes because it belonged to a god and not to a mortal (see also *N. D.* 3.49; Ando 2008, 7–10; Petrakou 1997, 218–23 n. 308 = Sherk 1984, 85–86 n. 70).

89 et Helenum filium et Cassandram filiam divinantes: The prophecies of Cassandra (on whom see 66n. *ubi illa paulo ante sapiens virginali modestia?*) were ignored; those of Helenus were heeded. Helenus's skill in divination by bird signs is noted by Hom., *Il.* 6.76. Once captured by Odysseus, Helenus revealed to the Greeks that they could take Troy only with the assistance of Pyrrhus and Philoctetes (Soph., *Phil.* 604–13). After Troy fell, Pyrrhus followed Helenus's advice to return home by land and so avoided the shipwrecks that killed many returning Greeks.   **Marcios quosdam fratres nobili loco natos**: *Nobili loco* = "to a noble station." Q. slips some Roman historical material into a catalog of Greek mythical *exempla*. The introduction of the Marcii as a rare instance of inspired prophets at Rome elevates them to the status of the great prophets of Greek antiquity and, at the same time, equates legendary figures with those who are unequivocally historical. The most famous account of a prophecy of Marcius, apparently a member of the aristocratic plebeian *gens Marcia*, comes from Liv. 25.12.1– 15. In 212 BCE, two prophecies of Marcius came to public attention. Because one was recognized, in retrospect, to have predicted the disaster at Cannae, greater authority was granted to the second, which promised the removal of Hannibal from Italy if games were held in honor of Apollo. The episode gives us a *terminus ante quem* for Marcius, but more detailed speculation as to his identity (e.g., the assertion of Wiseman [1994, 59] that he belongs to the first college of plebeian augurs in 300) should not be taken too far. Under the emperors of Rome, a collection of prophecies of Marcius was kept in the temple of Palatine Apollo along with the Sibylline books (Serv., *A.* 6.72). Ancient writers are not consistent on the number of Marcii. While some later authors mention multiple Marcii (Serv., *A.* 6.70, 72; Symm., *Ep.* 4.34.3), most record only a single prophetic Marcius (Fest. 162L; Plin., *Nat.* 7.119; Macr., *Sat.* 1.17.25; Amm. Marc. 14.1.7). C. refers to multiple Marcii here and at 2.113 but only to one at 1.115.   **Polyidum Corinthium**: like Amphiaraus and Amphilocus, a member of the family of Melampus (Paus. 1.44.5). Polyidus is most famous for bringing back to life Glaucus, son of Minos (Apollod. 3.3.1–2).   **filio . . . mortem praedixisse**: *Il.* 13.663– 72.   **rerum**: genitive object of *potiebantur*.   **ut enim sapere, sic divinare regale ducebant**: "They considered divination as much the proper domain of kings as wisdom." *Ut* and *sic* are coordinating conjunctions (*G&L* 482.4 n.). Q. frequently uses *sapere* and *sapiens* in regard to political leaders (e.g., 28, 36, 84), and diviner-kings have appeared throughout (Romulus, Deiotarus, Amphilocus, and Mopsus). The kings of Rome combined supreme civil and religious authority, including the right to take auspices.   **privati**: After the kings were expelled from Rome, most of their religious responsibilities were divided among the public priests (the augurs, the pontiffs, and the *rex sacrorum*). Public priests were not elected by the people until the late republic but, rather, were co-opted to their office; that is, new priests were selected by current members of the priesthood. Thus priests who did not concurrently hold political office remained *privati*.   **religionum auctoritate**: "by the authority of their religious duties." A similar phrase is found at 92. On the elasticity of Latin *religio*, see 7n. *auspiciis rebusque divinis religionique*. The plural *religionum* refers to the priests' actions, not their personal beliefs (*contra* Wardle and Timpanaro *ad loc.*). Roman priests were not "men of god" chosen for the depth of their devotion and the closeness of their personal connection to the divine. Their authority derived from their expertise in religious law and their proper performance of the ritual obligations imposed on them by their office.

90–100 Divination among the Nations of the World

This passage embellishes sections 2–4 of C.'s introduction, where he emphasized the universal practice of divination among the nations of the world. The long catalog of national *exempla* is capped by a discussion of divination at Rome, reinforcing Rome's pride of place within the community of civilized societies. Q. also takes up the relationship between geographical variation and the variety of national divinatory practices first addressed at 79.

90 Eaque divinationum ratio: "And this organizing principle for various forms of divination." For the plural, see 34n. *divinationum*. The *exempla* that follow make it clear that the *ratio* is a combination of ruling power and divinatory authority.   **ne in barbaris quidem gentibus**: Cf. the similar statement by C. at 2.   **siquidem**: Cf. 47n. *siquidem*.   **Druidae sunt, e quibus ipse Divitiacum Haeduum ... cognovi**: A good deal of what we know of the Druids, the most prominent priests of Gaul, comes from Caesar's *De Bello Gallico* (*BG*) 6.13.1–14.6, which is based partly on an account of the Celts by Posidonius (see 6n. *noster Posidonius*; Rankin 1987, 49–82) and partly on personal observation and perhaps on information from Divitiacus (spelled Diviciacus in the manuscripts of Caesar) himself. Divitiacus, a close acquaintance of Caesar, was the leader of the pro-Roman faction of Aedui, one of the Celtic tribes in Gaul. The Cicerones probably first met him when

he came to Rome in 61 to ask for the Senate's help as his people resisted
German incursions on their territory (*BG* 6.12.5).   **naturae rationem,
quam φυσιολογίαν Graeci appellant**: The same gloss for the study of the
natural world (including physics, metaphysics, and theology) appears at *N. D.*
1.20 (cf. Vitr. 1.1.7). The importance of φυσιολογία to the Druids is attested
by Caesar, who lists topics they were expected to study and teach: *multa
praeterea de sideribus atque eorum motu, de mundi ac terrarum magnitudine,
de rerum natura, de deorum immortalium vi ac potestate disputant et iuventuti
tradunt* (*BG* 6.14.6).   **partim auguriis partim coniectura**: Cf. D. S.
5.31.3. On *coniectura*, see 12n. *animadversa et notata*.   **magi**: See 46n.
magi.   **congregantur in fano**: *Fanum* is used in its technical sense of
a sacred area open to the sky (cf. 48n. *quae esset in fano Iunonis Laciniae*).
Herodotus's statement that the Persians did not have monumental temples
(1.131.1–2; cf. *Rep.* 3.14 and *Leg.* 2.26) is confirmed by archaeological
evidence, at least down to the late fifth and fourth centuries BCE. See De Jong
1997, 94–97.   **quod etiam idem vos quondam facere Nonis solebatis**:
The Nones fell on either the fifth or the seventh day of each month. The only
other reference to a monthly meeting of the augural college comes from *De
Amic.* 7, where C. describes it as taking place in a private garden belonging to
one of the augurs. See Linderski 1985, 212–13. Q. has already lamented that
M. and his augural colleagues no longer rigorously maintain the practice of
their discipline (see 25n. *quae quidem nunc a Romanis auguribus ignorantur*).

91 huic scientiae: sc. divination.   **Telmesus in Caria**: There were two
places called Telmessus in the area that is now the west coast of Turkey: the
larger, more famous Telmessus in Lycia and this town (or, rather, collection
of villages; Q. overstates its prominence by calling it an *urbs*, prompting Pease
to assert [*ad loc.*] that C. had obviously never visited the place), the site of an
oracle of Apollo, who was thought to have established a family of priests there.
For a summary of the evidence, see Bean and Cook 1955, 152–53; Parke 1985,
184–85. Arrian claims that all the inhabitants of the region had the gift of
prophecy (*Anab.* 2.3.2–4), and he recounts numerous true prophecies by the
most famous diviner from Carian Telmessus, Aristander, who accompanied
Alexander (e.g., 1.11.2, 25.6–8; 2.26.4–27.2). Various forms of divination
are associated with the Telmessians, including extispicy, ornithomancy, and
the interpretation of dreams and portents.   **Elis . . . familias duas certas
habet**: Elis, in northwestern Greece, was the home of three of the four most
important families of diviners in Greece: the Telliadae and the two mentioned
here, the Iamidae, descendants of the prophet Iamus (himself a son of Apollo),
and the Clytidae, descendants of Clytius. The only prominent family of
diviners not from Elis is the Melampodidae (on whom see 88n. *Amphilochus*

et Mopsus Argivorum reges fuerunt sed iidem augures . . .). From at least
the fifth century BCE until the third century CE, the Iamidae and Clytidae
maintained hereditary priesthoods at the temple of Zeus at Olympia, where
they practiced divination by examining cracks in the burnt skin of sacrificed
animals. The priesthood provided employment for only one member of each
family in each generation; other relatives became itinerant diviners of high
status. Membership in a famous family of diviners implied access to secret
knowledge, years of apprenticeship under master tutors, and an exceptional
innate ability to perceive signs in the natural world. See Flower 2008a, 37–
50.   **in Syria Chaldaei**: Cf. 2n. *qua in natione Chaldaei non ex artis sed ex
gentis vocabulo nominati.*

92 de caelo tacta: a common idiom meaning "lightning
strikes."   **scientissume**: "extremely knowledgably."   **eademque**:
nominative singular; antecedent is *Etruria*.   **monstris atque portentis**:
more classifications of signs (cf. *ostentum* in 73 and *portentum* in 76), the
precise meaning of which cannot be recovered. See Moussy 1977.   **senatus
tum cum florebat imperium decrevit**: *Tum cum* = "at that time when." Cf.
Val. Max. 1.1.1b. This vague statement has generated a great deal of scholarly
speculation on the date of this decree (the major positions are summarized
in Wardle *ad loc.*). It is a reasonable conclusion that the decree was issued in
a year for which there is no extant account by Livy, whose interest in such
matters it would surely have attracted. Wardle rightly points out that *tum
cum florebat imperium* stresses the Senate's concern for Rome's relationship
with the gods in good times and bad.   **de principum filiis x ex singulis
Etruriae populis in disciplinam traderentur**: "ten young men chosen from
among the sons of leading families from each of the peoples of Etruria should
be given over to studying haruspicy." *X* is the subject of *traderentur*. The text
presented here follows Pease and Timpanaro and represents the best, if still
imperfect, effort to reconcile the manuscripts of *Div.* with what is known
about the peoples of Etruria and the *ordo haruspicum*. All the manuscripts
read *filiis sex*, but Val. Max. 1.1.1, clearly relying on this passage, records
the number of youths as ten (x). Ten young men selected from each of the
twelve *populi Etruriae* (e.g., Liv. 1.8.3, 4.23.5; Fest. 492L) would yield a pool
of 120, a number twice the size of the *ordo haruspicum* recorded in several
early imperial inscriptions (e.g., *CIL* 6.2161–62, 32439). The discrepancy
between 120 and 60 may indicate that not all of the young men trained
in the *Etrusca disciplina* practiced it officially. However, we do not know
if an *ordo* or *collegium haruspicum* existed in the republic (Rawson 1978,
140): Tacitus (*Ann.* 11.15) reports that the emperor Claudius proposed the
organization of a *collegium haruspicum* in 47 CE. Q. continues to emphasize

elevated social status (*de principum filiis*). Cf. 88n. *qui sui quaestus causa fictas suscitant sententias.*   **propter tenuitatem hominum**: "on account of a shortage of men."   **a religionis auctoritate**: See 89n. *religionum auctoritate.*   **Phryges autem et Pisidae et Cilices et Arabum natio**: The first three groups frequently appear elsewhere in *Div.* (esp. 2, 25). Arabs are mentioned again only at 94.   **significationibus**: dative with *obtemperant.*   **factitatum**: "was regularly done."   **Umbria**: a region on the central east coast of Italy. There is little written evidence for the indigenous culture of Umbria, whose inhabitants Pliny called the *gens antiquissima Italiae* (*Nat.* 3.112). By far the most important documents of Umbrian society are the Iguvine Tablets, a set of seven bronze plaques containing a liturgical text (including instruction for augury) discovered in the fifteenth century at Iguvium, modern Gubbio, where they are now on display in the municipal museum. See Ancillotti and Cerri 1997; Poultney 1959.

93 divinationum oportunitates: "circumstances suited to various forms of divination." For the plural *divinationum*, see 34n. *divinationum.*   **in camporum patentium aequoribus**: "on the wide-open plains"; a poetic turn of phrase. *Aequor* first appears in this sense in Ennius's *Annales* (124 Skutsch) and was imitated by Lucretius and Vergil.   **quod . . . hostias immolabant . . . quodque . . . de caelo apud eos multa fiebant, et quod . . . multa invisitata . . . oriebantur**: the three main areas of haruspicial expertise. See 3n. *haruspicum disciplina.*   **religione inbuti**: "filled with reverence." Roman sources often emphasize the devotion of the Etruscans to their gods (e.g., Liv. 1.34.9, 5.1.6; Sen., *Nat.* 2.32.2; Arnob., *Adv. Nat.* 7.26).   **propter aëris crassitudinem**: The causes of lightning and thunder were subjects of philosophical speculation from the pre-Socratics onward. Many of the hypotheses preserved in the sources begin with a thickening of air, which creates clouds that, in turn, produce the flash and rumble (as well as other celestial phenomena). The cause of the light and noise varies among, for example, movement of the clouds, the release of kernels of fire that the clouds have absorbed from the sun, or a cloud rupture that releases a hot and fast-moving wind. Cf. Lucr. 6.96–422; Sen., *Nat.* 2.30.3–4; Plin., *Nat.* 2.136.   **partim e caelo alia ex terra oriebantur quaedam etiam**: *Partim, alia,* and *quaedam* are all coordinated and dependent on *oriebantur. Alia* has replaced a corresponding *partim* (*OLD*, s.v. *partim* 1c). *Partim e caelo* refers to prodigious rains of substances such as blood (Liv. 39.46.5), meat (Liv. 3.10.6), or stones (Liv. 7.28.6–8, 22.36.7, 29.10.4–5). Somehow the thickness of the air in Etruria can also cause abnormalities to arise out of the ground, such as hot water flowing from cold springs (Liv. 22.36.7) and rivers flowing with blood (Liv. 22.1.10).   **etiam ex hominum pecudumve conceptu et satu**: Q. adds a third category alongside *e caelo* and *ex terra*. Common in prodigy lists are prodigious births, such as hermaphrodites (there is an excellent discussion and a collection of references in MacBain 1982, 127–35), humans giving birth to animals (Obs. 57), and animals of one species giving birth to another (Liv. 23.31.15). Other portentous events include changes of sex among humans (Plin. *Nat.* 7.36–7) and animals (Liv. 22.1.13), speaking infants (Liv. 21.62.2; Phleg., *Olym.* frag. 13), talking cattle (Liv. 35.21.4–5, 41.13.1–3), and animals appearing outside their usual habitats (cf. 73n. *examen apium*).   **quorum:** refers to *signa* generally.   **ut tu soles dicere**: On C.'s enthusiasm for Latin etymologies, see 1n. *a divis . . . a furore.*   **quia enim ostendunt portendunt monstrant praedicunt, ostenta portenta monstra prodigia dicuntur**: Similar etymological lists can be found in *N. D.* 2.7; Var. ap. Serv., *A.* 3.366; Fest. 122L, 284L; Non. 693–4L, 701–2L; Aug., *Civ. D.* 21.8; Isid., *Etym.* 11.3.2. For the difficulty in reconstructing these divinatory categories, see 76n. *portentum.*

94 campos et montes hieme et aestate: Note the *abab* arrangement of pastures and their respective seasons. Transhumance is a very old human activity, characteristic of most ancient Mediterranean societies, in which herdsmen keep their flocks in low-lying warmer pastures during the cold months and move them up into the mountains in the summer, seeking greener, cooler places.   **quos ante dixi**: at 91.

95 in optuma quaque re publica . . . quis rex . . . quis populus: Q. notes, as did C. in the introduction (2), that divination is practiced by civilized nations of all types. It is important that divination is not exclusive to less sophisticated, more ancient cultures, like those described at 90–94; it is also valued and practiced by the rulers of the most enlightened states.   **certamen et discrimen salutis**: "critical contest for survival." For rendering the hendiadys, see 20n. *artis scripta ac monumenta volutans.*   **omitto nostros, qui . . . [dum habent auspicia]**: The text presents the reading of the majority of manuscripts, but it is difficult to make sense of *dum habent auspicia. Dum* may be a corruption of *domi* (so Pease and Timpanaro *ad loc.*), which would make a chiastic arrangement, *in bello sine extis . . . sine auspiciis domi.* The sentence is close to C.'s statement in 3: *nam ut omittam ceteros populos, noster quam multa genera conplexus est.*   **externa videamus**: A similar transition is found at 46.   **divinos quosdam sacerdotes, quos μάντεις vocant**: There is ample evidence for the high prestige of the diviners consulted regularly by the Athenian Assembly and by the annually elected board of generals in the classical and Hellenistic periods (Flower 2008a, 122–31). It is not clear to what extent these individuals were supported by public funds, as opposed to being hired by prominent individuals privately. Some diviners were active in Athenian politics in their own right, such as Lampon, who helped found a colony at Thurium in 443/3, signed the Peace of Nicias in 421, and was a close associate of Pericles. **Lacedaemonii regibus suis augurem adsessorem dederunt**: *Adsessorem* is in apposition to *augurem*. As at Athens, diviners at Sparta enjoyed high status and were intimately involved in state decision making. The best documented examples come from a branch of the Iamids (see 91n. *Elis . . . familias duas certas habet*) that settled at Sparta and served the city over several generations (Flower 2008b). Tisamenus the Iamid was given the rare honor of being granted Spartan citizenship and went on to be one of the victorious commanders, alongside the kings of Sparta, at Plataea in 479 BCE (Herodot. 9.33.2–35.2). His grandson Agias assisted Lysander in the defeat of the Athenians at Aegospotami in 405 (mentioned at 75), perhaps even capturing the Athenian fleet himself (Paus. 3.11.5). **senibus**: the γερουσία, a group of thirty, composed of the two kings of Sparta and the twenty-eight men, aged sixty or older, who served as their council (Herodot. 6.57.5; Plu., *Lyc.* 26.1). **aut Delphis oraclum aut ab Hammone aut a Dodona petebant**: Sparta relied more heavily on oracles, especially that of Apollo at Delphi, than any other Greek state (so Parker 1989, 154–63 with Robinson 1992). Delphic Apollo approved both the Spartan law code (see next note) and the dual Spartan kingship, and he continued to advise the Spartan kings regularly through officials called *Pythioi*, whose job was to consult him on public business. Pausanias notes also the Spartans' special attention to Ammon at Siwa in the Libyan desert (3.18.3), and several Spartan consultations of the oracle of Zeus at Dodona are recorded (e.g., D. S. 15.72.3).

96 Lycurgus: the traditional, possibly mythical, founder of Sparta's laws and constitution. Sources vary as to whether these were given to him directly by Apollo at Delphi (Herodot. 1.65.2–4) or were brought by him from Crete and then endorsed by the god through his oracle (Plu., *Lyc.* 6.1). **quas cum vellet Lysander commutare**: Lysander, the victor over Athens at Aegospotami, wanted to change the rules for eligibility for the Spartan kingship so that he could hold the office himself (Plu., *Lys.* 24.2–26.4; D. S. 14.13.2–4). Aware of the radical nature of what he proposed, he sought endorsement of the oracle at Delphi and then, having failed there, tried equally unsuccessfully at Dodona and at the oracle of Ammon. **eadem . . . religione** "by that same oracle." **qui praeerant Lacedaemoniis non contenti vigilantibus curis in Pasiphaae fano . . . somniandi causa excubabant**: an unusual use of *excubare* ("to sleep outdoors") for the specific ritual practice referred to in English as incubation (sleeping at a shrine in order to receive instructions from the god in a dream). The practice is most famously associated with Asclepius, but it was used frequently at shrines of many other gods throughout the Greek world, where those seeking aid slept indoors. Sleeping under the stars is unusual. See Renberg, forthcoming, chap. 5). The imperfect tense of *excubabant* implies that the ephors, an elected board of five men who functioned as the chief administrative officers in the city, no longer regularly consulted the oracle of Pasiphaë at Thalamai in Messenia (Paus. 3.26.1 identifies it as an oracular shrine of Ino with a statue of Pasiphaë). There is epigraphic evidence that Spartan ephors consulted the shrine in the second century CE, but it is not clear whether this was a continuation or a revival of the practice (*IG* 5.1.1314–15 and 5.1.1317 with Cartledge and Spawforth 1989, 196).

97 Ad nostra iam redeo: Cf. the transition at 55.   **ad libros ire**: a form of the usual idiom (sometimes with *adire*) for consultation of the Sibylline books. Cf. 4n. *furoris divinationem . . . contineri arbitrati.*   **⟨quantis in rebus quamque saepe responsis haruspicum paruit!⟩**: "How often and about what important matters did the Senate heed the answers of the *haruspices*!" *Quam* is adverbial; supply *senatus* as the subject of *paruit.* The manuscript tradition places this sentence at the end of 98, but all modern editors restore it here.   **et cum**: The repetition of *et cum* (six times in this section) indicates Q.'s building excitement as he piles up *exempla*; it is matched in the following section by the repetition of *quid* to introduce five different sets of prodigies. In 97 and 98, Q. refers to twenty different signs that, he says, the Romans dealt with by consulting both the *haruspices* and the Sibylline books. To the extent that his claim can be checked against other sources, Q. seems to be correct (see MacBain 1982, 21–24). Many of these prodigies occurred multiple times over the centuries (citations are available in Pease and Wardle *ad loc.*); they were handled sometimes by *haruspices* and sometimes by the *quindecimviri*. In dire situations, it was not unusual for the Senate to order both groups of priests to be consulted. Agreement between the *haruspices* and the *quindecimviri* reinforced the authority of both groups and, of more immediate value to Q., of divination itself. The ultimate source for Q.'s list may be C.'s contemporary L. Cornelius Sisenna, who is explicitly cited as the source for five prodigies at 99. Sisenna's history, of which only about 140 brief fragments remain, dealt with contemporary events, beginning with the Social War (to which the prodigies listed in this passage pertain) and ending with the death of Sulla in 78 BCE. See also Rawson 1979.   **cum duo visi soles essent et cum tres lunae**: The parhelion (or sun dog) is an atmospheric phenomenon that causes bright spots of light (either one or two) to appear in the sky as light from the sun is refracted through ice crystals in the clouds. A parallel phenomenon, the paraselene (or moon dog), creates the appearance of multiple moons (cf. *tres lunae*). The *exemplum* of the double suns sets a somber, foreboding tone maintained throughout the catalog. The parhelion was always treated by the Romans as a sign of impending doom (e.g., Liv. 28.11.3, 29.14.3; Obs. 14, 32, 43, 68, 70). C. highlighted the parhelion of 129 in *Rep.* 1.15 and 1.31, treating it as a sign of deep division within the *res publica*, and again in *N. D.* 2.14, as foretelling the death of Scipio Aemilianus later that year.   **faces**: Cf. 18.   **e caelo fremitus auditus**: Cf. 35n. *saepe fremitus saepe mugitus saepe motus.*   **globi**: Reports of fireballs or disks in the sky (e.g., Sen., *Nat.* 1.1.2; Oros. 5.18; Obs. 54) are thought to refer to bolides, large meteors that explode in the atmosphere (see Stothers 2007, 84–86).   **delata etiam ad senatum**: The Senate at Rome was the ultimate religious authority in the city and for outlying areas under Roman control, including Privernum (modern Priverno).   **magna . . . bella perniciosaeque seditiones**: Given the frequency with which the prodigies in this catalog appear in the historical record, Q. need not have a single specific occurrence in mind for each item in the list. Wardle (*ad loc.*), however, takes *bella* and *seditiones* as rhetorical plurals and, pointing to MacBain's dating of many of the signs in this catalog to 117 and 91 (see 97n. *et cum*; MacBain 1982, 22), suggests that the phrase refers to the invasions by the Cimbri and Teutones and the Social War.

98 quid, cum Cumis Apollo sudavit Capuae Victoria: Cf. 16n. *Quid.* Both Apollo and Victoria are subjects of *sudavit.* This begins a second series of portents that were addressed by both the *haruspices* and the *quindecimviri* (see 97n. *et cum*). On sweating statues, see 74n. *in Herculis fano arma sonuerunt Herculisque simulacrum . . . manavit.*   **ortus androgyni**: The Graecism *androgynus* (man-woman) appears in republican and early imperial literature (e.g., Lucr. 5.839; Val. Max. 8.3.1; Liv. 27.11.4) but eventually gave way to another, more common Graecism, *hermaphroditus.* Hermaphrodites appear with surprising frequency in the lists of prodigies from the republic, with fourteen instances between 209 and 92 BCE (plus another two possible occurrences), always at times of great crisis. By the imperial period, they were no longer seen as prodigious but came to be treated as freaks of nature to be collected by the emperor, along with dwarves and other humans with physical oddities (see Dench 2005, 280–83). The best discussion of hermaphroditic prodigies remains MacBain 1982, 127–35. See also Brisson 2002, 24–40.   **quid, quod fluvius Atratus sanguine fluxit**: *Quid quod* = "what about the fact that." The location of the river is unknown.   **saepe . . . non numquam . . . interdum . . . quondam**: Q. orders this group of *exempla* from most to least common. Rains of substances other than water (including precious metals, bricks, fish, and frogs) appear frequently in prodigy lists (see Wardle and Pease *ad loc.*). Cf. 93n. *partim e caelo alia ex terra oriebantur quaedam etiam.*   **in Capitolio ictus Centaurus e caelo**: refers to a statue, otherwise unknown. Cf. 16n. *e caelo* and 19.   **Romaeque Pietatis**: "and at Rome, the temple of Pietas." Vowed in 191 by M'. Acilius Glabrio for his victory at Thermopylae in 191 (Liv. 40.34.4–6), this temple sat in the Forum Holitorium (Rome's vegetable market). If it has been properly identified as one of the three republican temples incorporated into the medieval church of San Nicola in Carcere, it sat next to the temple of Juno Sospita that appears in the next *exemplum.* Obs. 54 confirms that the temple was struck by lightning in 91. See *NTDAR* 290, s.v. "Pietas, Aedes (2)"; P. Ciancio Rossetto, *LTUR* 4.86, s.v. "Pietas, Aedes in Foro Holitorio / in Circo Flaminio."   **[quotiens ... paruit]**: See 97n. ⟨*quantis in rebus quamque saepe responsis haruspicum paruit!*⟩.

99 Caeciliae Q. f. somnio ... restitutum: Cf. 4n. *templum ... somnio.*   **modo Marsico bello**: *Modo* is temporal, meaning "recently." This is another way to refer to the Social War, in which the Marsi, a people from mountains of central Italy, played a prominent role in the fight against Rome.   **quod ... somnium ... mirifice ad verbum cum re convenisse**: "the dream corresponded to the event with amazing precision"; *oratio obliqua* dependent on *disputavisset.*   **Sisenna cum disputavisset ... tum ... disputat**: "although he had said that ... he says." When correlative *cum* and *tum* each have their own verbs and when the verb with *cum* is in the subjunctive, the *cum* clause often has a concessive force (*G&L* 588.2). On awkward repetition such as that of *disput-* (to which can be added another *disputat* in the next sentence), see 2n. *quid ... significaretur.* On Sisenna, see 97n. *et cum.* C. approved the style of Sisenna's work, more than its content (*Leg.* 1.7; *Brut.* 228, 259).   **ab Epicureo aliquo inductus**: Cf. 62n. *Epicurum igitur ... namque Carneades?* There is no conclusive evidence that Sisenna was an adherent of Epicureanism, and we have very little evidence for his philosophical and religious leanings (see Rawson 1979, 341).   **somniis**: dative object of the impersonal passive *credi.*   **ex occulto**: "from a mysterious source."   **quod haruspicibus tristissumum visum esset**: The antecedent of *quod* is *Lanuvii clipeos ... a muribus esse derosos.*

100 quid quod in annalibus habemus: Q. is no longer discussing Sisenna, who wrote only *Historiae*, a monograph covering a relatively short period of time rather than an annalistic history (Rawson 1979, 330–32).   **lacus Albanus**: This episode is a major element in the tradition about Rome's war with Veii (406–396). For accounts, see Liv. 5.15.1–17.10; D. H. 12.10–15; Val. Max. 1.6.3; Plu., *Cam.* 3.1–4.7. M. rebuts this *exemplum* at 2.69. The *lacus Albanus* (modern *lago Albano*) is a small lake in a volcanic crater near

ancient Alba Longa, at the base of the Mons Albanus (on which see 18n.
nam primum . . . perempta est). It is now overlooked by the papal retreat
of Castel Gandolfo.   **praeter modum**: "excessively."   **Veientem
quendam . . . hominem nobilem**: The aristocratic status of the informant
increases his authority. Cf. 92n. *de principum filiis x ex singulis Etruriae
populis in disciplinam traderentur.*   **ex fatis**: perhaps the Etruscan *libri
fatales*. Cf. 20n. *artis scripta ac monumenta volutans.*   **dum lacus is
redundaret**: proviso clause. When the adjective *is* follows its noun, it usually
serves a deictic purpose (*lacus is* = "that lake").   **lapsu et cursu**: "by its
trajectory and path."   **sin**: "if, however"; a conditional particle (originally
composed of *si* and *ne*) with a strong adversative sense.   **ex quo**: Cf. 32n.
ex quo.   **illa mirabilis . . . deductio**: *Deductio* refers to the draining of
the lake by an underground tunnel (*cuniculus, emissarium*) that still provides
enough drainage to keep the lake at a consistent level. The tunnel at the Alban
Lake is just one of a series of ancient underground man-made channels
running beneath northern Latium. It cannot be securely dated to the time
of Rome's war with Veii on the basis of archaeological evidence alone, but
the traditional date of the early fourth century BCE is possible (see Judson
and Kahane 1963).   **dixisse dicitur**: a polyptoton that appears also at
76.   **sexennio post Veios captos**: that is, 390.

101–8 Prophetic Utterances and Auspices

101 Fauni auditi: Q. continues on the topic of predictions related to the
Gallic sack of Rome, smoothly shifting from written to spoken prophecies.
The Fauni are vaguely defined woodland gods, famous for their prophetic
powers (cf. Lucr. 4.580–83; Verg., *E.* 6.27–28; Verg., *G.* 1.10–12; Verg., *A.*
8.314). Varro identifies them as Faunus and Fauna, gods worshipped by the
Latins (*L.* 7.36), and derives their names from *fari* (cf. Serv., *A.* 7.81). See
Wiseman 2006. Faunus is often associated with other rustic deities: Inuus,
Silvanus, and Pan (D. H. 1.80.1; Ov., *F.* 2.267–424, 5.97–102; Serv., *A.* 6.775).
Fauna is sometimes identified with the Bona Dea and Ops (e.g., Macr., *Sat.*
1.12.21–22).   **veridicae**: appears only a handful of times in classical Latin,
always in the context of prophecy.   **cuius generis duo sint ex multis
exempla**: The subjunctive stipulates a condition for the sake of argument,
akin to that at 42.   **non multo ante urbem captam**: Liv. 5.32.6–7 dates this
to the year before the Gallic sack and recounts that the divine warning was
heard by M. Caedicius, who tried to warn the *tribuni plebis*. The magistrates
shunned Caedicius, however, because of his low status (cf. Plu., *Cam.* 14.2–
4).   **exaudita vox est**: introduces both the indirect command *ut muri*

et portae reficerentur (an element of the story preserved only here) and the indirect statement beginning *futurum esse.*   **a luco Vestae**: Vesta's grove is otherwise unknown from literary sources. Artistic and archaeological evidence suggests that a symbolic remnant of the grove, perhaps only a single tree, was preserved through the imperial period. See R. T. Scott, *LTUR* 5.129–30, s.v. "Vesta, lucus"; *NTDAR* 413, s.v. "Vesta, Lucus."   **novam viam**: This ran from the Porta Mugonia on the northern slope of the Palatine along the base of the hill until, at the northwest end, it turned at a right angle toward the Velabrum, an area between the Palatine and Capitoline hills. See R. Santangeli Valenzani and R. Volpe, *LTUR* 3.346–49, s.v. "Nova Via"; *NTDAR* 268–69, s.v. "Nova Via."   **devexus est**: "extended down to."   **Aio Loquenti**: At 2.69, M. pokes fun at the god who stopped speaking as soon as he was named "Sayer Speaker." An identity between Aius Locutius (the more common form of his name) and Faunus (on whom see 101n. *Fauni auditi*) has been proposed by J. Aronen (*LTUR* 1.29, s.v. "Aius Locutius").   **quam saeptam videmus**: The altar of Aius Locutius, like many other public open-air altars, was surrounded by a wall.   **exadversus eum locum**: "opposite this place," that is, across the Nova Via from the *lucus Vestae*.   **ut sue plena procuratio fieret**: "an expiatory offering of a pregnant sow should be performed." This indirect command is dependent on *vocem . . . extitisse*, a construction parallel to *exaudita vox est* a few lines above. **sue plena**: instrumental ablative (cf. 42n. *exsacrificabat hostiis balantibus*). Although the warning came from Juno's temple, it is unlikely that Juno (or Juno alone) was the recipient of the sacrifice. The sow was an appropriate choice to expiate an earthquake: pigs were commonly (but not exclusively) offered to chthonic deities such as Ceres and Mars. A pregnant sow was sacrificed annually to Ceres and Tellus at the *feriae Sementivae* in January and to Terra Mater at the occasion of the Secular Games.   **ab aede Iunonis ex arce**: the temple of Juno Moneta on the Capitoline, vowed by L. Furius Camillus (usually identified as the son or grandson of the famous Camillus; see *MRR* 1.131, s.a. 345) during a war with the Aurunci (Liv. 7.28.4–6; Ov., *F.* 6.183–86; G. Giannelli, *LTUR* 3.123–25, s.v. "Iuno Moneta, Aedes").   **quocirca Iunonem illam appellatam Monetam**: Q. implies an etymological link between Moneta and *monere*. The temple was also the site of the mint of republican Rome (C., *Att.* 8.7.3 = *SBA* 155.3; Liv. 6.20.13; *NTDAR* 215, s.v. "Iuno Moneta, Aedes"), and *moneta* came to mean "mint" and "money." The *Suda* (s.v. Μονῆτα) combines these two threads (and changes the date of the episode), claiming that Juno advised the Romans to establish the mint at her temple in order to ensure success in their war against Pyrrhus (280–275 BCE).

102 voces . . . hominum, quae vocant omina: Timpanaro (*ad loc.*) suspects that C. is playing with a supposed etymological link between *homines* and *omina*. *Omen*, the technical term for prophetic speech in Latin, is more commonly derived by the ancients from *os* (Var., *L.* 6.76; Paul. ex Fest. 213L; Don., *Ter. Andr.* 200.1). The examples that follow are rebutted by M. at 2.83.   **Pythagorei**: Cf. 5n. *Pythagoras*. Pythagoras's interest in speech that foreshadowed events is attested by D. L. 8.20 and Iambl., *Vit. Pyth.* 149.   **omnibus rebus agendis**: ablative of circumstance.   **"quod bonum, faustum, felix fortunatumque esset"**: *Esset* is a jussive subjunctive. The collocation of near synonyms is a common feature of Roman religious language (cf. the response of the *coniectores* at 45). This exact phrase appears elsewhere only at Pl., *Trin.* 41, but variations are amply attested in both literature (seven times in Livy alone) and inscriptions dating well into the imperial period. It was regularly used at public assemblies by the presiding magistrate (see, e.g., Liv. 1.17.10 with Ogilvie's commentary and 39.15.1).   **ut "faverent linguis" . . . ut "litibus et iurgiis se abstinerent"**: indirect commands dependent on *imperabatur*. *Favere linguis* (*favete ore*, *favete vocibus*, *parcito linguam*) is an admonition to avoid words of ill omen by keeping silent, equivalent to Greek εὐφήμειν (e.g., Non. 693–94L; Paul. ex Fest. 78L, 249L; Sen., *Vit. B.* 26.7). At public sacrifices, a flute player (*tibicen*) was employed to help drown out potentially inauspicious noises. C. includes the injunction against *lites et iurgia* on *feriae* in his ideal law code in *Leg.* 2.19 and 2.29 (cf. *Leg.* 2.55). See also Macr., *Sat.* 1.16.9–11.   **inque feriis imperandis**: "in proclaiming holidays." *Feriae imperativae* were celebrated on dates announced annually by magistrates, rather than on a fixed date.   **in lustranda colonia . . . lustraret**: Q. refers to the procession of a ram, a pig, and a bull around the army or the people of a city or colony before the animals were sacrificed, a ritual called *suovetaurilia* (77n. *exercitu lustrato*).   **bonis nominibus qui hostias ducerent eligebantur**: *Bonis nominibus* = names of good omen (ablative of description), such as *Valerius* or *Salvius* (similar to *valere* and *salvus*). *Ducerent* is subjunctive in a relative clause of purpose.   **in dilectu**: "when holding a levy."   **primus miles**: To ensure that any undertaking began as positively as possible, the first person or unit called forth for a public reckoning needed to have a name with positive connotations. Presiding magistrates would summon first a man *bono nomine* for military service or census registration. Similarly, the region of the Lacus Lucrinus (seemingly derived from *lucrum*) was called first for tax collection (Paul. ex Fest. 108L). It was also considered a good omen if the unit chosen by lot to vote first in consular elections (the *centuria praerogativa*) had a fortunate sounding name. Cf. Plin., *Nat.* 28.22.

103 quae quidem a te scis . . . esse servata: The word order is somewhat jumbled. The connecting relative *quae*, the antecedent of which is the customs in the previous sentence, comes first; *a te* is then moved forward, out of the indirect statement, to emphasize that M. has taken part in these rituals himself; finally, *scis* governs the following *oratio obliqua*.   **summa cum religione**: "with the greatest scrupulousness." As consul of 63, C. presided over elections for the following year. In a letter to Atticus (5.20.2 = *SBA* 113.2), he mentions performing a *lustratio exercitus* in his capacity as governor of Cilicia at the military camp at Iconium in August 51, in preparation for a campaign against the Parthians.   **praerogativam**: sc. *centuriam*. C. makes much of the importance of the omen of the prerogative century in his political speeches (e.g., *Planc.* 49).   **iustorum**: "legitimate."   **L. Paulus consul iterum**: The year is 168, on the eve of the Third Macedonian War against Perseus. Although this story had probably been part of the tradition of the war for some time, it appears first here. Cf. Plu., *Aem.* 10.6–8; Plu., *Mor.* 197F—198A; Val. Max. 1.5.3.   **ea ipsa die**: *Dies* is feminine when referring to a specific time.   **ad vesperum**: "toward evening."   **filiolam ... tristiculam**: Diminutives are common in informal speech and contribute to the intimate feel of the episode. By emphasizing the young age of Tertia (note also *quae tum erat admodum parva*), Q. implies a guilelessness that strengthens the prophetic impact of her statement.   **Tertia**: In formal contexts, women were known by the feminine version of the paternal nomen (e.g., C.'s daughter was called "Tullia"). Within the household, daughters were referred to by a numerical designation marking birth order: Tertia presumably had two older sisters. In some circumstances, women of a particular *gens* were further distinguished from one another by the addition of the genitive form of their husbands' or fathers' nomina or cognomina, as in the case of Caecilia Metelli in 104 below.   **Persa perit**: The statement is prophetic because the puppy's name is close to that of the ruler of Macedonia, King Perseus. Naming pets after places was not unusual. See Toynbee 1948, 29.   **"Accipio ... omen"**: Omens, like prodigies, had to be accepted by the proper authority in order to be significant. As consul, Paullus had the authority to approve the omen on behalf of the *res publica* and did so, using the proper formula (cf. Liv. 1.7.11, 5.55.2, 9.14.8; Tac., *Ann* 2.13; Tac., *Hist.* 1.62).

104 L. Flaccum flaminem Martialem: The *flamen Martialis* was a priest of patrician stock dedicated to the worship of Mars. We know little about his duties, but the prominence of the priesthood is made clear in our sources: along with the *flamen Dialis* (a priest of Jupiter, the *flamen* about whom we are best informed) and the *flamen Quirinalis* (the priest of Quirinus, the deified Romulus), the *flamen Martialis* was one of three major *flamines* out of a group of twelve. The precise identity of L. Valerius Flaccus is not certain, but it is probable that he was the consul of 100 (*MRR* 1.577, s.a.; C., *Att.* 8.3.6 = *SBA* 153.6; Var., *L.*6.21), son of the homonymous consul of 131, who had served as *flamen Dialis*. Although Flaccus's own rank and priesthood make him an authoritative source, it is likely that his importance as the source for this particular story comes from some tie to the women involved. The tale has the feel of family lore: it deals with domestic matters that have no significance for the *res publica*.   **Caeciliam Metelli**: On the form of her name, see 103n. *Tertia*. It is possible that Q. here means "Caecilia, the daughter of Metellus" (cf. *ex Caeciliae Baliarici filiae somnio* at 4), but Val. Max. 1.5.4, following this passage, identifies her as his wife. She is otherwise unknown. Though not a widespread practice, it was neither unusual nor scandalous for a Roman woman to marry within her own *gens*.   **sororis suae filiam**: Though primarily the duty of a young person's parents, the search for a suitable match was often taken on by the extended family and circle of friends. The interest of women in their siblings' offspring was formalized by the festival of the Matralia, held in honor of Mater Matuta each June, at which aunts prayed for the continued well-being of their nieces and nephews (Ov., *F.* 6.559–62; Plu., *Cam.* 5.2; Plu., *RQ* 17 = *Mor.* 267e).   **ominis capiendi causa**: Caecilia and her niece go to the shrine for guidance in selecting a husband for the younger woman. This ritual, about which nothing else is known, is distinct from the *auspicia nuptiarum* mentioned at 28.   **puellam defatigatam petisse a matertera**: still dependent on *cum diceret* in the previous sentence.   **meas sedes**: Plural *sedes* is frequently interchangeable with the singular. Caecilia's statement is ambiguous: *sedes* can mean both a seat and one's home.   **deos non putare**: subject of *est*. Q. argues (as he did at 10) that this is the equivalent of *quae ab iis significantur contemnere*.

105 Quid de auguribus loquar: Q. shifts from an easily dismissed *exemplum* to a topic more difficult for M. to explain away.   **tuae ... tuum ... tibi**: Q. draws attention to the fact that he has to defend augury before M., the augur, and he stresses M.'s own role in the *exemplum* that follows.   **tibi Ap. Claudius augur consuli**: The chiastic word order presents M. and Claudius, consul and augur, as a unit. On Claudius, see 29n. *Appius collega tuus*.   **addubitato salutis augurio**: "because the augury of the welfare of the state was in doubt." Through the *augurium salutis*, the Romans asked the gods' permission to ask further for prosperity for the people (Dio Cass. 37.24.1–2).   **paucis ... paucioribus**: Q. stresses both the speed with which Claudius's prediction of civil discord (= the Catilinarian conspiracy) came true and the speed of M.'s response.   **decantandi augurii**: "droning on through an augury."   **collegae tui**: the other augurs, although C. was technically not yet a member of the augural college in 63. Q. takes a rather dim view (cf. 25) of Roman augurs of his own day.   **tum Pisidam tum Soranum augurem**: *Tum ... tum* = "sometimes ... at other times." On

Pisidian ornithoscopy (praised by Q. at 25 but a target for M. at 2.80), see 2n. *Cilicum . . . et Pisidarum gens et . . . Pamphylia.* Sora is a small town in Latium in the same region as C.'s hometown of Arpinum, originally inhabited by Volscians, but under Roman control by the late fourth century BCE. Nothing is known of Sora's particular affinity for augury, but many editors point to its proximity to the territory of the Marsi, whose augurs are too suspect even for Q. (132).   **ad opinionem imperitorum esse fictas religiones** "religious rituals were made up to influence the ignorant." On the difficulty of translating *religiones*, see 7n. *auspiciis rebusque divinis religionique.* The sentiment is repeated at 107.   **haec calliditas**: *Haec* is equivalent to *tanta*, to introduce the result clause. Cf. 35n. *calliditas.*   **religionis simulacra**: "sham rituals."   **sed difficultas laborque discendi disertam negelentiam reddidit**: Q. accuses M.'s fellow augurs of preferring to dismiss augury rather than undertaking the arduous task of learning the discipline.   **malunt enim disserere nihil esse in auspiciis quam quid sit ediscere**: The apparent sophistication of contemporary augurs is really mere laziness.

106 divinius: Cf. 57n. *divinius.*   **in Mario**: Very little of C.'s epic poem *Marius* survives: to this fragment can be added only another two, unconnected lines preserved in *Leg.* 1.2 and Isid., *Orig.* 19.1.20. The only other mention of the poem is in *Leg.* 1.1–5, where the *Marius* serves as the vehicle for a debate about the relationship between poetry and reality. Its date of composition is unknown; proposals range widely, with a date in the fifties seeming most likely. Arguments are summarized in Dyck 2004, 57–58. The placement of this fragment in the midst of a discussion of Romulus's augurate is awkward but can be explained as an attempt by Q. to transfer some of the authority of Marius's historical augurate to Romulus's. On Marius himself, see 59n. *C. Marium cum fascibus laureatis.*   **ut utar potissumum auctore te**: Q. again appeals to M. himself as the most authoritative source, a tactic that not only strengthens Q.'s position but also serves to draw the figure of the author closer to the argument for divination (cf. 17–23 from *Consulatus Suus*). For a different understanding of the decision to have Q. quote the *Marius*, see Wardle *ad loc.*   **hic Iovis . . .** : This passage takes as its model *Il.* 12.200–207 (cf. *Od.* 15.160–78). The motif of conflict between eagles and snakes is very old and widespread among ancient societies (evidence, mostly archaeological, is collected in Wittkower 1939). Homer's powerful image was taken up by many later writers, including Aristophanes (*Knights* 197–201) and Vergil (*A.* 11.751–56). C.'s version is very close to its Homeric and Ennian models. The first four lines of this fragment are close renderings of Homer's Greek, filtered through the vocabulary of Ennius (see below); thus C. elevates the conflict between Marius and Sulla to an epic level. But C.'s

snake, unlike Homer's, does not defend itself before it is dropped into the
sea. The change shifts the focalization from the snake (whose fate in Homer
presages the Trojans' defeat) to the eagle, strongly associated with Marius (see
Plin., *Nat.* 10.16; Plu., *Mar.* 36.8; App., *BC* 1.75). Q. has earlier linked Sulla
to snake signs at 72. The passage quoted here also has a strong resemblance
to C.'s translation of a fragment Aeschylus's *Prometheus Unbound* in *Tusc.*
2.24.   **Iovis altisoni:** a rendering of the Homeric phrase Ζεὺς ὑψιβρεμέτης.
Goldberg (1995, 142) points out that C. gives Jupiter an epithet that Ennius
uses for things (e.g., *altisonum cael, Ann.* 586 Skutsch). Ennian *altitonantis*,
used by C. at 19, does not fit metrically here.   **pinnata satelles:** that is, an
eagle. Cf. 26n. *aquilae admonitus volatu. Satelles*, a word that appears almost
exclusively in poetic contexts, is picked up by *ipsa* two lines below. At 2.73,
M. refers to *interpres et satelles Iovis.*   **arboris e trunco . . . subrigit:** "rises
from the trunk of the tree." The bird already has the snake in its talons (and
has been bitten) when Marius sees it. In Wardle's translation, the bird "swoops
down from a tree trunk" to attack, but in both the Homeric model and here,
the struggle between the eagle and snake takes place in midair.   **saucia:**
modifies *satelles.*   **semanimum et varia graviter cervice micantem:**
"half-alive, with its colorful neck glistening menacingly"; an imitation of
semianimesque micant oculi (Enn., *Ann.* 484 Skutsch).   **animos:** Greek
accusative.   **abiecit:** present tense, as is indicated by the short penult.
Cf. Lucr. 2.951.   **ecflantem:** "expiring."   **seque obitu a solis nitidos
convertit ad ortus:** The change in the bird's course to an eastward direction
represents a positive change in Marius's fortunes (cf. 28n. *sinistra* and 45). As
Wardle points out (*ad loc.*), C. has cast the image in proper augural terms.
obitu a solis: The unusual word order and the elision of *obitu a* create a line
of alternating dactyls and spondees. **nitidos . . . ad ortus:** Cf. 20n. *claros
spectaret in ortus.*   **praepetibus pinnis lapsuque:** "on favorable wing and
course." Here, as in the passage from Ennius at 108, *praepes* is used in its
augural sense of "favorable, boding well" (Fest. 224L), rather than in the more
general, poetic sense of "swift." Cf. Verg., *A.* 6.14–15 with Gel. 7.6.1–12; Ov.,
H. 8.38.   **conspexit Marius . . . augur:** Marius was probably co-opted (i.e.,
chosen by the current members) into the augural college in 97. See *ad Brut.*
1.5.3 = *SBQ Brut.* 9.3; *MRR* 2.8–9, s.a. 97.   **partibus . . . sinistris:** Cf. 28n.
sinistra.

107 atque ille Romuli auguratus pastoralis non urbanus fuit: Q. returns
to the discussion he left at 105, echoing a sentiment expressed first by C.
in the introduction (2), that urbane refinement is antithetical to belief in
divination.   **apud Ennium:** The passage that follows, *Ann.* 72–91 Skutsch,
is linked to the previous episode by its emphasis on *aves praepetes appearing*
on the left. Drawing on another fragment of Ennius, quoted by Varro (*R.*

3.1.2) and Suetonius (*Aug.* 7.2 = *Ann.* 155 Skutsch), scholars identify the sign sent to Romulus in this fragment as the *augurium augustum*. **curantes magna cum cura tum cupientes | regni**: "diligently taking care and desirous of rule." Note the polyptoton of *curantes . . . cum cura*. **auspicio augurioque**: datives with *dant operam*. These are two separate actions (*contra* Skutsch *ad loc.*). The twins needed to perform the act of auspication (ensuring that the gods approved that day for the founding of the city) before they could perform the act of inauguration at the site, that is, the founding of the city itself. See 28n. *multa auguria multa auspicia*. **in monte | "Remus auspicio se devovet atque secundam**: This appears as a single line in the manuscripts, but it is too long for hexameter, and the vague *in monte* does not balance the specific *in alto . . . Aventino* in the next two lines. Many editors have tried to resolve the problem by removing *in monte* from the line and attributing the phrase to Q. Skutsch (followed by Jocelyn 1971, 60–61; Wiseman 1995, 7; and Schäublin and Wardle *ad loc.*) replaces *in monte* with *in Murco*, a name given to part of the Aventine originally identified as a separate hill. **se devovet**: This probably means "committed himself (to an extreme degree, to the point of being willing to die)"; cf. *TLL* 5.882.57–58, s.v. *devoveo* IIA. Cf. similar uses at *Dom.* 145 and *Red.* 1, where the notions of extraordinary, complete commitment and self-sacrifice are at play but the specific ritual of *devotio* is not. There is no need to alter the text (*contra* Skutsch and Wardle *ad loc.*). Even if this phrase is used in its technical sense (cf. 51n. *devovit se*), we are to understand that Remus "made a bargain with the underworld gods, according to which they were either to help him to the kingship by giving a certain auspice or to claim him for their own" (Jocelyn 1971, 63, accepted by Wiseman 1995, 12–13). **servat**: "watches for." **Romulus pulcher**: Cf. 40n. *homo pulcher*. **in alto . . . Aventino**: Serv., *A.* 3.46 confirms that this is not a textual error but in fact represents an alternate tradition to the more widely known version that puts Romulus on the Palatine (Liv. 1.6.4; D. H. 1.86.2; Ov., *F.* 4.815–18). **genus altivolantum**: not an augural phrase, but a poetical alternative to *avem* (so Skutsch *ad loc.*). *Altivolans* is a calque on ὑψιπέτης. **certabant urbem Romam Remoramne vocarent**: Ennius shifts from the present to the imperfect tense because he now describes an earlier situation that led to the event in the previous four lines. The name of Remus's proposed city is preserved only here, possibly coined by Ennius (so Skutsch and Timpanaro *ad loc.*). It was common in the ancient world to derive the name of a city from its founder, not just in the case of mythological founders (e.g., Ilium from *Ilus* and Rome from *Romulus*; cf. Paul. ex Fest 327L), but also in the case of historical individuals, such as Alexander the Great (Alexandria) and Constantine (Constantinople). Remus's name was thought to be related to *remorari* (*Origo* 21.4; Fest. 344L). In a variant tradition, Remor(i)a/Remuria is the location where Remus wanted to found his city and where he was later

buried (D. H. 1.85.6–87.2; *Origo* 23; Paul. ex Fest. 345). It is sometimes located
on the Aventine hill (Plu., *Rom.* 9.4), but other sources put it about five miles
from Rome along the Tiber (*Origo* 23.1; D. H. 1.85.6). The debate has not yet
been settled. Wiseman (1995, 114–17) would put Remuria on the *Mons Sacer*,
Coarelli (2003) in the Grove of the Dea Dia maintained by the Arval Brethren
on the outskirts of Rome. It is odd that no ancient source connects Remus or
Remor(i)a to the *remores aves* mentioned at Paul. ex Fest. 345: *remores aves in
auspicio dicuntur, quae acturum aliquid remorari conpellunt.*   **induperator**:
This alternate form of *imperator* is a neologism used for metrical reasons. The
archaic preposition *endo* (*indu*) = *in*. The heavy, archaizing sound made this
form attractive to Lucretius, but not to Vergil.   **exspectant, veluti consul
cum mittere signum / volt**: The subject of *exspectant* must be the followers
of Romulus and Remus whose presence was introduced by Ennius before this
fragment picks up. The magistrate presiding over public games would signal
the start of the horse-racing competition by dropping a cloth from a balcony
that sat above the *carceres* (e.g., Var., *L.* 5.153). This vivid image, which, unlike
most of Ennius's similes, seems to have no Greek model (Skutsch *ad loc.*),
is particularly apt here since everyone is waiting for Jupiter to give a sign
(*signum mittere*).   **ad carceris oras**: "toward the starting gate."

108 ore timebat / rebus: "on their faces they show fear for the situation."
Rebus is dative of reference with *timebat*.   **magni . . . regni**: objective
genitive with *victoria*.   **sol albus**: probably the morning star, which rises
a few hours before the sun; see Jocelyn 1971, 70–72. Augurs slept outside on
the night before taking the auspices, then arose and watched the skies in the
hours between first light and the rising of the sun (*aureus . . . sol* below), a
time when birds are especially active (e.g., Lucr. 2.144–56; Verg., *A.* 7.25–34).
On the timing of augural observation, see Vaahtera 2001, 114–16; Linderski
2006, 90.   **exin candida se radiis dedit icta foras lux**: "Then white light
gave itself forth, struck by rays." Skutsch points out that rays of the sun are
not seen. Rather, something is struck (the vault of the heavens?) by them and
radiates light.   **longe pulcherruma praepes / laeva volavit avis**: As the
sky begins to glow with the light of the sun, Remus receives an unequivocally
positive sign. *Pulcher praepes*, an asyndetic augural formula, is repeated
three lines below and appears also in Enn., *Ann.* 457 Skutsch. **laeva volavit
avis**: Note alliteration of *l* and *v* and assonance with *a*.   **simul aureus
exoritur sol**: Romulus receives his sign after the orb of the sun is visible in the
sky.   **cedunt de caelo ter quattuor corpora sancta**: Note the alliteration of
c and *t*. *Ter quattuor* is a periphrasis for the unmetrical *duodecim*.   **data . . .
esse priora**: not prior in time, but preeminent in rank. See Pease and Wardle

ad loc.   **auspicio regni stabilita scamna solumque**: "the throne and the
land of the kingdom had been confirmed by the auspices." *Stabilita* agrees
with *scamna* but has a long final syllable (see Skutsch, p. 57 and *ad loc.*).
Scamnum has two meanings, both at play here. A *scamnum* is something
that gives support from underneath, for example, a footstool or the pedestal
of a throne (cf. Cat., *Agr.* 10–14; Var., *L.* 5.168). In an agricultural context,
scamnum refers to land between two furrows and, by extension, to the
breadthwise dividing lines marking out parcels of land (Frontin., *De Agrorum
Qualitate* 10 with Dilke 1971, 94–95).

109–31 *The Causae of Divination*

Q. again dismisses the need for any sort of *ratio* (as at 12–16, 35, and 85–87),
but he goes on to recapitulate much of what he has already said about the
causes of divination. Only at 125, almost at the very end of his defense, does
Q. finally enumerates these causes: *a deo*, *a fato*, and *a natura*. He has already
addressed the first and third: he established divination as a result of the gods'
concern for mankind most fully at 82–84, and he has developed aspects of the
argument *a natura* (divination arises from the physical nature of the universe
and of the mortal soul) at 38, 60–71, and 79–81. His earlier treatment of the
ratio a natura focused on natural divination; here he expands the argument to
cover technical divination as well. The *ratio a fato*, which overlaps somewhat
with the *ratio a natura*, is introduced here. C. reserves extensive treatment of
the issue of fate for a separate dialogue, *De Fato*.

109 eodem: refers to the argument at 85.   **Epicuro Carneadive**:
Cf. 62n. *Epicurum igitur . . . namque Carneades.*   **divinae**: "divinely
inspired."   **observatione diuturna**: The same phrase appears at 2. Cf.
longinqua observatione below.

110 ut ante dixi: Cf. 11n. *duo . . . divinandi genera.*   **physica disputandi
subtilitate**: "the subtle arguments of natural philosophy."   **ad naturam
deorum, a qua . . . haustos animos et libatos habemus**: Q. made
this argument about the nature of the mortal soul at 64 (see n. *quippe
qui deorum cognatione teneatur*) and 70. M. repeats this definition at
2.26.   **mente divina**: C. often uses this phrase for divine intelligence
in his philosophical works, as at *Sen.* 78 and *Leg.* 1.23. In his speeches, it
usually refers to exceptional human perceptiveness (e.g., *Mil.* 21; *Rab.* 29;
Phil. 3.3).   **cognatione**: This correction of the manuscripts' *cognitione* is

preferred by most editors over the alternative emendation *contagione*. At 64, Q. follows Posidonius in attributing the soul's prophetic power to its *deorum cognatione*.

111 rarum est quoddam genus: introduces a digression (through the end of 113) on the distinction between two different causes of foreknowledge: one is the result of an exceptional level of scientific understanding, and the other is truly the result of divine inspiration. Only the latter is really divination. **horum sunt auguria non divini impetus sed rationis humanae**: *Auguria* is used in a non-technical sense, equivalent to "predictions." Cf. 3n. *optumus augur*. As examples of professions whose foreknowledge is scientific (rather than inspired, like that of seers and other diviners), Q. names the same professions that were grouped with (rather than distinguished from) divination at 24 as *artes* that rely on the subjective interpretation of signs. **deflagrationem futuram aliquando caeli atque terrarum**: The substantive *deflagratio* is very rare, appearing only a handful of times in classical Latin—all in C. The Stoic concept of ἐκπύρωσις dictated that the entire universe would be reduced to fire and that a new universe would arise from it when all the celestial bodies returned to their exact original positions (an interval lasting 12,960 years; see de Callataÿ 1996, 1–58). **ut de Atheniensi Solone accepimus**: The early sixth-century lawgiver of Athens is credited with having foreseen the tyranny of Pisistratus (Val. Max. 5.3 ext. 3b; Plu., *Solon* 29.3). **prudentes . . . id est providentes**: Cf. 24n. *prudentia.* **Milesium Thalem**: like Solon, one of the Seven Sages, a group of philosophers and statesmen of the late seventh and early sixth centuries considered to be the wisest men in the Greek world (see Pl., *Protag.* 343a; C., *Rep.* 1.12). For this story with some variation of detail, see Arist., *Pol.* 1.4.5 = 1259a; D. L. 1.26; Plin., *Nat.* 18.273 (where the feat is attributed to Democritus).

112 quae Astyage regnante facta est: The date of the eclipse is generally agreed to be 585 BCE. The *locus classicus* for this story is Herodot. 1.74, which identifies the Median king as Cyaxares, the father of Astyages. For more detailed discussion of the difficulties of chronology and of how Thales may have made the prediction, see Wardle *ad loc.* **ab Anaximandro physico**: Anaximander of Miletus (d. c. 547) was thought to have been a pupil of Thales and is most famous for having invented the *gnomon*, the piece of a sundial that casts a shadow to mark time. He was also the first to make a map of the earth and sea (D. L. 2.1–2) and the first Greek to write a prose treatise on natural history. The only other source for this story is Plin.,

Nat. 2.191, which relies on this passage.   **armatique**: The inclusion of this detail prompted Pease (*ad loc.*) and others to identify the earthquake predicted by Anaximander with one recorded by several sources (e.g., Thuc. 1.101; D. S. 11.63.1; Plu., *Cim.* 16.4–5) during the revolt of the helots in 464, a date well after Anaximander's death. The chronological difficulties cannot be surmounted. Either Q. has attributed the prediction to the wrong natural philosopher, or there is some other explanation (now lost) for the weapons.   **terrae motus instaret**: Earlier references to earthquakes (35, 78, 101) have dealt with their interpretation after the fact as signs of impending disaster. Their appearance here as a regular, predictable phenomenon of the natural world illustrates the difficulty, amply exploited by M. in Book 2, of determining whether or not an unusual event is indeed a predictive sign.   **Pherecydes . . . Pythagorae magister**: another sixth-century figure, whose floruit seems to have been about a generation later than Anaximander. It is not certain whether claims that he taught Pythagoras are accurate: the two may have been linked in the tradition solely on the basis of their shared belief in the immortality of the soul. Pherecydes's predictive powers were famous (e.g., D. L. 1.116–18; additional sources for this tale are collected in Wardle *ad loc.*). He also authored a prose work titled *On Nature* and a genealogy of the gods.   **de iugi puteo**: "from a well of ever-flowing water," that is, a spring-fed well as opposed to a groundwater well (one dug deeply enough to reach the water table). Water from this latter type is stagnant and often has an unpleasant taste, like the water from cisterns. Cf. Hor., *Epist.* 1.15.15–16 and *Sat.* 2.6.1–3.

113 ea duo genera a Dicaearcho probantur et ut dixi a Cratippo nostro: It was actually C. who noted this in the introduction (5), which makes this another instance of the difficulty even C. had in keeping separate the authorial voice and the voice of Q.'s character.   **si propterea**: refers back to the previous sentence (that Dicaearchus and Cratippus approve of these two types of divination).   **sint summa sane**: The subjunctive indicates a concession for the sake of argument; that is, "we might well consider them the best." Cf. 42n. *sit sane etiam illud commenticium*.   **modo ne**: C. is particularly fond of this unusual form of the negative proviso.   **putant . . . tollunt**: Dicaearchus and Cratippus are the subjects.   **vitae ratio**: "guiding principle of life"; refers not only to the service of augurs and haruspices to the state but also to the myriad forms of divination that shaped quotidian decision making at all levels of society. This phrase, appearing first in Lucretius (1.105, 5.9), is rare in classical Latin and is restricted almost entirely to philosophical and moralizing texts.   **dant**: Dicaearchus and Cratippus are still the

subjects.   [**vaticinationes cum somniis**]: All modern editors identify this
awkward phrase as a gloss.   **nihil est quod**: "there is no reason that"; cf.
G&L 525.1 n. 2.

114 Ergo et: returns to the discussion of natural divination at the end
of 110.   **ardore aliquo inflammati**: The first subcategory of natural
divination to be explained is inspired prophecy.   **qui sono quodam
vocum et Phrygiis cantibus incitantur**: Cf. 80. Among the ancients, musical
forms (or modes) were identified by their geographical origins—Lydian,
Dorian, Ionian, and so on—and each was thought to have its own particular
psychological effect. The Phrygian mode was generally thought to evoke a
passionate, frenzied response. Aristotle (*Pol.* 8.7.9–10 = 1342b) describes
it as exciting and emotional, suitable to Bacchic frenzy. Phrygian rhythms
were a key element in the ecstasy of Cybele's worshippers (Lucr. 2.618–
23).   "**eheu videte . . .** : Cassandra is the speaker in this fragment from
Ennius's *Alexander* (on which see 42n. *mater gravida . . .* with Jocelyn 1967,
217–20); the passage is from a later point in the play than the fragment
quoted at 67 (cf. 2.112).   **iudicavit . . . adveniet**: This is the unanimous
manuscript reading, and it should be preserved. The shift in tense has
caused some editors (e.g., Pease) to change the perfect to *iudicabit*, but other
fragmentary prophecies from the same play are also expressed in the perfect
tense (see Jocelyn 1967, 80–81). C. writes as if he understood this whole
passage to refer to the future.   **Lacedaemonia mulier**: Helen.   **verbis**:
To make sense of the contrast with *versibus* below, this must mean "in prose,"
even though this use is unattested elsewhere.   **versibus quos olim Fauni
vatesque canebant**: from Ennius's *Annales* (207 Skutsch; cf. C., *Brut.* 71, 75;
C., *Orat.* 171; *Origo* 4.5); identified as part of the proem to Book VII, in which
Ennius seems to have distanced himself from the Saturnians (the *versibus*
here) of Naevius. Cf. 101n. *Fauni auditi.*

115 Marcius et Publicius vates: See 89n. *Marcios quosdam fratres
nobili loco natos.* Publicius (mentioned again at 2.113) is otherwise
unknown.   **anhelitus quosdam fuisse**: This issue was addressed
at 38.   **Atque haec quidem vatium ratio est, nec dissimilis sane
somniorum**: introduces a discussion that closely follows that at 60–
67.   **qui quia vixit ab omni aeternitate**: *Qui = animus.* The source for
this passage has long been debated. Since the notion of an eternal, individual
soul is not Stoic (Glucker 1999, 31–32 n. 5), Posidonius or any other Stoic
is unlikely to be C.'s source. The Stoics believed that the soul was born and
later died (on which see 111n. *deflagrationem futuram aliquando caeli
atque terrarum*). Because both Plato and Pythagoras argue for an immortal

soul, Glucker (1999) suggests that C. is relying on a "Pythagoreanizing Platonist" whose identity is now lost. Building on some of the key points of Glucker's argument, Tarrant (2000) identifies Cratippus as the source.   **innumerabilibus animis**: The idea seems to be that individual souls can communicate with each other and share their knowledge.

116 sunt enim explanatores, ut grammatici poetarum: Cf. 34n. *ut grammatici poetarum*. This phrase is marked as a gloss by Pease and Schäublin because it repeats almost verbatim what Q. said at 34, but Timpanaro and Wardle rightly point out that this passage is rife with repetition of earlier sections and that *explanator* ("one who explains"), which does not appear in the earlier passage, is a Ciceronian word unlikely to have occurred to an ancient commentator. Indeed, *explanator* appears only twice more in classical Latin, both times in C. (*Div.* 2.131; *Rep.* 3.27).   **nam ut**: introduces a simile, picked up by *sic cum omni utilitate* below. The need for interpretation of oracles, dreams, and waking prophecies complicates the simplistic division of artificial and natural divination, and even though the skill of interpretation is divinely granted (the point made here), the need for interpretation introduces the possibility of human error into the process of communication from the divine to mortals. At 24–25, Q. admitted that sometimes the interpretation of divine messages is incorrect (he admits this again at 118 below), but he has also devoted much of his speech (esp. 26–59) to arguing for the general accuracy and authority of various diviners.   **item igitur somniis vaticinationibus oraclis**: The *ratio a deo*—that foreknowledge is a beneficial gift bestowed on mankind by the gods who cherish them—was made at 82–83. It is addressed at much greater length in *N. D.* 2.4–12, 162–66.

117 magna quaestio est: The same formulation appeared at 38.   **continet enim totam hanc quaestionem ea ratio quae est de natura deorum, quae a te secundo libro est explicata dilucide**: Q. points out that C.'s earlier work has made part of his case for him. At the beginning of his speech (9–10), Q. expressed his desire to follow up on the Stoic argument of Book 2 of *N. D.* that he felt had dealt insufficiently with the question of divination (on this point, see 9n. *Sed quod praetermissum est in illis libris . . .*). For the relationship between the Stoics' conception of divinity and their belief in the validity of divination, see 10n. *ut et si divinatio sit, di sint, et si di sint, sit divinatio*.   **quam si obtinemus**: sc. the whole argument of *N. D.* 2.   **de quo agimus**: explained by the following *oratio obliqua*.

118 non placet Stoicis: At 12, Q. made it clear that Panaetius, who doubted the validity of divination (6), had mocked the idea that each individual sign was the result of divine intervention. The argument that the gods are not concerned with small matters is more prominent in *N. D.* (2.167, 3.90, 3.93), though admittedly not with regard to divination.   **sed ita a principio . . . in furentium vocibus**: Q. here identifies the same physical phenomenon as the ultimate cause of both natural and technical divination. Timpanaro (*ad loc.*) posits that Posidonius would have been the first to articulate this principle.   **falsa sunt**: probably the perfect passive of *fallo*, continuing the passive of *falluntur*.   **esse quandam vim divinam hominum vitam continentem**: explains *hoc autem posito atque concesso* and repeats the point made at 12 and 80.   **ad hostiam deligendam potest dux esse vis quaedam sentiens**: In his rebuttal at 2.35, M. repeats this phrase almost verbatim, leaving out only *potest*: another instance of his removing the careful qualification of Q.'s argument in order to make it easier to attack. Cf. 9n. *quae est earum rerum quae fortuitae putantur praedictio atque praesensio.*   **velis**: indefinite second person.

119 maximo . . . argumento: The following example is doubly authoritative because it was a recent occurrence pertaining to the highest power in the state and because the impending danger it signaled was swiftly realized. In addition, Q. and M. may well have witnessed the event, making it even more difficult to dismiss the episode.   **quod paulo ante . . . contigit**: This episode is an essential part of the tradition surrounding Caesar's death repeated by numerous authors (e.g., Plin., *Nat.* 11.186; Val. Max. 1.6.13; Suet., *Iul.* 77; App., *B. Civ.* 2.116; Plu., *Caes.* 63).   **primum in sella aurea sedit et cum purpurea veste processit**: just two out of a long series of exceptional honors heaped on Caesar in the last eighteen months of his life. Dio Cassius seems to date both to the year 44, though he says (44.4.1) that he has grouped all the honors together without strict regard for chronology. Efforts to determine the precise occasion to which Q. refers have not been successful (for a summary, see Wardle *ad loc.*). Q.'s emphasis on the fact that it was the first time Caesar used his golden chair (a more regal version of the standard *sella curulis*, restricted to magistrates of high rank) underscores the speed with which the gods indicated their displeasure with his imperious behavior. In the Roman mind, clothing of all purple was strongly identified with foreign kings and, during the Roman Empire, with the emperors of Rome. Other Roman aristocrats wore purple, but less of it: equestrians wore togas decorated with a narrow purple stripe; the stripe on a senatorial toga was wider. During the republic, the only individual entitled to a completely purple toga, or *toga picta* (cf. Fest. 228L), like the one granted to Caesar, was a victorious general on the day of his triumphal procession, a sign that the general was, for that one day, the embodiment of Jupiter himself (Liv. 10.7.9–10 with Oakley's commentary). Wearing the *toga picta* outside the triumphal context was viewed as an assertion of absolute power and caused offense, as the general Marius discovered when he failed to remove his special garb before entering the *curia* after his triumph over Jugurtha in 104 (Plu., *Mar.* 12.7).   **bovis opimi**: "choicest bull"; an exceptionally beautiful, well fed animal intended for sacrifice. *Bos* is gender neutral, but the animal is identified as a *taurus* at 2.36–37. Cf. Fest. 202L with Paul. ex Fest. 203L.   **cor non fuit**: Caesar also received this most improbable sign in 45 when preparing to fight the remnants of Pompey's forces in Spain (App., *BC* 2.116; Polyaen. 8.23.33).   **qua † ille rei novitate perculsus**: *Ille* = Caeasar. In light of Caesar's well documented disdain for predictive sciences (e.g., 2.52; Suet., *Iul.* 59; App., *B. Civ.* 2.116), especially haruspicy, editors agree that a negative has fallen out of this phrase.   **Spurinna**: a member of an aristocratic Etruscan family. Several *Spurinnae* are among the *haruspices* known from epigraphic sources (see Torelli 1975). It is not clear if Spurinna is present at the event as a *haruspex* employed by the Roman state or in some other capacity. It is also not certain if he is the *summus haruspex* whose prediction Caesar dismisses at 2.52. He was an acquaintance of C. and seems to have been in Rome still in 43 (*Fam.* 9.24.2 = *SBF* 362.2). For more discussion, see Rawson 1978.   **proficisci, ****: Some editors reasonably posit a lacuna here based on the similarity of this passage to the version in Suet., *Iul.* 77, which includes a fuller account of Caesar's response.   **caput in iecore**: On the importance of the liver in extispicy, see 16n. *quid fissum in extis, quid fibra valeat.* The absence of the *caput* (a lobe identified as the *processus caudatus* in Wardle *ad loc.*) was commonly taken to be a sign of dire things to come (e.g., Val. Max. 1.6.9; Plin., *Nat.* 11.189–90).   **ut videret interitum non ut caveret**: This statement, with its two contrasting but parallel purpose clauses (a common structure in C.), contradicts earlier parts of Q.'s argument, such as the statements that signs *nuntiant eventura nisi provideris* (29) and that people will be more wary if they have foreknowledge (82). Wardle attempts to absolve Q. of inconsistency by reading these as two result clauses, but the natural reading of *ut videret interitum* (and, by extension, of *non ut caveret*) is as a purpose clause. Pease accepts the contradiction, attributing it to a switch in sources. Timpanaro acknowledges the contradiction and rightly sees the statement here as a strong anti-Caesarian statement: the gods wanted Caesar's death. In any case, this statement is a digression: Q. has been arguing that *vis quaedam sentiens* is involved in technical divination, but now he touches momentarily on a new topic, that is, whether mortals can alter the course of events forecast to them (to which M. vigorously objects at 2.22–25).

120 divina mens: Cf. 110n. *mente divina.*   **alites . . . oscines**: "birds that provide auspices by flight . . . birds that provide auspices by song." The *locus classicus* for these technical augural terms is Fest. 214L with Paul. ex. Fest. 3L. See also Serv., *A*. 1.394, 4.462.   **prono obliquo supino**: Pease renders this phrase as "forward, sideways, backward."   **quanto id deo est facilius**: because *divina mens* permeates the entire world and all things contained in it. Cf. *N. D*. 3.92. This raises the issue of free will, but Q. does not take it up.

121 quale scriptum illud: points forward to the following series of three predictions, each expressed as a future more vivid conditional statement in *oratio obliqua* (*G&L* 595 r. 1). This passage is evidence for the influence of Near Eastern omen series on Roman divination: each of the three predictions listed has close parallels in the extant remains of such lists. See Jacobs 2010. In presenting these *exempla* and the two that follow (Croesus's son and Servius Tullius), Q. seems to lose sight of his immediate point—that there are diviners whose psychological state makes them exceptionally accurate interpreters of signs in the natural world—and slips into another catalog of signs proven accurate by later events. Q. does not name or even mention the interpreters of any of these signs.   **si luna paulo ante solis ortum defecisset in signo Leonis**: It is not possible to pinpoint a specific episode in the reign of Darius III (336–330) to which this pertains. There is no real correspondence between accounts of the battle of Gaugamela in 331 BCE, with which this eclipse has long been associated, and the details preserved here. Pease and Wardle (*ad loc.*) follow the argument of Boll (1910, 168–70), that this refers to the eclipse of February 338.   **[proelio]**: Timpanaro (*ad loc.*) omits this on the basis of its redundancy with *armis* above. Pease and Wardle remove it on the basis of the date (338) to which they assign the eclipse: since Darius's reign did not begin until 336, the prediction must refer not to a single battle but to the whole of Darius's military efforts. It is also possible that C. simply has the date wrong.   **et si mulier leonem peperisse visa esset**: picks up *in signo Leonis* above, thus framing this group of signs. Cf. 40n. *visus . . . videbar . . . videtur.* There is a series of pregnancy dreams at 39–46. Agariste, the mother of Pericles, had this dream (Herodot. 6.131; Plu., *Peric.* 3.3).   **quod scribit Herodotus**: Herodot. 1.85–86 (also in Plin., *Nat.* 11.270). The story is given a different, non-divinatory interpretation at Val. Max. 5.4 ext. 6 and Gell. 5.9.1–4.   **infans**: here with its primary meaning of "not speaking, mute."   **ostento**: Cf. 73n. *ostentum.*   **caput arsisse Servio Tullio dormienti**: The most famous account is Liv. 1.39.1–4 (see Pease *ad loc.* for other citations and a list of similar tales about other individuals). This rounds off the series of royal *exempla* and moves the conversation back to a Roman context.   **Ut igitur . . .**: Q. finally returns to the point he had been arguing (see 121n. *quale scriptum illud*). He reasserts that the freedom of the soul from the concerns of the body gives rise to both natural and technical divination.

122 de Socrate: The logical connection to what immediately precedes is loose. Q. has just argued that the state of a person's soul can make him a more accurate interpreter of forms of technical divination; he here reverts to an authoritative example of someone whose purity of soul made him more receptive to natural divination.   **in libris Socraticorum**: Cf. 5n. *cum Socrates . . . cumque*.   **quod δαιμόνιον appellat**: refers to the divine sign sent to Socrates (in the form of a sound or voice) by a god, probably Apollo, to guide him in matters great and small (Pl., *Apol.* 40a). The δαιμόνιον was an important aspect of Socrates's religiosity and appears prominently in the arguments attributed to him by Plato (esp. *Apol.* 31c–32a) and Xenophon (*Mem.* 1.1.4–5). It was also the subject of philosophical works by Plutarch (*De Genio Socratis = Mor.* 575a–598f), Apuleius (*De Deo Socratis*), and the late second century CE philosopher Maximus of Tyre (*Or.* 8 and 9). For extended discussion, see the contributions to Destrée and Smith 2005.   **numquam impellenti, saepe revocanti**: In Plato, the role of Socrates's δαιμόνιον is entirely deterrent: it only restrains Socrates from taking an unfavorable course of action on which he has already decided (*Apol.* 31d; *Phdr.* 242b–c). In Xenophon, the δαιμόνιον sometimes provides positive advice as well (e.g., *Mem.* 1.1.4).   **Xenophonti consulenti sequereturne Cyrum**: Cf. 52n. *in ea militia*. This story is told by Xenophon in *Anab.* 3.1.5 and *Mem.* 1.1.6.   **exposuit quae ipsi videbantur**: "he laid out what seemed right to him (Socrates)." Cf. *OLD*, s.v. *video* 23. The pronoun *ipse* can be used as an emphatic reflexive (*G&L* 311.2). It is used here to stress that Socrates has just laid out his own opinion. This is borne out by the direct quote that follows.   **ad quem etiam Athenienses publice de maioribus rebus semper rettulerunt**: Cf. statements at 3, 37, and 95.

123 scriptum est item: The source for this story, preserved only here, is not known.   **Critonis sui familiaris**: a wealthy, devoted friend of Socrates mentioned in several works of Plato, including the dialogue that bears his name. In the *Apologia*, he visits Socrates regularly in prison, stands surety for Socrates's fine, and is present at his trial.   **qua soleo**: Supply *uti* (brachylogy). Xenophon asserts that Socrates's δαιμόνιον often gave him advice that pertained to his friends (e.g., *Mem.* 1.1.4); Plato depicts the δαιμόνιον as concerned only with Socrates's actions.   **cum apud Delium male pugnatum esset**: Socrates fought in the Peloponnesian War. Plato (*Apol.* 28e) mentions his service in the siege of Potidaea (432–430/29 BCE), this battle at Delium in Boeotia (424), and the battle of Amphipolis (422). This story is also told in Plu., *Gen. Soc.* 581e. In the version of Strabo 9.2.7 and D. L. 2.22–3, he saved Xenophon's life at Delium. **Lachete praetore**: Laches, son of Melanopus, was elected στρατηγός (of which *praetor* is the standard Latin rendering) in 427/6 (Thuc. 3.86.1). This is the only evidence that he might have held the same position in 424, and it should be set aside. Since Thucydides does not mention Laches's reelection for 424, it is more likely that this small confusion is a result of C.'s hasty composition. See Develin 1989, 133, s.a. 424/3. In the Platonic dialogue bearing his name, Laches gives high praise to Socrates's efforts in that battle (181b). **qua ceteri**: Supply *fugerant*. **Antipatro**: Cf. 6n. *Antipater*. It is not clear if he is the source for the preceding Socratic anecdotes.

124 tamen: Q. cannot help adding this last Socratic *exemplum*. It is not immediately relevant to the primary point (demonstrating Socrates's prophetic powers), but it does highlight the extraordinary quality of his soul that is the cause of those powers. **quod**: "namely that." **impiis sententiis**: Q. makes not Socrates but the jury guilty of impiety, thus inverting the charge against him. **aequissimo animo se dixit mori**: taken from Pl., *Apol.* 40a–c and 41d. Q. mentioned Socrates's foreknowledge of his death at 52. **illud suggestum**: refers to the βῆμα, or speaker's platform. **Equidem sic arbitror**: Q. returns to the argument he began at 118 (cf. 24). **aut arte aut coniectura**: Q. distinguishes between forms of technical divination that interpret signs and those that are applied to direct communication from the gods (e.g., dream interpretation). Cf. 116. **signum dubie datum**: This could apply to any sign that would support more than a single interpretation, such as a vague oracular pronouncement. See Wardle *ad loc.* for a discussion of *auspicia incerta*. **potest aliquod latuisse aut ipsum aut quod esset illi contrarium**: "it is possible that some sign lies hidden, either the sign itself or another sign that counters the first." *Aut quod* is in place of *aut aliud quod*. Serv., *A.* 3.374 reports that greater auguries trumped lesser ones (see also Gell. 13.15.1–7). **Mihi autem ad hoc . . . et praedicta reperiri**: a more moderate version of the position attributed to Cratippus at 71: *satis est ad confirmandam divinationem semel aliquid esse ita divinatum ut nihil fortuito cecidisse videatur.*

125 Quin etiam hoc non dubitans dixerim . . . esse omnibus confitendum: "I would not even hesitate to say that if any single thing should have been foretold and preconceived in such a way that, when it happens, it occurs just as it was predicted and there is nothing in it that appears to have occurred by chance or accident, then divination exists, and everyone ought to admit it." The use of *dixerim* as a potential subjunctive that is, in essence, present is not common in early Latin but expands from C.'s time forward (*G&L* 257.2 n. 1). There is hysteron proteron (a reversal of the logical order of events) in *praedictum praesensumque*. **a deo . . . deinde a fato, deinde a natura vis omnis divinandi ratioque repetenda**: This clear articulation of the various causes of divination is much delayed. Q. has already laid out explanations of divination *a deo*, as a manifestation of the gods' concern for mankind (esp. 82–83, where it is attributed to the Stoics, particularly Chrysippus, Diogenes, and Antipater), and *a natura*, as a function of the physical nature of the human soul (60–64). At 118, he returned to and expanded on the *ratio a natura* to include the physical nature of the universe. Only in what follows will he turn to the explanation *a fato*. The triple causation applies to both natural and technical divination, although some explanations are more easily applied to one or the other (see 130n. *hanc quidem rationem difficile est fortasse traducere ad id genus divinationis, quod ex arte profectum dicimus*). Posidonius's tripartite division is in keeping with the general Stoic argument. For further discussion, see Edelstein and Kidd 1988–89, frag. 103 and 107. **Fieri igitur omnia fato ratio cogit fateri**: Note the consonance of *f* and *t* and the possible etymological pun on *fato* and *fateri*. The orthodox Stoic position is that all things happen through antecedent causes that were themselves ultimately set in motion by the divine intelligence that permeates the universe. Causes bring about events that, in their turn, cause further events, and so on. This unending series of events is fate and is foreseen in its entirety by *divina mens*. **seriemque causarum, cum causae causa nexa**: The polyptoton and the consonance of *c* and *s* illustrate the close intricate linking of causes. **quod non futurum fuerit**: "which would not have happened." *Fuerit* is a potential subjunctive.

126 Ex quo intellegitur, ut: *Intellegere* with a substantive result clause is unusual in classical Latin; it is more commonly followed by an indirect statement. **ut fatum sit non id quod superstitiose sed id quod physice dicitur, causa aeterna rerum**: For the Stoics, the physical nature of the universe gives rise to the existence of fate. See 125n. *Fieri igitur omnia fato ratio cogit fateri*. Cf. *N. D.* 3.92. **causa aeterna rerum**: This is explained further by the following three-part indirect question. **plerumque . . . etiamsi non semper (nam id quidem adfirmare difficile est)**: *Plerumque* is adverbial, meaning "generally." A similar caveat appears at 128. **veri simile est**: "it is likely"; a mild anacoluthon. Distracted by the preceding parenthetical statement, Q. has forgotten that he is still in a substantive result clause that requires a subjunctive verb. This phrase, associated more strongly with Academics than with Stoics (see Glucker 1995), is awkward here. Since 118, Q. has been asserting without qualification that natural divination and technical divination both arise from the predictable relationship between predetermined signs and the events they precede.

127 alio loco ostendetur: Presumably Q. steps out of character to refer to C.'s next project, *De Fato*, which, in its extant form, does not, in fact, present the Stoic position on fate; it offers only an attack. An explanation for the omission is not far to seek: in the introduction to *De Fato* (1), C. tells his reader that the political upheaval that followed Caesar's death prevented him from structuring that work as a dialogue like *N. D.* and *Div.*   **conligationem**: "the binding together"; a rare word that appears almost exclusively in philosophical contexts.   **nisi deus**: The omniscience of the gods is taken as a given at 82.   **quasi rudentis explicatio**: The metaphor of the uncoiling rope aptly illustrates the Stoic notion of the eternal interweaving and linking of causes. It seems to be original with C. See Hankinson 1996.   **nihil novi efficientis et primum quicque replicantis**: "bringing about nothing new and unrolling each thing for the first time." *Nihil novi* = nothing that is completely outside the endless series of causes and events. Cf. 125. After the great conflagration that marks the end of the *annus magnus* (see 111n. *deflagrationem futuram aliquando caeli atque terrarum*), everything in the cosmos returns to its original position, and the same series of causes begins again. Thus these causes are not truly new.

128 Non est igitur ut mirandum sit ea praesentiri a divinantibus quae nusquam sint: sunt enim omnia, sed tempore absunt: Q. finally answers the question he raised at 117. Diviners cannot see anything novel, that is, anything that is outside the endless series of causes and events. They can see things within that series that may be greatly distant in time.   **ut in seminibus vis inest**: For other instances of this analogy, see *N. D.* 2.58, 81, 127; *Sen.* 52. Seed imagery is essential to Stoic cosmology (the creative force of the universe is the σπερματικὸς λόγος) and moral theory. For a good discussion, see Horowitz 1998, 26–34.   **consequentiam**: This appears to be a Ciceronian neologism.

129 A natura: Q. returns to the last of his three sources of divination listed at 125. This brief section repeats the argument made first and more extensively at 60–64.   **Ut enim deorum animi . . . sentiunt inter se quid quisque sentiat . . . sic animi hominum . . . cernunt**: *Quisque* must refer to mortals and not to other gods (*contra* Wardle *ad loc.*); otherwise the following parenthetical statement makes little sense. The comparison is between the mechanism by which gods receive communication from mortals and that by which mortals receive information from the gods.   **sine oculis sine auribus sine lingua**: Stoic gods are not anthropomorphic (D. L. 7.147).

130 hanc quidem rationem naturae difficile est fortasse traducere ad id genus divinationis, quod ex arte profectum dicimus: The apparent contradiction of this statement with 109 (*Quid, si etiam ratio exstat artificiosae praesensionis facilis, divinae autem paulo obscurior?*) is resolved by recognizing that Q. treats different aspects of the *ratio a natura* for technical divination at each locus. At 109, he distinguishes between the readily observable pattern of signs in the natural world (and the events that follow them) and the physical properties of the mortal soul that allow it, under certain conditions, to perform natural divination. Here, *hanc rationem* refers again to the argument that the physical nature of the human soul gives rise to natural divination. The difficulty comes in building the argument that the soul's physical nature also makes some people particularly perceptive of signs in the natural world that require the application of *ars* for accurate interpretation. Q. asserted this at 121 but did not adduce any supporting material that was directly relevant.   **signa**: This probably refers to all kinds of signs in the natural world rather than only to meteorological signs (so Pease *ad loc.*). The *exempla* that follow include extispicy.   **Ceos accepimus ortum Caniculae diligenter quotannis solere servare**: Cean worship of Sirius, the Dog Star, is explained by a story preserved in several sources (Callimach., *Aetia* 75.32–37; Apoll. Rhod. 2.498–527; D. S. 4.82.1–3; Hyg., *Astr.* 2.4). Aristaeus, the son of Apollo and the nymph Cyrene, was instructed by the oracle at Delphi to visit the small Cycladic island of Cos, where he would be worshipped by the inhabitants. Upon his arrival, Aristaeus discovered that the Dog Star was causing a plague among the Ceans. He instituted new sacrifices to Zeus Ikmaios and appeased Sirius by putting murderers to death. The plague lifted, and in gratitude, the Ceans worshipped Aristaeus as the god of moisture and propitiated the Dog Star each year. The association of the star with widespread illness is well documented in ancient sources, both Greek and Roman (see Brosch 2008, 20–27). The ancients believed that heat and drought were major causes of plague. In antiquity, Sirius, the brightest object in the sky apart from the sun, moon, and Venus, first rose above the horizon before sunrise in July and August—the hottest, driest part of the year.   **Ponticus Heraclides**: Cf. 46n. *Ponticus Heraclides.*   **concretum esse caelum**: Cf. 18n. *concreto lumine.*

131 Democritus: See 5n. *Democritus.*   **Quae si a natura profecta**: that is, the various forms of technical divination.   **dies**: "the passage of time"

(OLD, s.v. 10). **ille Pacuvianus qui in Chryse physicus inducitur**: *Ille Pacuvianus* = "that character of Pacuvius." On Pacuvius, see 24n. *profectione laeti . . . occaecat nigror.* The *Chryses*, now known only from a handful of fragments, probably told the story of the flight of Orestes, Pylades, and Iphigenia from Thoas, king of the Taurians. They escaped to the island of Sminthe, where they encountered Chryses, son of Chryseis and Agamemnon; until their arrival, he did not know his true parentage. Sophocles also wrote a *Chryses*, now largely lost; the story is elsewhere preserved in detail only in Hyg., *Fab.* 120–21. We know neither the identity of the *physicus* nor how he fit into the plot (see Schierl 2006, 192–239, esp. 203–4 and 228–30, with D'Anna 1967, 71–83, 198–203). For an analysis of the play as a whole, see Slater 2000.   **"nam isti qui . . .**: The first line of this fragment of iambic senarii is only partial. The sense, however, should be complete, since *nam* introduces a new thought. The grammatical connection of *isti* to what follows is dropped (anacoluthon).   **ex suo**: For Greeks and Romans, the human liver was the seat of emotion and thought.   **magis audiendum quam auscultandum censeo**: "I think they ought to be heard more than heeded." *Audiendum* and *auscultandum* are impersonal.   **cur, quaeso . . .**: Q. addresses the *physicus*.   **omniumque idemst pater**: that is, *Aether*. Note the heavy use of elision in this line and the next.   **cur . . . cur**: Q. repeats *cur* to remind his listener of the question he began before the long circumstantial clause intervened.   **cumque animi hominum semper fuerint futurique sint**: Cf. 115n. *qui quia vixit ab omni aeternitate.*

132 Quintus Reveals His Personal Opinion

Having defended every form of divination, Q. ends by stepping back from the orthodox Stoic position he has been arguing. Echoing his argument at 87–92, Q. concludes by voicing his personal prejudice against certain types of lower-class diviners, some of whom he had defended earlier: the validity of their service to private clients is tainted by their desire for profit. Q. distances himself from the Stoic position again at 2.100 (*tamen etiam mea sponte nimis superstitiosam de divinatione Stoicorum sententiam iudicabam*), which is reinforced by M.'s response at 2.101: *Non ignoro . . . Quinte te semper ita sensisse, ut de ceteris divinandi generibus dubitares, ista duo furoris et somnii, quae a libera mente fluere viderentur, probares.*

132 Nunc illa testabor: Q. announces that he is no longer speaking as the advocate for Stoicism but offering his own opinion.   **non . . . neque . . . ne . . . quidem**: articulates an ascending tricolon.   **sortilegos**: itinerant lot diviners, or at least those not associated with prominent oracular sites. See 34n. *sortes quas e terra editas* and Klingshirn 2006. **hariolentur**: See 4n. *hariolorum . . . praedictiones.* **psychomantia**: C. has transliterated the Greek word for consultation of the dead for information not available to mortals, the most famous example of which is Odysseus's journey to the underworld in Hom., *Od.* 11. The term appears in Latin only here and at *Tusc.* 1.115. This branch of necromancy caps the first list of diviners for hire because they are the most authoritative: Appius Claudius endorsed them. **Appius amicus tuus**: See 29n. *Appius collega tuus.* At 105, Q. spoke favorably of Claudius's attitude toward divination. **non habeo . . . nauci Marsum augurem**: "I don't consider a Marsian augur worth anything"; or, with more humor, "I think a Marsian augur ain't worth nothin'." *Naucum* is an uncommon word, appearing almost exclusively in Roman comedies of the second century. By the late republic, it required explanation (so Fest. 166L, citing C.'s contemporary L. Ateius Philologus). Through its comic association, Q. injects levity into the conclusion of his speech. In later Latin, *naucum* appears only at Apul., *Apol.* 91. On the basis of the strong association of *naucum* with earlier Latin, some editors (including Wardle) unnecessarily identify this sentence as a quotation or a paraphrase from a source—unknown, but probably Ennian. The repetition of *non* throughout this sentence underscores the many types of diviner Q. disapproves. **Marsum augurem**: See 105n. *tum Pisidam tum Soranum augurem.* **vicanos haruspices**: "village haruspices." Plautus pairs these low-status *haruspices* (not to be confused with the aristocratic *haruspices* brought in by the Roman state) with *harioli* at *Amph.* 1132, *Mil.* 693 (where they are female), and *Poen.* 791. Cato (*Agr.* 5.4) includes them in a list of diviners whom the *vilicus* must avoid. **de circo astrologos**: The area around the Circus Maximus (P. Ciancio Rossetto, *LTUR* 1.272–77, s.v. "Circus Maximus"; *NTDAR* 84–87, s.v. "Circus Maximus") was notorious for fortune-tellers who catered to a less affluent clientele (Hor., *Sat.* 1.6.113–14; Juv. 6.582–91). **Isiacos coniectores**: It is not certain that the cult of Isis in Italy included rites of incubation, though this can be assumed since it is known that worshippers in the Greek East and Egypt sought medical cures from the goddess in dreams (e.g., D. S. 1.25.2–5; Paus. 10.32.13). It is possible that the goddess also offered oracular pronouncements in dreams. **"superstitiosi vates**: "superstitious prophets." Q. is drawing on the contemporary, heavily negative meaning of *superstitiosus* here, although it would have been a more neutral term in Ennius's day. See 66n. *missa sum superstitiosis hariolationibus.* This is probably where the quotation from Ennius's *Telamon* begins (so Ax and Timpanaro), although Pease includes the preceding *sed.* Schäublin (*ad loc.*) and Jocelyn (1967, 128 with 397–98) attribute this partial line to Q.

and begin the quotation at *aut inertes aut insani*. These lines largely repeat
what Q. has already argued, so the quotation serves primarily to lend the
authority of Ennius to Q.'s personal opinion.   **insani**: that is, mentally
disturbed rather than enduring the divinely inspired madness that gives rise
to true prophecy.   **atque haec quidem Ennius**: Supply *scribit*.   **"sed
eos non curare" opinatur "quid agat humanum genus"**: still part of the
relative clause introduced by *qui paucis ante versibus*. This sentiment is
distinctive of the Epicureans and forms part of their argument that divination
does not exist (see 5n. *Xenophanes unus . . . reliqui vero omnes praeter
Epicurum*).   **levitate vanitate malitia**: an ascending tricolon. Q. ends
with a flourish.   **"praeclare tu quidem" inquam paratus . . .** : M., who
has not spoken since 11, reenters the dialogue. The text breaks off with this
incomplete sentence, but it is unlikely that much of any real significance has
been lost.

Bibliography

Allen, J. 2005. "The Stoics on the Origin of Language and the Foundations of Etymology." In Frede and Inwood 2005, 14–35.

Ancillotti, A., and R. Cerri. 1997. *The Tables of Iguvium*. Perugia: Jama.

Ando, C. 2008. *The Matter of the Gods: Religion and the Roman Empire*. Berkeley: University of California Press.

André, J. 1985. *Les Noms de Plantes dans la Rome Antique*. Paris: Les Belles Lettres.

Arrighetti, G. 1973. *Epicuro Opere*. 2nd ed. Turin: Einaudi.

Artigas, E. 1990. *Pacuviana: Marco Pacuvio en Cicerón*. Barcelona: Universitat de Barcelona.

Astin, A. E. 1978. *Cato the Censor*. Oxford: Clarendon.

Babcock, C. L. 1965. "The Early Career of Fulvia." *AJP* 86: 1–32.

Barton, T. 1994. *Ancient Astrology*. London: Routledge.

Bean, G. E., and J. M. Cook. 1955. "The Halicarnassus Peninsula." *ABSA* 50: 85–171.

Beard, M. 1986. "Cicero and Divination: The Formation of a Latin Discourse." *JRS* 76: 33–46.

Bicknell, P. J. 1969. "Democritus' Theory of Precognition." *REG* 82: 318–26.

Bodel, J. 1994. *Graveyards and Groves: A Study of the* Lex Lucerina. AJAH 11 (1986) [pub. 1994]. Cambridge, MA.

Boëls-Janssen, N. 1993. *La Vie Religieuse des Matrones dans la Rome Archaïque*. CEFR 176. Rome: École Française de Rome.

Boll, F. 1910. "Paralipomena I." *Philologus* 69: 161–77.

Bosworth, A. B. 1998. "Calanus and the Brahman Opposition." In *Alexander der Grosse: Eine Welteroberung und ihr Hintergrund*, ed. W. Will, 173–203. Bonn: Habelt.

Bowden, H. 2005. *Classical Athens and the Delphic Oracle: Divination and Democracy*. Cambridge: Cambridge University Press.

Boyle, A. J. 2006. *An Introduction to Roman Tragedy*. London: Routledge.

Brennan, T. C. 2000. *The Praetorship in the Roman Republic*. 2 vols. Oxford: Oxford University Press.

Brisson, L. 2002. *Sexual Ambivalence: Androgyny and Hermaphroditism in Graeco-Roman Antiquity*. Trans. J. Lloyd. Berkeley: University of California Press.

Brittain, C. 2005. "Common Sense: Concepts, Definition, and Meaning in and out of the Stoa." In Frede and Inwood 2005, 164–209.

Broad, W. J. 2006. *The Oracle: The Lost Secrets and Hidden Message of Ancient Delphi*. New York: Penguin.

Brosch, N. 2008. *Sirius Matters*. Astrophysics and Space Science Library 354. Dordrecht: Springer Science and Business Media B. V.

Cardauns, B. 1976. *M. Terentius Varro: Antiquitates rerum divinarum*. 2 vols. Mainz: Steiner.

Carney, T. F. 1967. "The Changing Picture of Marius in Ancient Literature." *PACA* 10: 5–22.

Cartledge, P., and A. Spawforth. 1989. *Hellenistic and Roman Sparta: A Tale of Two Cities*. London: Routledge.

Casson, L. L. 2001. *Libraries in the Ancient World*. New Haven: Yale University Press.

Casson, L. L. 1974. *Travel in the Ancient World*. Toronto: Hakkert.

Chaplin, J. D. 2000. *Livy's Exemplary History*. Oxford: Oxford University Press.

Coarelli, F. 2007. *Rome and Environs: An Archaeological Guide*. Trans. J. J. Clauss and D. P. Harmon. Berkeley: University of California Press.

Coarelli, F. 2003. "Remoria." In *Myth, History, and Culture in Republican Rome: Studies in Honour of T. P. Wiseman*, ed. D. Braund and C. Gill, 41–55. Exeter: University of Exeter Press.

Coleman, R. G. G. 1999. "Poetic Diction, Poetic Discourse, and the Poetic Register." In *Aspects of the Language of Latin Poetry*, ed. J. N. Adams and R. Mayer, 21–93. Oxford: Oxford University Press.

Connors, C. 1994. "Ennius, Ovid, and Representations of Ilia." *MD* 32: 99–112.

Courtney, E. 2003. *The Fragmentary Latin Poets*. Oxford: Oxford University Press.

Craig, C. P. 1993. *Form as Argument in Cicero's Speeches: A Study of Dilemma*. Atlanta: Scholars Press.

Crawford, M., ed. 1996 *Roman Statutes*. 2 vols. Bulletin of the Institute of Classical Studies Suppl. 64. London: Institute of Classical Studies.

D'Anna, G. 1967. *M. Pacuvii fragmenta*. Poetarum Latinorum reliquiae: Aetas rei publicae 3.1. Rome: Athenaeum.

de Callataÿ, G. 1996. *Annus Platonicus*. Louvain-la-Neuve: Université Catholique De Louvain.

de Cazanove, O. 1995. "Rituels Romains dans les Vignobles." In *In Vino Veritas*, ed. O. Murray and M. Tecusan, 214–23. London: British School at Rome.

de Grummond, N. T. 2006. "Prophets and Priests." In de Grummond and Simon 2006, 27–44.

de Grummond, N. T., and E. Simon, eds. 2006. *The Religion of the Etruscans*. Austin: University of Texas Press.

De Jong, A. 1997. *Traditions of the Magi: Zoroastrianism in Greek and Latin Literature.* Leiden: Brill.

Dench, E. 2005. *Romulus' Asylum: Roman Identities from the Age of Alexander to the Age of Hadrian.* Oxford: Oxford University Press.

Denyer, N. 1985. "The Case against Divination: An Examination of Cicero's *De Divinatione.*" *PCPhS* 31: 1–10.

Destrée, P., and N. D. Smith, eds. 2005. "Socrates' Divine Sign: Religion, Practice, and Value in Socratic Philosophy." *Apeiron* 38.

Develin, R. 1989. *Athenian Officials, 684–321 B.C.* Cambridge: Cambridge University Press.

Devillers, O., and V. Krings. 2006. "Le songe d'Hannibal: Quelques réflexions sur la tradition littéraire." *Pallas* 70: 337–46.

Dickie, M. W. 2001. *Magic and Magicians in the Greco-Roman World.* London: Routledge.

Diels, H., and W. Kranz. 1967. *Die Fragmente der Vorsokratiker.* 12th ed. Berlin: Weidmann.

Dilke, O. A. W. 1971. *The Roman Land Surveyors.* New York: Barnes and Noble.

Dillon, J. 2003. *The Heirs of Plato: A Study of the Old Academy (347–274 BC).* Oxford: Clarendon.

Dover, K. 1993. *Aristophanes:* Frogs. Oxford: Clarendon.

Durand, R. 1903. "La Date du *De Divinatione.*" In *Mélanges Boissier,* ed. A. Fontemoing, 173–83. Paris: Fontemoing.

Dyck, A. R. 2004. *A Commentary on Cicero,* De Legibus. Ann Arbor: University of Michigan Press.

Dyck, A. R. 1996. *A Commentary on Cicero,* De Officiis. Ann Arbor: University of Michigan Press.

Eckstein, A. M. 1979. "The Foundation Day of Roman 'Coloniae.'" *CSCA* 12: 85–97.

Edelstein, L., and I. G. Kidd. 1988–89. *Posidonius.* 2nd ed. 3 vols. Cambridge: Cambridge University Press.

Edlund-Berry, I. 2006. "Hot, Cold, or Smelly: The Power of Sacred Water in Roman Religion, 400–100 BCE." In Schultz and Harvey 2006, 162–80.

Edwards, C. 1993. *The Politics of Immorality in Ancient Rome.* Cambridge: Cambridge University Press.

Engels, D. 2007. *Das römische Vorzeichenwesen (753–27 v. Chr.): Quellen, Terminologie, Kommentar, historische Entwicklung.* Potsdamer Altertumswissenschaftliche Beiträge 22. Stuttgart: Steiner.

Erasmo, M. 2004. *Roman Tragedy: Theatre to Theatricality.* Austin: University of Texas Press.

Ewbank, W. W. 1933. *The Poems of Cicero.* London: University of London Press.

Fantham, E. 2004. *The Roman World of Cicero's* De Oratore. Oxford: Oxford University Press.

Fantham, E. 2003. "Pacuvius: Melodrama, Reversals, and Recognitions." In *Myth,*

History, and Culture in Republican Rome: Studies in Honour of T. P. Wiseman, ed. D. Braund and C. Gill, 98–118. Exeter: University of Exeter Press.

Fantham, E. 2002. "Orator and/et Actor." In *Greek and Roman Actors: Aspects of an Ancient Profession*, ed. P. Easterling and E. Hall, 362–76. Cambridge: Cambridge University Press.

Fantham, E. 1972. *Comparative Studies in Republican Latin Imagery*. Phoenix Suppl. 10. Toronto: University of Toronto Press.

Fauth, W. 1976. "Der Traum des Tarquinius." *Latomus* 35: 469–503.

Flower, M. A. 2008a. *The Seer in Ancient Greece*. Berkeley: University of California Press.

Flower, M. A. 2008b. "The Iamidae: A Mantic Family and Its Public Image." In *Practitioners of the Divine: Greek Priests and Religious Officials from Homer to Heliodorus*, ed. B. Dignas and K. Trampedach, 187–206. Hellenic Studies 30. Washington, DC: Center for Hellenic Studies.

Frede, D., and B. Inwood. 2005. *Language and Learning: Philosophy of Language in the Hellenistic Age; Proceedings of the Ninth Symposium Hellenisticum*. Cambridge: Cambridge University Press.

Frede, M. 1987. *Essays in Ancient Philosophy*. Minneapolis: University of Minnesota Press.

Freyburger, G., and J. Scheid. 2004. *Cicéron: De la Divination*. 2nd ed. Paris: Les Belles Lettres.

Fridh, A. 1990. "*Sacellum, Sacrarium, Fanum*, and Related Terms." In *Greek and Latin Studies in Memory of Cajus Fabricius*, ed. S.-T. Teodorsson, 173–87. Gothenburg: University of Gothenburg.

Gagarin, M. 2002. *Antiphon the Athenian: Oratory, Law, and Justice in the Age of the Sophists*. Austin: University of Texas Press.

Gargola. D. J. 1995. *Lands, Laws, and Gods: Magistrates and Ceremony in the Regulation of Public Lands in Republican Rome*. Chapel Hill: University of North Carolina Press.

Garnsey, P. 1999. *Food and Society in Classical Antiquity*. Cambridge: Cambridge University Press.

Gaster, T. H. 1973. "A Hang-up for Hang-ups: The Second Amuletic Plaque from the Arslan Tash." *Bulletin of the American Schools of Oriental Research* 209: 18–26.

Gee, E. 2001. "Cicero's Astronomy." *CQ* 51: 520–36.

Giannantoni, G. 1990. *Socrates et Socraticorum reliquiae*. Naples: Bibliopolis.

Glinister, F. 2000. "Sacred Rubbish." In *Religion in Archaic and Republican Rome and Italy*, ed. E. Bispham and C. Smith, 54–70. Chicago: Fitzroy Dearborn.

Glucker, J. 1999. "A Platonic Cento in Cicero." *Phronesis* 44: 30–44.

Glucker, J. 1995. "*Probabile, Veri Simile*, and Related Terms." In Powell 1995, 115–43.

Goldberg, S. 2000. "Cicero and the Work of Tragedy." In Manuwald 2000, 49–59.

Goldberg, S. 1995. *Epic in Republican Rome*. Oxford: Oxford University Press.

Gottschalk, H. B. 1980. *Heraclides of Pontus*. Oxford: Clarendon.

Graf, F. 2005. "Rolling the Dice for an Answer." In Johnston and Struck 2005, 51–97.

Grottanelli, C. 2006. *Le De divinatione de Cicéron et les théories antiques de la divination*. Collection Latomus 298. Brussels: Latomus.

Grottanelli, C. 2005. "*Sorte Unica pro Casibus Pluribus Enotata*: Literary Texts and Lot Inscriptions as Sources for Ancient Kleromancy." In Johnston and Struck 2005, 129–46.

Grottanelli, C. 1999. "On the Mantic Meaning of Incestuous Dreams." In *Dream Cultures: Explorations in the Comparative History of Dreaming*, ed. D. Shulman and G. G. Stroumsa, 143–68. New York: Oxford University Press.

Grottanelli, C. 1984. *Philosophe et augure: Recherches sur la théorie cicéronnienne de la divination*. Collection Latomus 184. Brussels: Latomus.

Guillaumont, F. 2006. *Le De divinatione de Cicéron et les théories antiques de la divination*. Collection Latomus 298. Brussells: Latomus.

Guillaumont, F. 1984. *Philosophe et augure: recherches sur la théorie cicéronnienne de la divination*. Collection Latomus 184. Brussells: Latomus.

Guittard, C. 1986. "La Songe de Tarquin." In *Le Divination dans le Monde Étrusco-Italique*, 2:47–67. Caesarodunum Suppl. 54. Tours: Université de Tours.

Gunderson, E. 2000. *Staging Masculinity: The Rhetoric of Performance in the Roman World*. Ann Arbor: University of Michigan Press.

Halporn, J. W., M. Ostwald, and T. G. Rosenmeyer. 1963. *The Meters of Greek and Latin Poetry*. London: Methuen.

Hankinson, R. J. 1996. "Cicero's Rope." In *Polyhistor: Studies in the History and Historiography of Ancient Philosophy*, ed. K. Algra et al., 185–205. Leiden: Brill, 185–205.

Hankinson, R. J. 1988. "Stoicism, Science, and Divination." In *Method, Medicine, and Metaphysics: Studies in the Philosophy of Ancient Science*, ed. R. J. Hankinson, 123–60. *Apeiron* 21.

Harris, W. V. 2009. *Dreams and Experience in Classical Antiquity*. Cambridge, MA: Harvard University Press.

Harte, V. 2005. "Conflicting Values in Plato's *Crito*." In *Plato's Euthyphro, Apology, and* Crito, ed. R. Kamtekar, 229–59. Lanham, MD: Rowman and Littlefield.

Haynes, S. 2000. *Etruscan Civilization: A Cultural History*. Los Angeles: J. Paul Getty Museum.

Hays, S. 1987. "*Lactea Ubertas:* What's Milky about Livy?" *CJ* 82: 107–16.

Hersch, K. K. 2010. *The Roman Wedding: Ritual and Meaning in Antiquity*. Cambridge: Cambridge University Press.

Hickson, F. V. 1993. *Roman Prayer Language: Livy and the* Aneid [*sic*] *of Vergil*. Stuttgart: Teubner.

Hillard, T. W. 1996. "Death by Lightning, Pompeius Strabo, and the People." *RhM* 139: 135–45.

Hinz, V. 2001. *Nunc Phalaris doctum protulit ecce caput: Antike Phalarislegende und Nachleben der Phalarisbriefe*. Munich: Saur.

Horowitz, M. C. 1998. *Seeds of Virtue and Knowledge*. Princeton: Princeton University Press.

Huffman, C. A. 1999. "The Pythagorean Tradition." In *The Cambridge Companion to Early Greek Philosophy*, ed. A. A. Long, 66–87. Cambridge: Cambridge University Press.

Hyland, A. 1990. *Equus: The Horse in the Roman World*. New Haven: Yale University Press.

Iriarte, A., et al. 1997. "A Votive Deposit of Republican Weapons at Gracurris." *JRMES* 8: 233–50.

Isaac, B. 2004. *The Invention of Racism in Classical Antiquity*. Princeton: Princeton University Press.

Jacobs, J. 2010. "Traces of the Omen Series *Šumma izbu* in Cicero, *De Divinatione*." In *Divination and Interpretation of Signs in the Ancient World*, ed. A. Annus, 317–39. Chicago: Oriental Institute of the University of Chicago.

Jaeger, M. 2006. "Livy, Hannibal's Monument, and the Temple of Juno at Croton." *TAPA* 136: 389–414.

Jaeger, M. 2002. "Cicero and Archimedes' Tomb." *JRS* 92: 49–61..

Jannot, J.-R. 2005. *Religion in Ancient Etruria*. Trans. J. K. Whitehead. Madison: University of Wisconsin Press.

Jocelyn, H. D. 1984. "Urania's Discourse in Cicero's Poem *On His Consulship*: Some Problems." *Ciceroniana* 5: 39–54.

Jocelyn, H. D. 1973. "Greek Poetry in Cicero's Prose Writing." *YCS* 23: 61–111.

Jocelyn, H. D. 1971. "*Urbs Augurio Augusto Condita*: Ennius ap. Cic. *Div.* 1.107 (= *Ann.* 77–96 V²)." *PCPhS* 17: 44–74.

Jocelyn, H. D. 1967. *The Tragedies of Ennius*. Cambridge: Cambridge University Press.

Johnston, S. I. 2008. *Ancient Greek Divination*. Malden, MA: Wiley-Blackwell.

Johnston, S. I., and P. T. Struck. 2005. *Mantikê: Studies in Ancient Divination*. Leiden: Brill.

Jordan, H. [1860] 1967. *M. Catonis Praeter Librum de Re Rustica Quae Exstant*. Leipzig: Teubner.

Judson, S., and A. Kahane. 1963. "Underground Drainageways in Southern Etruria and Northern Latium." *PBSR* 31: 74–99.

Kany-Turpin, J. 2004. *Cicéron: De la divination / De Divinatione*. Paris: Flammarion.

Kany-Turpin, J., and P. Pellegrin. 1989. "Cicero and the Aristotelian Theory of Divination by Dreams." In *Cicero's Knowledge of the Peripatos*, ed. W. W. Stambaugh and P. Steinmetz, 220–45. Rutgers University Studies in Classical Humanities 4. New Brunswick, NJ: Transaction.

Kaster, R. A. 2006. *Cicero: Speech on Behalf of Publius Sestius*. Oxford: Clarendon.

Kelly, G. P. 2006. *A History of Exile in the Roman Republic*. New York: Cambridge University Press.

Kirk, G. S. , J. E. Raven, and M. Schofield. 1983. *The Presocratic Philosophers*. 2nd ed. Cambridge: Cambridge University Press.

Klingshirn, W. E. 2006. "Inventing the *Sortilegus*: Lot Divination and Cultural Identity in Italy, Rome, and the Provinces." In Schultz and Harvey 2006, 137–61.

Konrad, C. F. 2004. "*Vellere Signa*." In *Augusto Augurio: Rerum humanarum et divinarum commentationes in honorem Jerzy Linderski*, ed. C. F. Konrad, 169–203. Stuttgart: Steiner.

Krevans, N. 1993. "Ilia's Dream: Ennius, Virgil, and the Mythology of Seduction." *HSPh* 95: 257–71.

Krostenko, B. 2000. "Beyond (Dis)belief: Rhetorical Form and Religious Symbol in Cicero's *De Divinatione*." *TAPA* 130: 353–91.

Kubiak, D. P. 1990. "Cicero and the Poetry of Nature." *SIFC* 8: 198–214.

Lacey, W. K. 1986. "*Patria Potestas*." In *The Family in Ancient Rome*, ed. B. Rawson, 121–44. Ithaca, NY: Cornell University Press.

Lebek, W. D. 1996. "Moneymaking on the Roman Stage." In *Roman Theater and Society*, ed. W. J. Slater, 29–48. E. Togo Salmon Papers 1. Ann Arbor: University of Michigan Press.

Lefkowitz, M. 1981. *The Lives of the Greek Poets*. Baltimore: Johns Hopkins University Press.

Levick, B. 1982. "Sulla's March on Rome in 88 B.C." *Historia* 31: 503–8.

Linderski, J. 2006. "Founding the City." In *Ten Years of the Agnes Kirsopp Lake Michels Lectures at Bryn Mawr College*, ed. S. B. Faris and L. E. Lundeen, 88–107. Reprinted, with slight revision, as "Founding the City: Ennius and Romulus on the Site of Rome," in *Roman Questions II: Selected Papers*, 3–19. Stuttgart: Steiner, 2007.

Linderski, J. 1995. *Roman Questions: Selected Papers*. Stuttgart: Steiner.

Linderski, J. 1986. "The Augural Law." *ANRW* II.16.3: 2146–312.

Linderski, J. 1985. "The *Libri Reconditi*." *HSCP* 89: 207–34. Reprinted in Linderski 1995, 496–523.

Linderski, J. 1982. "Cicero and Roman Divination." *PP* 37: 12–38. Reprinted in Linderski 1995, 458–84.

Lintott, A. 1999. *The Constitution of the Roman Republic*. Oxford: Clarendon.

Livi, V. 2006. "Religious Locales in the Territory of Minturnae: Aspects of Romanization." In Schultz and Harvey 2006, 90–116.

Lomas, K. 1993. *Rome and the Western Greeks, 350 BC–AD 200*. London: Routledge.

Long, A. A.1986. *Hellenistic Philosophy*. 2nd ed. Berkeley: University of California Press.

MacBain, B. 1982. *Prodigy and Expiation: A Study in Religion and Politics in Republican Rome*. Collection Latomus 177. Brussels: Latomus.

MacDowell, D. M. 1978. *The Law in Classical Athens*. Ithaca, NY: Cornell University Press.

MacInnes, D. 2000. "*Dirum ostentum*: Bee Swarm Prodigies at Roman Military

Camps." In *Studies in Latin Literature and Roman History* 10, ed. C. Deroux, 56–69. Collection Latomus 254. Brussels: Latomus.

Magie, D. 1950. *Roman Rule in Asia Minor to the End of the Third Century after Christ*. 2 vols. Princeton : Princeton University Press.

Malcovati, E. 1976. *Oratorum Romanorum Fragmenta Liberae Rei Publicae*. 4th ed. Corpus Scriptorum Latinorum Paravianum. Aug. Taurinorum: Milan and Pavia.

Malkin, I. 1987. *Religion and Colonization in Ancient Greece*. Leiden: Brill.

Manuwald, G. 2001. *Fabulae Praetextae*. Munich: Beck.

Manuwald, G., ed. 2000. *Identität und Alterität in der frührömischen Tragödie*. Würzburg: Ergon.

Margel, S. 2006. "*Religio/Supertitio*: La crise des institutions, de Cicéron à Augustin." *RTP* 138: 193–207.

Marshall, A. J. 1984. "Symbols and Showmanship in Roman Public Life: The Fasces." *Phoenix* 38: 120–41.

Mastrocinque, A. 1983. "La cacciata di Tarquinio il Superbo: Tradizione romana e letteratura greca." *Athenaeum* 61: 457–80.

May, J. M. 1980. "The Image of the Ship of State in Cicero's *Pro Sestio*." *Maia* 32: 259–64.

Mayor, A. 2000. *The First Fossil Hunters: Paleontology in Greek and Roman Times*. Princeton: Princeton University Press.

McDermott, W. C. 1938. *The Ape in Antiquity*. Johns Hopkins University Studies in Archaeology 27. Baltimore: Johns Hopkins University Press.

Mirhady, D. C. 2001. "Dicaearchus of Messana: The Sources, Text, and Translation." In *Dicaearchus of Messana: Text, Translation, and Discussion*, ed. W. W. Fortenbaugh and E. Schütrumpf, 1–142. Rutgers University Studies in Classical Humanities 10. New Brunswick, NJ: Transaction.

Moede, K. 2007. "Reliefs, Public and Private." In *A Companion to Roman Religion*, ed. J. Rüpke, 164–75. Malden, MA: Blackwell.

Mommsen, T. 1898. *The History of Rome*. Trans. W. P. Dickson. 5 vols. New York: Charles Scribner.

Morford, M. 2002. *The Roman Philosophers*. London: Routledge.

Moussy, C. 1990. "Un Problème de Synonymie: *Ostentum* et *Portentum*." *RPh* 64: 47–60.

Moussy, C. 1977. "Esquisse de l'Histoire de *Monstrum*." *REL* 55: 345–69.

Moyer, I. 2003. "Thessalos of Tralles and Cultural Exchange." In *Prayer, Magic, and the Stars in the Ancient and Late Antique World*, ed. S. Noegel, J. Walker, and B. Wheeler, 39–56. University Park: Pennsylvania State University Press.

Nongbri, B. 2013. *Before Religion: A History of a Modern Concept*. New Haven: Yale University Press.

Nutton, V. 2004. *Ancient Medicine*. London: Routledge.

Obbink, D. 1992. "'What All Men Believe—Must Be True': Common Conceptions and *Consensio Omnium* in Aristotle and Hellenistic Philosophy." In *Oxford Studies in Ancient Philosophy*, vol. 10, ed. J. Annas, 193–231. Oxford: Clarendon.

Obbink, D. 1989. "The Atheism of Epicurus." *GRBS* 30: 187–223.

O'Brien-Moore, A. 1942. "M. Tullius Cratippus, Priest of Rome: *CIL* III, 399." *YCS* 8: 25–49.

Ogden, D. 2002. *Magic, Witchcraft, and Ghosts in the Greek and Roman Worlds*. Oxford: Oxford University Press.

Ogilvie, R. M. 1965. *A Commentary on Livy Books 1–5*. Oxford: Clarendon.

Page, D. L. 1981. *Further Greek Epigrams*. Cambridge: Cambridge University Press.

Parke, H. W. 1985. *The Oracles of Apollo in Asia Minor*. London: Croom Helm.

Parker, R. 1989. "Spartan Religion." In *Classical Sparta: Techniques behind Her Success*, ed. A. Powell, 142–72. London: Routledge.

Parpola, S. 2004. "National and Ethnic Identity in the Neo-Assyrian Empire and Assyrian Identity in Post-Empire Times." *JAAS* 18: 5–40.

Pendrick, G. J. 2002. *Antiphon the Sophist: The Fragments*. Cambridge: Cambridge University Press.

Petrakou, B. 1997. *Oi Epigraphes tou Oropou*. Athens: Archaiologike Etaireia.

Poltera, O. 2008. *Simonides lyricus: Testimonia und Fragmente*. Basel: Schwabe.

Poultney, J. W. 1959. *The Bronze Tables of Iguvium*. Baltimore: American Philological Association.

Powell, J. G. F., ed. 1995. *Cicero the Philosopher*. Oxford: Clarendon.

Powell, J. G. F., ed. 1988. *Cicero:* Cato Maior de Senectute. Cambridge: Cambridge University Press.

Purcell, N. 2003. "The Way We Used to Eat: Diet, Community, and History at Rome." *AJP* 124: 329–58.

Radden, J., ed. 2000. *The Nature of Melancholy: From Aristotle to Kristeva*. New York: Oxford University Press.

Rankin, H. D. 1987. *Celts and the Classical World*. London: Croom Helm.

Rawson, E. 1991. *Roman Culture and Society*. Oxford: Clarendon.

Rawson, E. 1985a. *Intellectual Life in the Late Roman Republic*. Baltimore: Johns Hopkins University Press.

Rawson, E. 1985b. "Cicero and the Areopagus." *Athenaeum* 63: 44–67. Reprinted in Rawson 1991, 444–67.

Rawson, E. 1979. "L. Cornelius Sisenna and the Early First Century BC." *CQ* 29: 327–46. Reprinted in Rawson 1991, 363–88.

Rawson, E. 1978. "Caesar, Etruria, and the *Disciplina Etrusca*." *JRS* 68: 132–52. Reprinted in Rawson 1991, 289–323.

Rawson, E. 1975. *Cicero: A Portrait*. London: Allen Lane.

Renberg, G. Forthcoming. *Where Dreams May Come: A Survey of Incubation Sanctuaries in the Greco-Roman World*.

Renberg, G. 2006–7. "Public and Private Places of Worship in the Cult of Asclepius at Rome." *MAAR* 51–52:87–172.

Renberg, G. 2003. "'Commanded by the Gods': An Epigraphical Study of Dreams and Visions in Greek and Roman Religious Life." Dissertation, Duke University.

Ribbeck, O. 1897. *Scaenicae Romanorum Poesis Fragmenta*. 3rd ed. 2 vols. Leipzig: Teubner.

Riedweg, C. 2005. *Pythagoras: His Life, Teaching, and Influence*. Trans. S. Rendall. Ithaca, NY: Cornell University Press.

Riginos, A. S. 1976. *Platonica: The Anecdotes concerning the Life and Writings of Plato*. Leiden: Brill.

Robinson, E. W. 1992. "Oracles and Spartan Religious Scruples." *LCM* 17: 131–32.

Roller, L. E. 1983. "The Legend of Midas." *CA* 2: 299–313.

Ross, D. O., Jr. 1969. *Style and Tradition in Catullus*. Cambridge, MA: Harvard University Press.

Ryberg, I. S. 1955. *Rites of the State Religion in Roman Art*. Memoirs of the American Academy in Rome 22. Rome: American Academy in Rome.

Santangelo, F. 2005. "The Religious Tradition of the Gracchi." *ARG* 7: 198–214.

Scarsi, M. 2005. "*Neque Attii Navii nomen memoria floreret tam diu.*" *BStudLat* 35: 401–39.

Schierl, P. 2006. *Die Tragödien des Pacuvius*. Texte und Kommentare 28. Berlin: de Gruyter.

Schofield, M. 1986. "Cicero for and against Divination." *JRS* 76: 47–65.

Schultz, C. E. 2009. "Argument and Anecdote in Cicero's *De Divinatione.*" In *Maxima Debetur Magistro Reverentia: Essays on Rome and the Roman Tradition in Honor of Russell T. Scott*, ed. P. B. Harvey, Jr., and C. Conybeare, 193–206. Bibliotheca di Athenaeum 54. Como: New Press Edizioni

Schultz, C. E. 2006. "Juno Sospita and Roman Insecurity in the Social War." In Schultz and Harvey 2006, 207–27.

Schultz, C. E., and P. B. Harvey, Jr., eds. 2006. *Religion in Republican Italy*. Yale Classical Studies 33. Cambridge: Cambridge University Press.

Schütrumpf, E., ed. 2008. *Heraclides of Pontus: Texts and Translation*. Rutgers University Studies in Classical Humanities 14. New Brunswick, NJ: Transaction.

Scullard, H. H. 1981. *Festivals and Ceremonies of the Roman Republic*. Ithaca, NY: Cornell University Press.

Sedley, D. 1997. "The Ethics of Brutus and Cassius." *JRS* 87: 41–53.

Shackleton Bailey, D. R. 1971. *Cicero*. New York: Scribner.

Sharples, R. W. 2001. "Dicaearchus on the Soul and on Divination." In *Dicaearchus of Messana: Text, Translation, and Discussion*, ed. W. W. Fortenbaugh and E. Schütrumpf, 143–73. Rutgers University Studies in Classical Humanities 10. New Brunswick, NJ: Transaction.

Shaw, B. 2001. "Raising and Killing Children: Two Roman Myths." *Mnemosyne* 54: 31–77.

Sherk, R. K. 1984. *Rome and the Greek East to the Death of Augustus*. Translated Documents of Greece and Rome 4. Cambridge: Cambridge University Press.

Slater, N. 2000. "Religion and Identity in Pacuvius's *Chryses*." In Manuwald 2000, 315–23.

Soubiran, J. 1972. *Cicéron: Aratea Fragments Poétiques*. Paris: Les Belles Lettres.

Stewart, R. 1997. "The Jug and Lituus on Roman Republican Coin Types: Ritual Symbols and Political Power." *Phoenix* 51: 170–89.

Stothers, R. B. 2007. "Unidentified Flying Objects in Classical Antiquity." *CJ* 103: 79–92.

Stothers, R. B. 2004. "Earthquake Prediction in Antiquity." *AHB* 3–4: 101–8.

Struck, P. 2005. "Divination and Literary Criticism?" In Johnston and Struck 2005, 147–65.

Tarrant, H. 2000. "Recollection and Prophesy in the *De Divinatione*." *Phronesis* 45: 64–76.

Taylor, C. C. W. 1999. *The Atomists: Leucippus and Democritus*. Phoenix Suppl. 36. Toronto: University of Toronto Press.

Thomas, R. 2000. *Herodotus in Context: Ethnography, Science, and the Art of Persuasion*. Cambridge: Cambridge University Press.

Torelli, M., ed. 2001. *The Etruscans*. New York: Rizzoli.

Torelli, M. 1975. *Elogia Tarquiniensia*. Florence: Sansoni.

Toynbee, J. M. C. 1948. "Beasts and Their Names in the Roman Empire." *PBSR* 16: 24–37.

Treggiari, S. 1991. *Roman Marriage: Iusti Coniuges from the Time of Cicero to the Time of Ulpian*. Oxford: Clarendon.

Turcan, R. 1988. *Religion Romaine*. Iconography of Religions 17.1. Leiden: Brill.

Ustinova, Y. 2009. *Caves and the Ancient Greek Mind*. Oxford: Oxford University Press.

Usubillaga, A., et al. 2005. "Anti-snake Venom Effect of *Aristolochia odoratissima* L. Aqueous Extract on Mice." *Acta Horticulturae* 677: 85–89.

Vaahtera, J. 2001. *Roman Augural Lore in Greek Historiography*. Historia Einzelschriften 156. Stuttgart: Steiner.

Valeton, I. M. J. 1890. "De Modis Auspicandi Romanorum II." *Mnemosyne* 18: 208–63, 406–56.

van der Eijk, P. J. 2005. *Medicine and Philosophy in Classical Antiquity*. Cambridge: Cambridge University Press.

van der Eijk, P. J. 2004. "Divination, Prognosis, and Prophylaxis: The Hippocratic Work 'On Dreams' (*De Victu* 4) and Its Near Eastern Background." In *Magic and Rationality in Ancient Near Eastern and Graeco-Roman Medicine*, ed. H. F. J. Horstmanshoff and M. Stol, 187–218. Leiden: Brill.

van der Eijk, P. J. 1994. *Aristoteles: De Insomniis, De Divinatione per Somnum*. Berlin: Akademie Verlag.

van der Eijk, P. J. 1993. "Aristotelian Elements in Cicero's *De Divinatione*." *Philologus* 137: 223–31.

Vander Waerdt, P. A. 1985. "The Peripatetic Interpretation of Plato's Tripartite Psychology." *GRBS* 26: 283–302.

van Straaten, M. 1962. *Panaetii Rhodii Fragmenta*. 3rd ed. Leiden: Brill.

Vasaly, A. 1993. *Representations: Images of the World in Ciceronian Oratory*. Berkeley: University of California Press.

Verbaal, W. 2006. "Cicero and Dionysios the Elder, or The End of Liberty." *CW* 99: 145–56.

von Albrecht, M. 2003. *Cicero's Style: A Synopsis*. Leiden: Brill.

von Arnim, H. 1905–24. *Stoicorum Veterum Fragmenta*. 4 vols. Leipzig: Teubner.

Wallace, R. 1996. "'Amaze Your Friends!': Lucretius on Magnets." *Greece and Rome* 43: 178–87.

Waterfield, R. 2009. *The First Philosophers: The Presocratics and Sophists*. Oxford: Oxford University Press.

West, M. L. 1992. *Iambi et Elegi Graeci*. 2nd ed. 2 vols. Oxford: Oxford University Press.

Willink, C. W. 1986. *Euripides: Orestes*. Oxford: Clarendon.

Wirszubski, C. 1950. Libertas *as a Political Idea at Rome during the Late Republic and Early Principate*. Cambridge: Cambridge University Press.

Wiseman, T. P. 2006. "Fauns, Prophets, and Ennius's *Annales*." *Arethusa* 39: 513–29.

Wiseman, T. P. 1995. *Remus: A Roman Myth*. Cambridge: Cambridge University Press.

Wiseman, T. P. 1994. *Historiography and Imagination: Eight Essays on Roman Culture*. Exeter: University of Exeter Press.

Wittkower, R. 1939. "Eagle and Serpent: A Study in the Migration of Symbols." *JWI* 2: 293–325.

Wood, N. 1988. *Cicero's Social and Political Thought*. Berkeley: University of California Press.

Wynne, J. P. F. 2008. "Cicero on the Philosophy of Religion: *De Natura Deorum* and *De Divinatione*." Dissertation, Cornell University.

Latin and Greek Index

Page references are to the commentary notes only.

People and Gods Index

Page references are to the commentary notes only. The interlocutors of the dialogue are not included here.

General Index

Page references are to the commentary notes only.